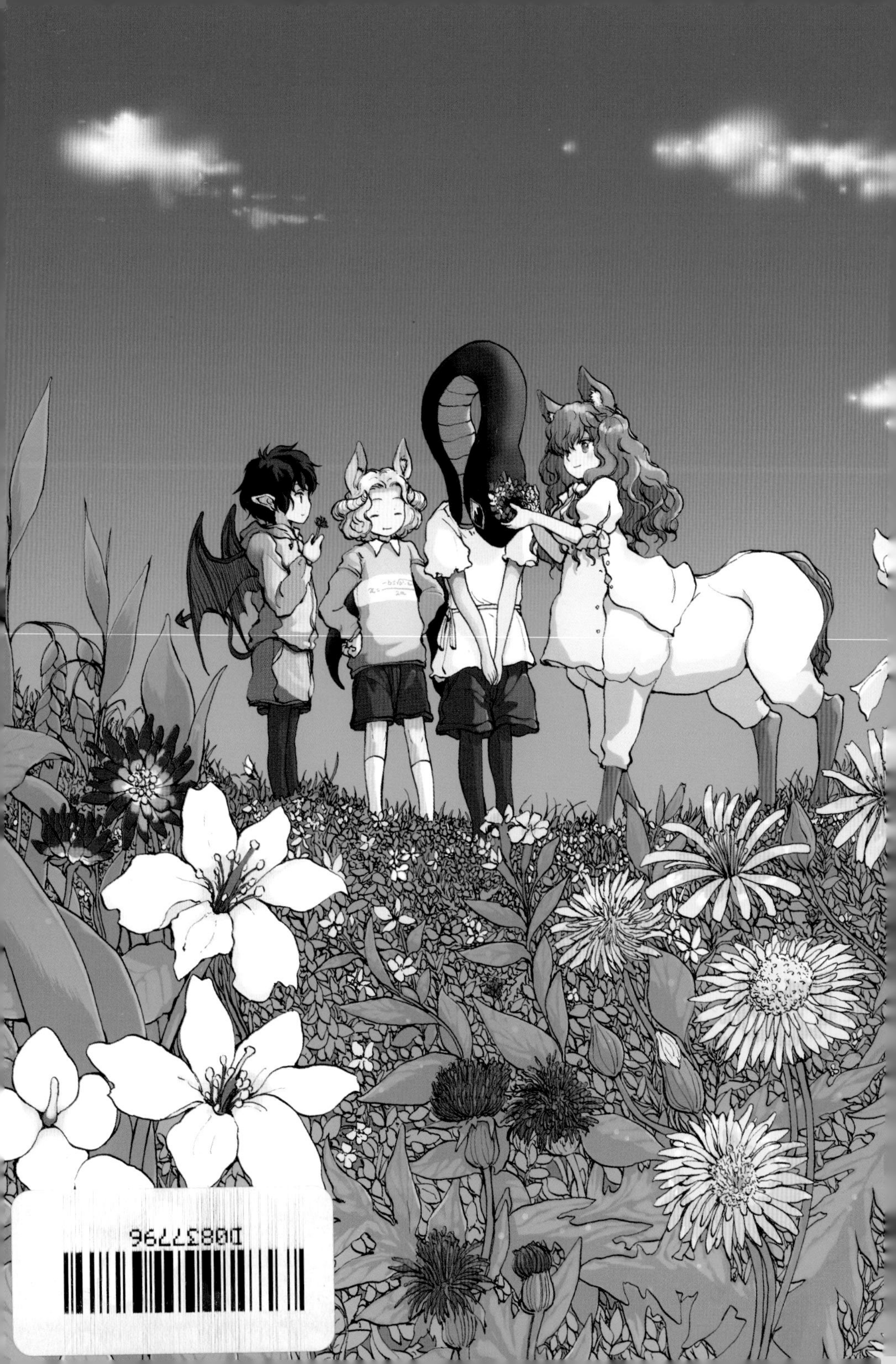

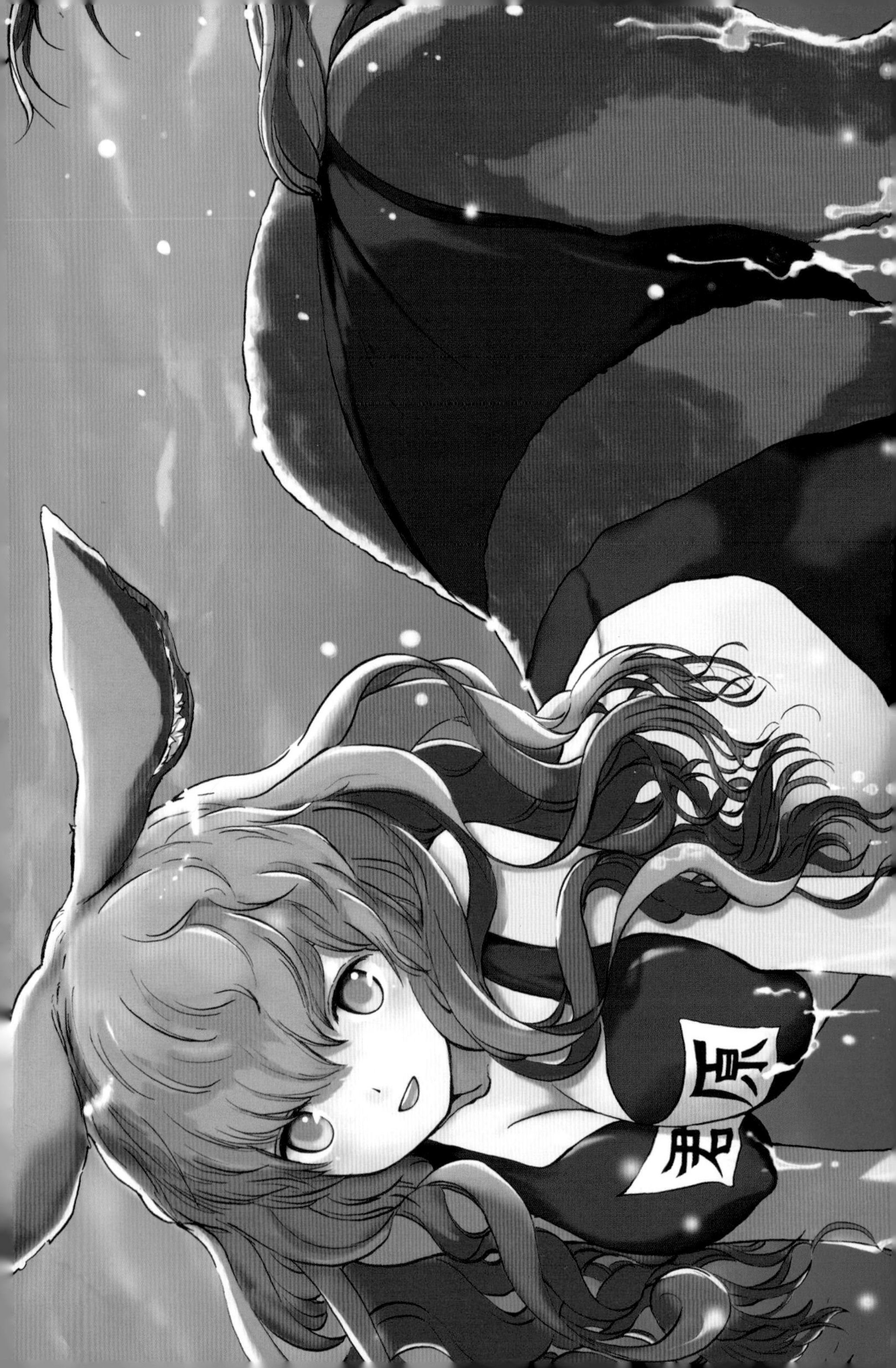

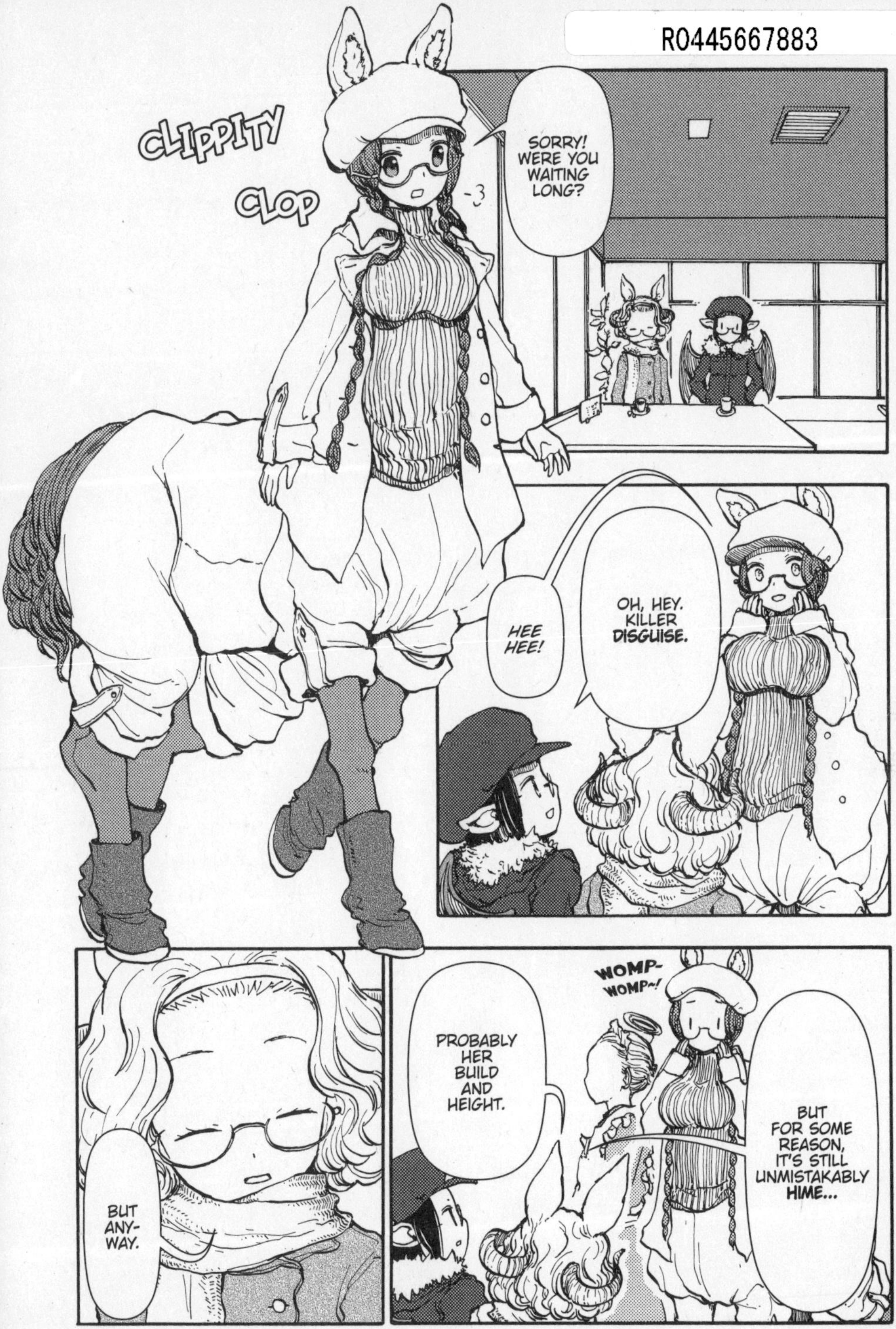
SORRY! WERE YOU WAITING LONG?
-3
OH, HEY. KILLER DISGUISE.
HEE HEE!
CLIPPITY
CLOP
WOMP-WOMP~!
BUT FOR SOME REASON, IT'S STILL UNMISTAKABLY HIME...
PROBABLY HER BUILD AND HEIGHT.
BUT ANY-WAY.

CHAPTER 45

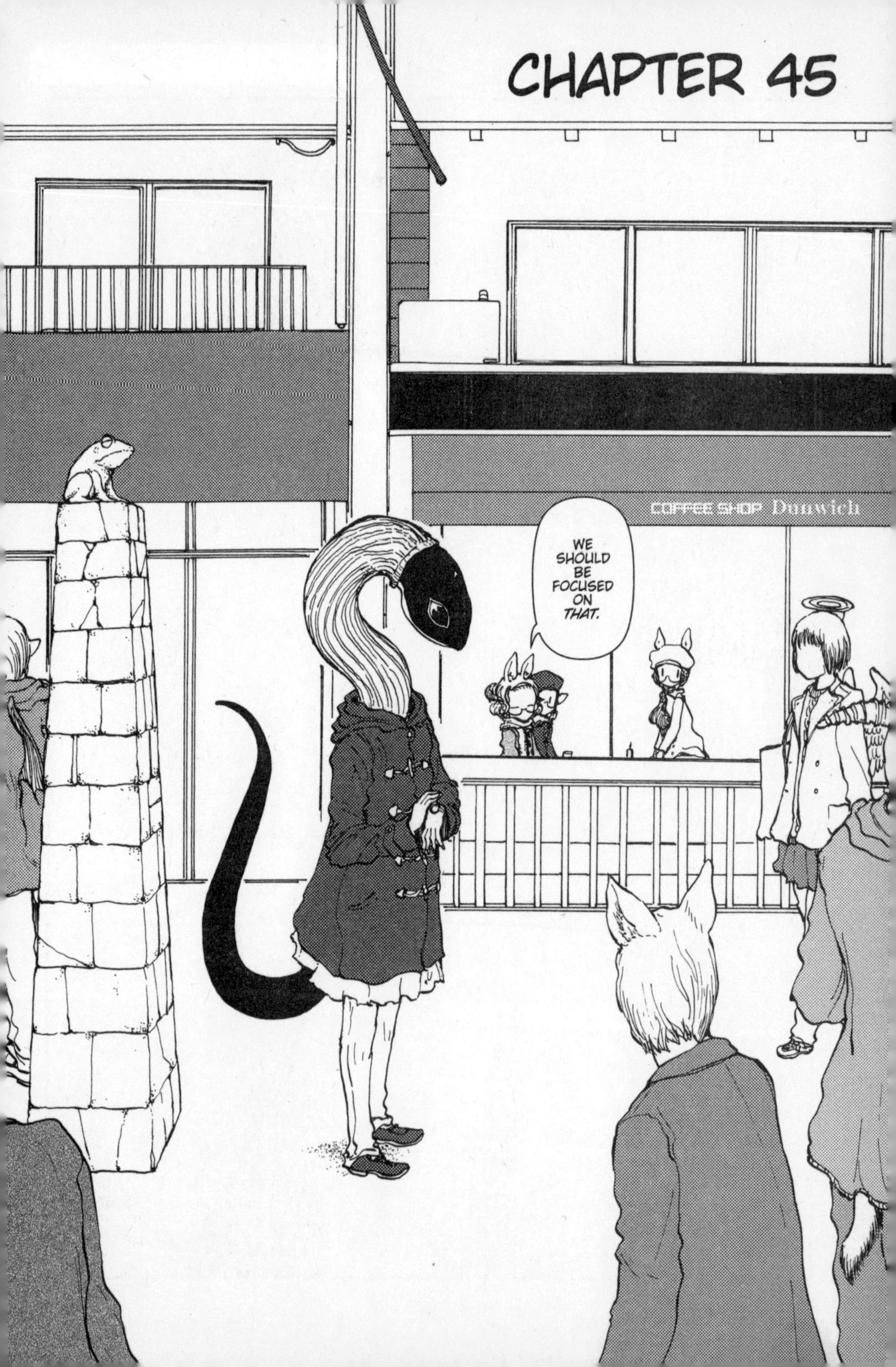

COFFEE SHOP Dunwich
WE SHOULD BE FOCUSED ON *THAT.*

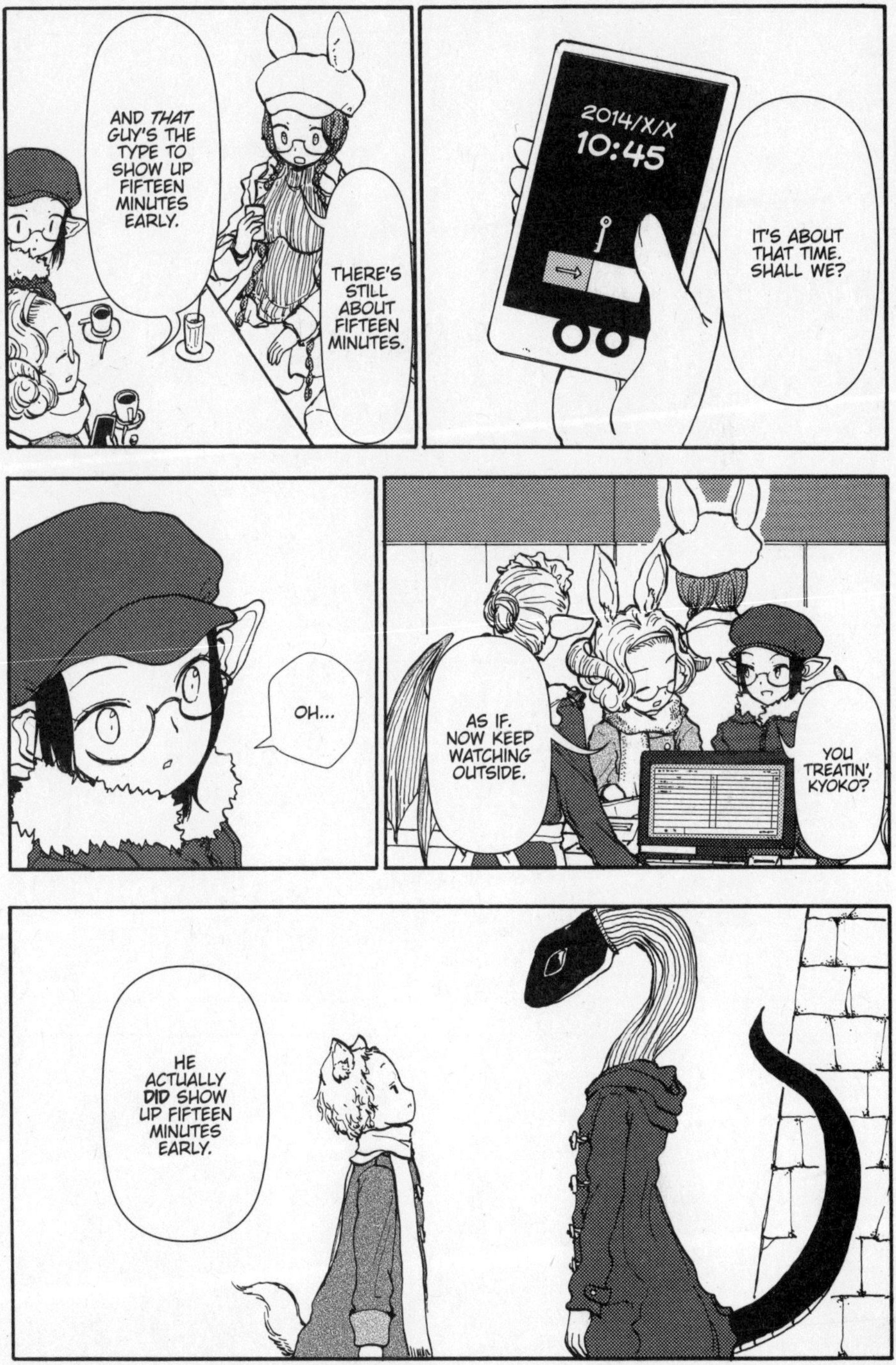
2014/X/X
10:45
IT'S ABOUT THAT TIME. SHALL WE?
THERE'S STILL ABOUT FIFTEEN MINUTES.
AND *THAT* GUY'S THE TYPE TO SHOW UP FIFTEEN MINUTES EARLY.
YOU TREATIN', KYOKO?
AS IF. NOW KEEP WATCHING OUTSIDE.
OH...
HE ACTUALLY **DID** SHOW UP FIFTEEN MINUTES EARLY.

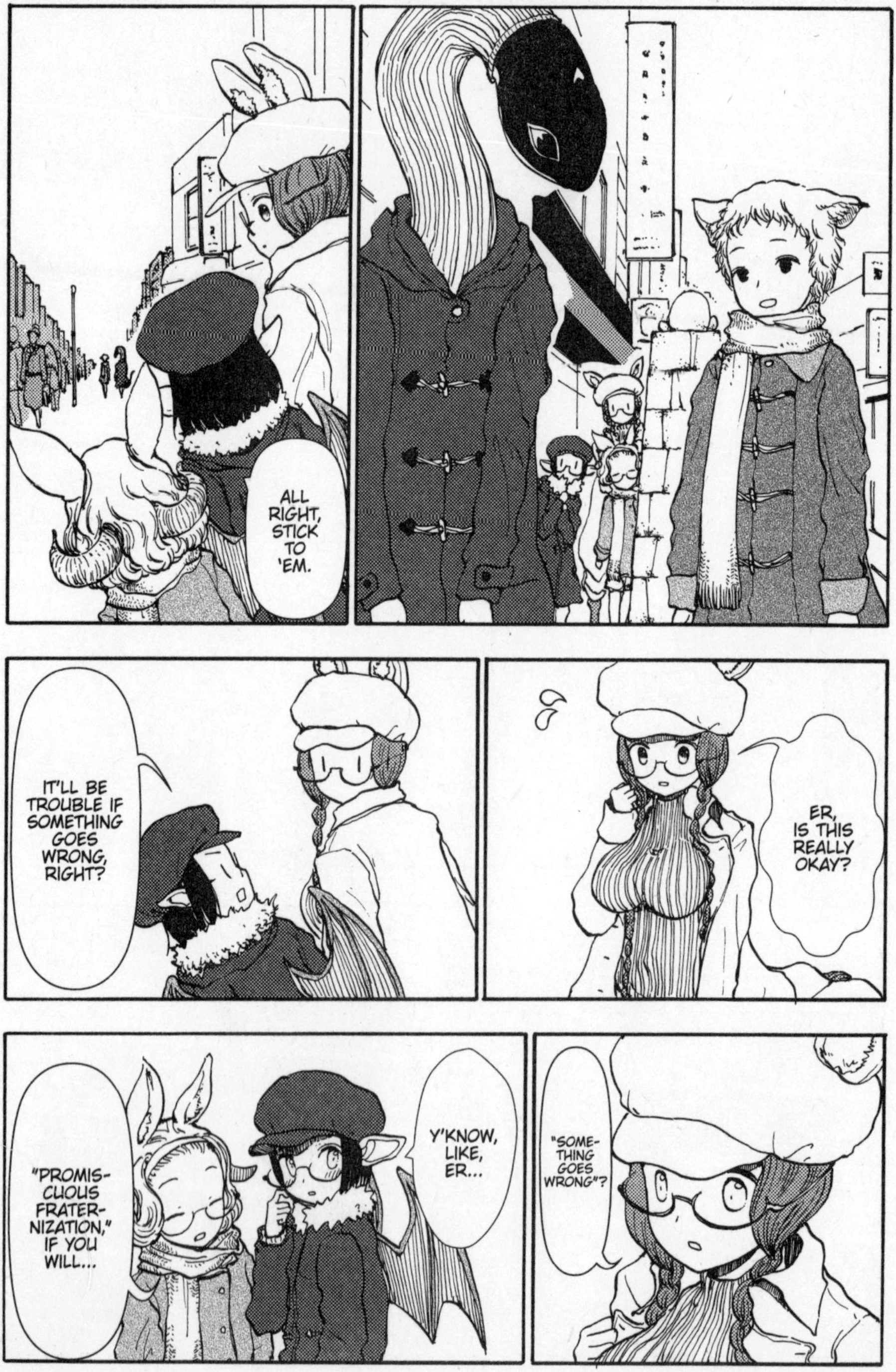
ALL RIGHT, STICK TO 'EM.
ER, IS THIS REALLY OKAY?
IT'LL BE TROUBLE IF SOMETHING GOES WRONG, RIGHT?
"SOMETHING GOES WRONG"?
Y'KNOW, LIKE, ER...
"PROMISCUOUS FRATERNIZATION," IF YOU WILL...

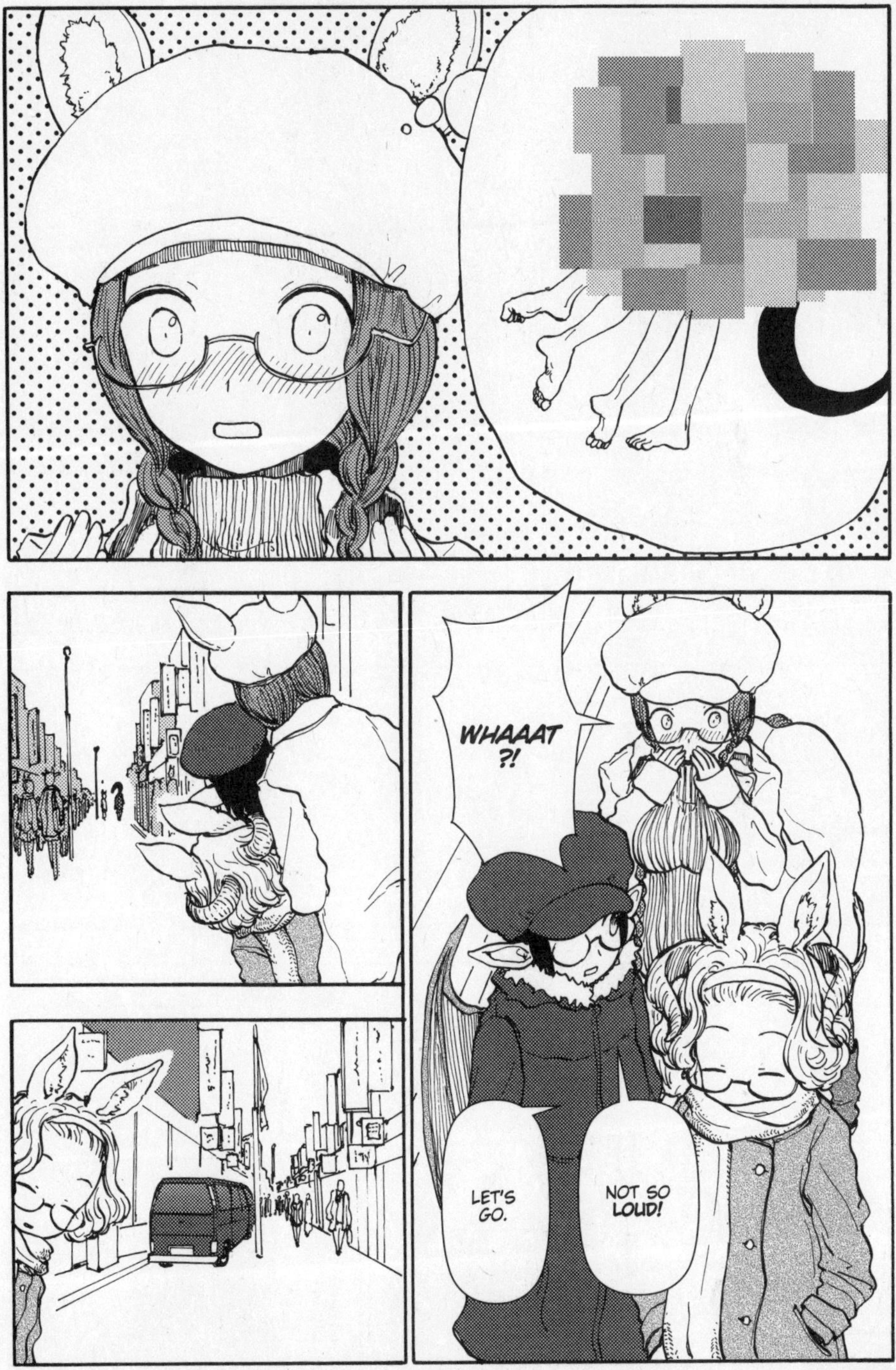
WHAAAT?!
NOT SO LOUD!
LET'S GO.

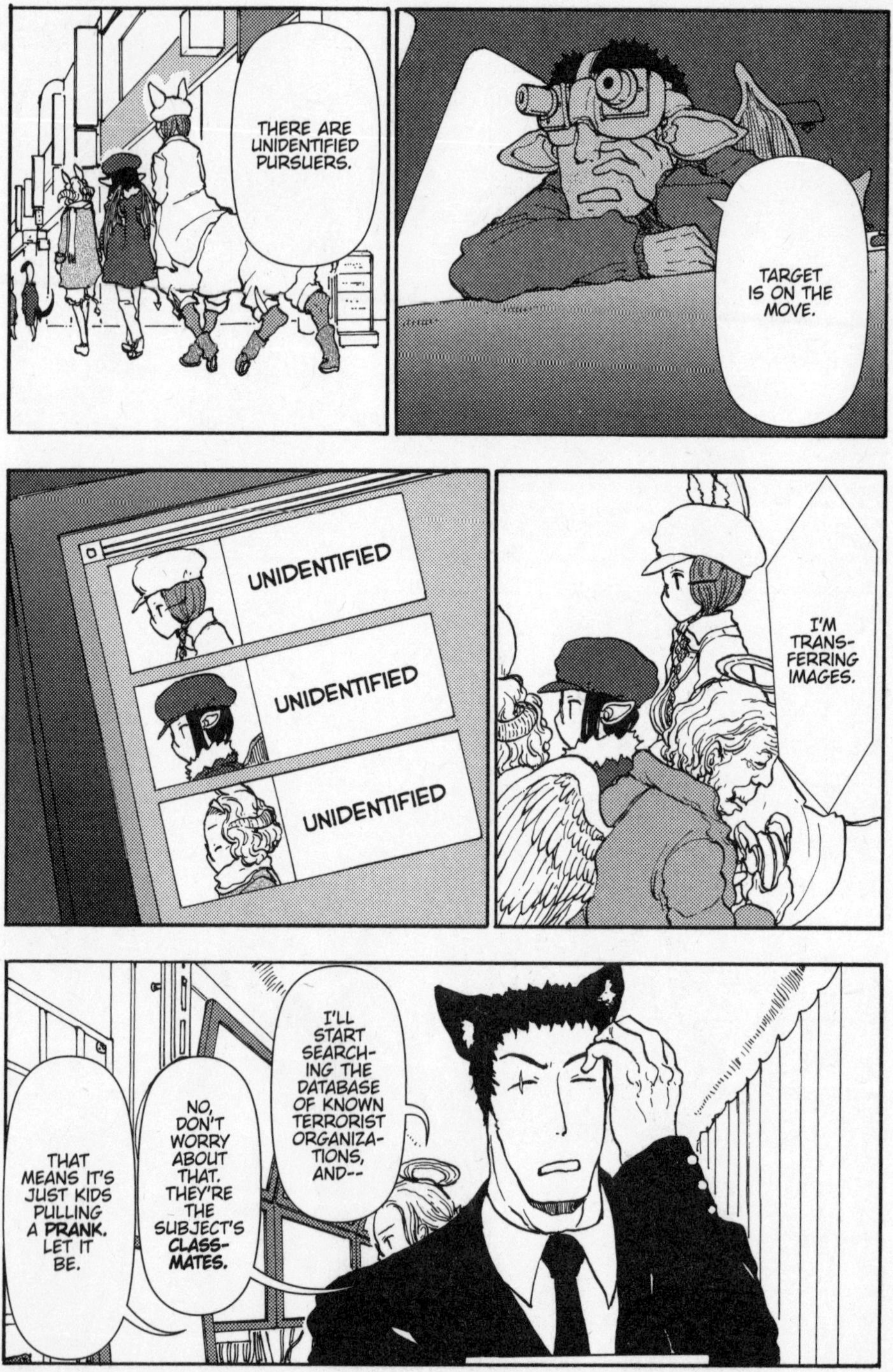
TARGET IS ON THE MOVE.
THERE ARE UNIDENTIFIED PURSUERS.
I'M TRANS-FERRING IMAGES.
UNIDENTIFIED
UNIDENTIFIED
UNIDENTIFIED
I'LL START SEARCHING THE DATABASE OF KNOWN TERRORIST ORGANIZA-TIONS, AND--
NO, DON'T WORRY ABOUT THAT. THEY'RE THE SUBJECT'S **CLASS-MATES.**
THAT MEANS IT'S JUST KIDS PULLING A **PRANK.** LET IT BE.

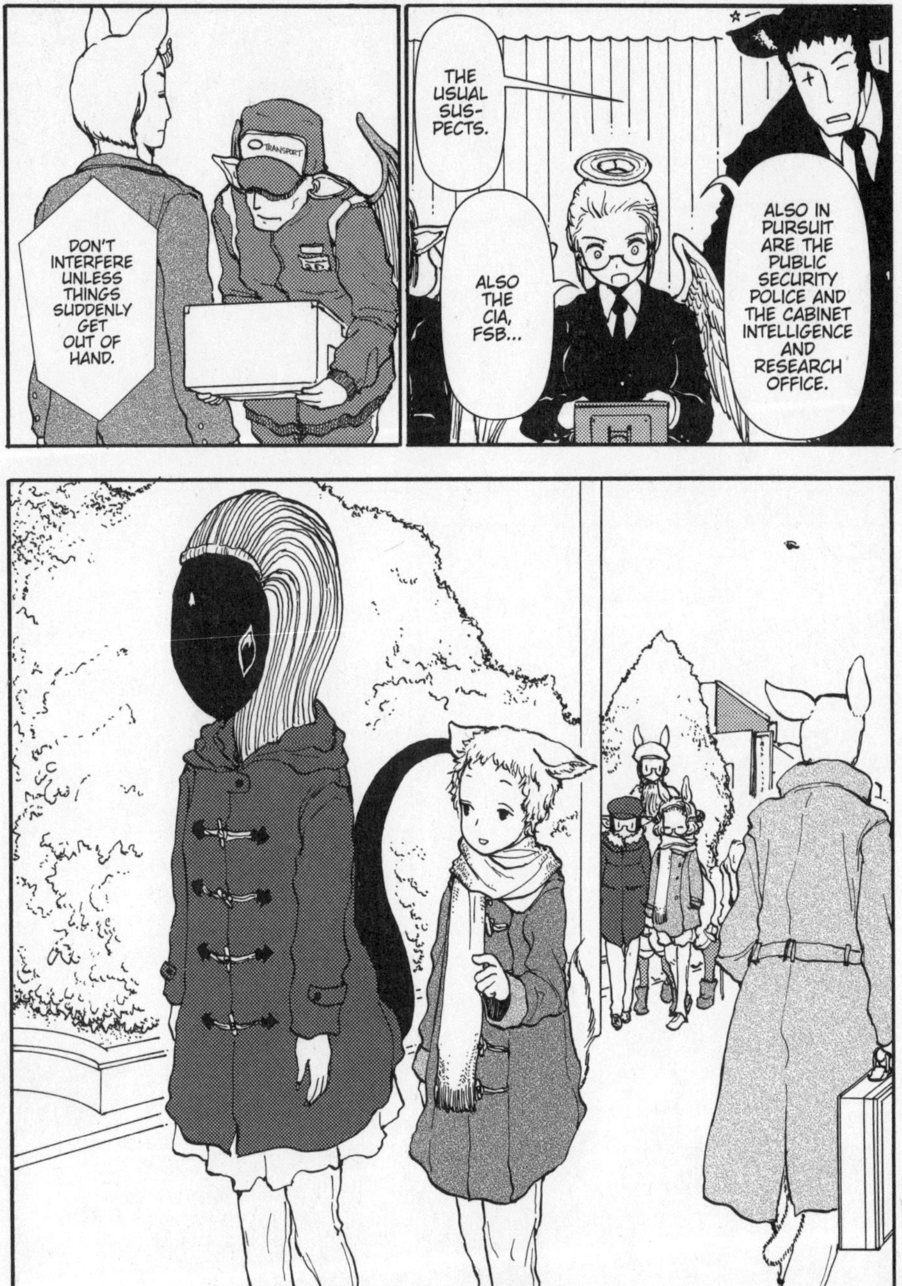
THE USUAL SUS-PECTS.
ALSO THE CIA, FSB...
ALSO IN PURSUIT ARE THE PUBLIC SECURITY POLICE AND THE CABINET INTELLIGENCE AND RESEARCH OFFICE.
TRANSPORT
DON'T INTERFERE UNLESS THINGS SUDDENLY GET OUT OF HAND.

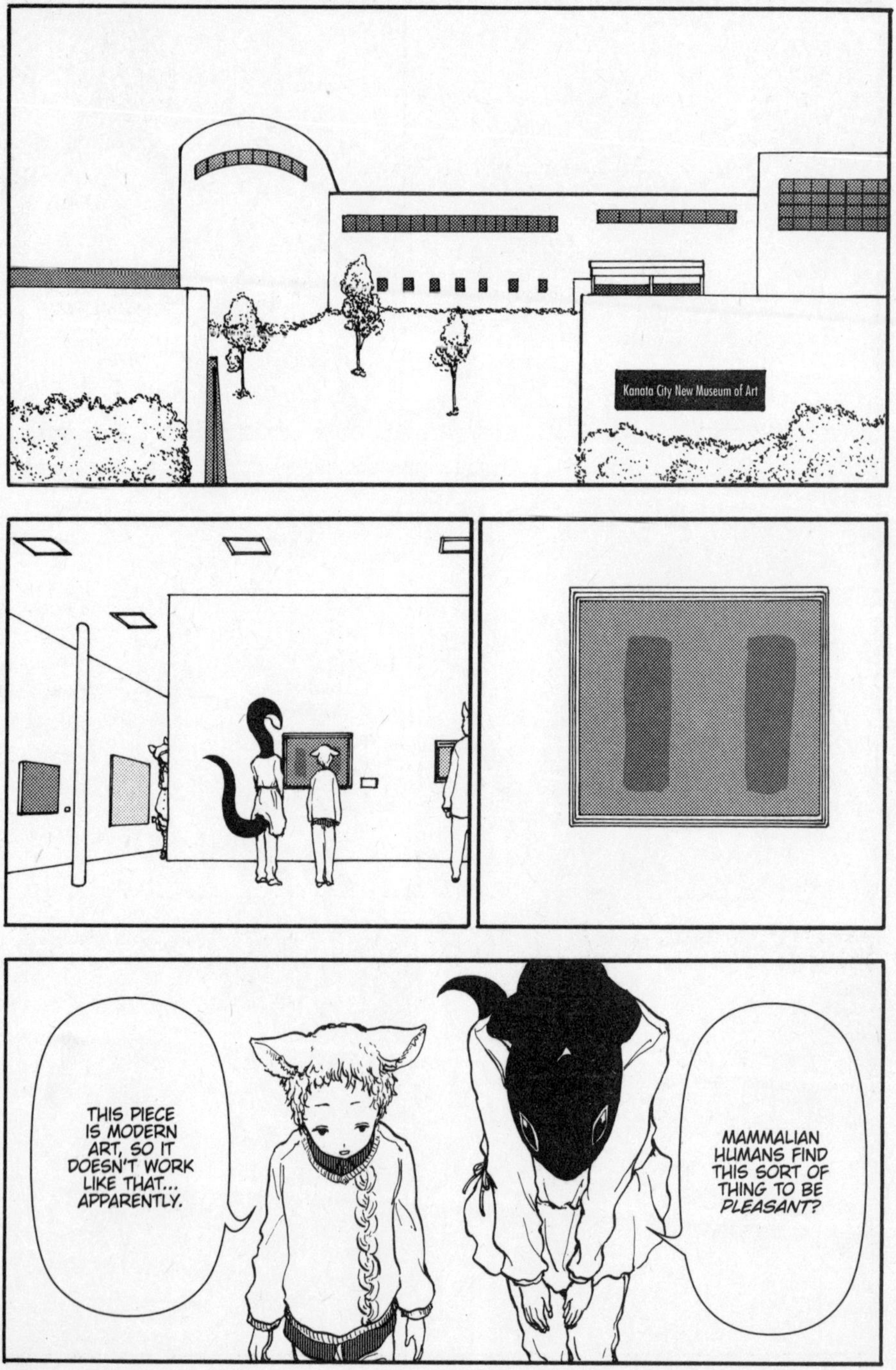
Kanata City New Museum of Art
MAMMALIAN HUMANS FIND THIS SORT OF THING TO BE *PLEASANT?*
THIS PIECE IS MODERN ART, SO IT DOESN'T WORK LIKE THAT... APPARENTLY.

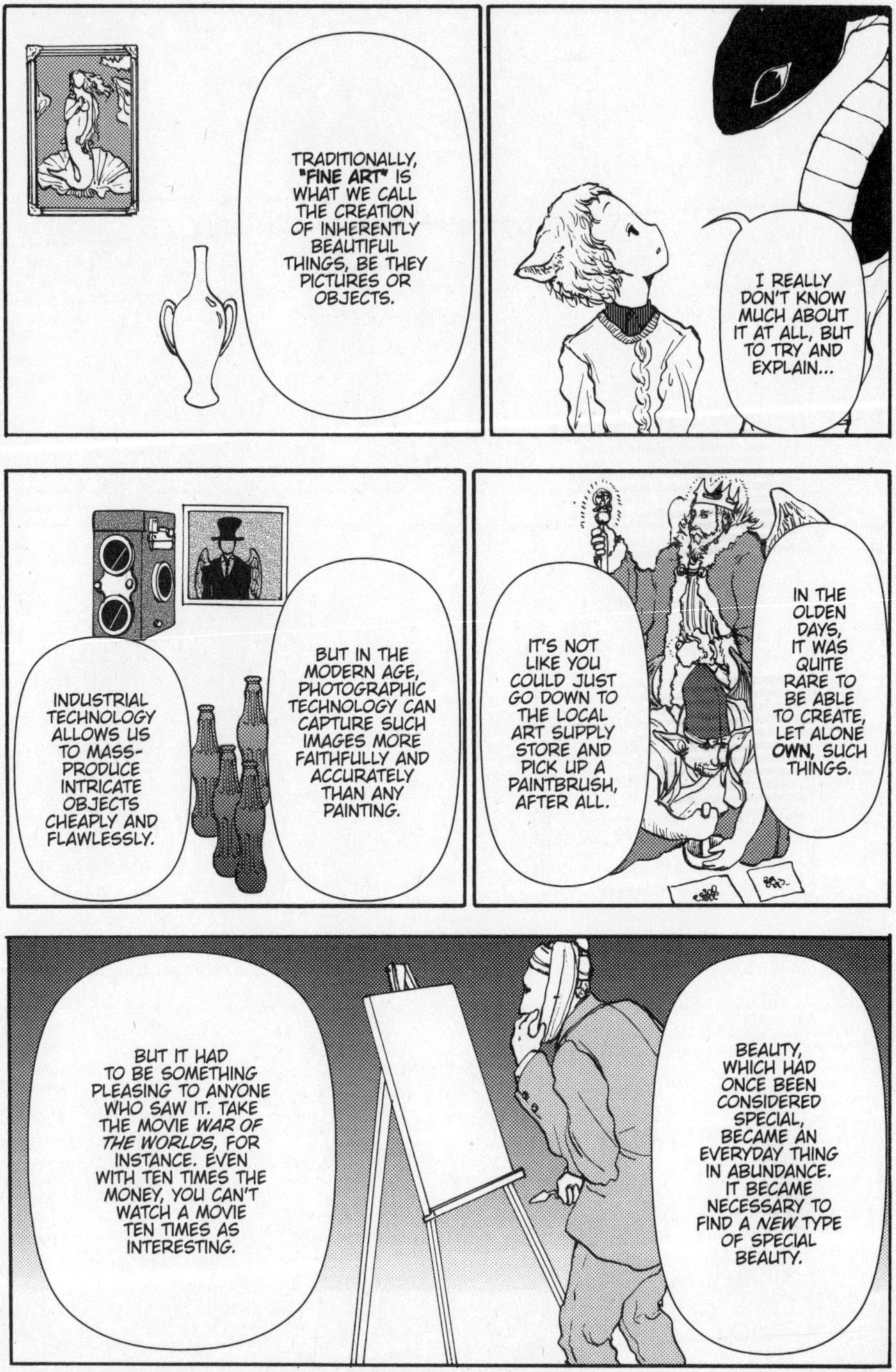
I REALLY DON'T KNOW MUCH ABOUT IT AT ALL, BUT TO TRY AND EXPLAIN...
TRADITIONALLY, **"FINE ART"** IS WHAT WE CALL THE CREATION OF INHERENTLY BEAUTIFUL THINGS, BE THEY PICTURES OR OBJECTS.
IN THE OLDEN DAYS, IT WAS QUITE RARE TO BE ABLE TO CREATE, LET ALONE **OWN**, SUCH THINGS.
IT'S NOT LIKE YOU COULD JUST GO DOWN TO THE LOCAL ART SUPPLY STORE AND PICK UP A PAINTBRUSH, AFTER ALL.
BUT IN THE MODERN AGE, PHOTOGRAPHIC TECHNOLOGY CAN CAPTURE SUCH IMAGES MORE FAITHFULLY AND ACCURATELY THAN ANY PAINTING.
INDUSTRIAL TECHNOLOGY ALLOWS US TO MASS-PRODUCE INTRICATE OBJECTS CHEAPLY AND FLAWLESSLY.
BEAUTY, WHICH HAD ONCE BEEN CONSIDERED SPECIAL, BECAME AN EVERYDAY THING IN ABUNDANCE. IT BECAME NECESSARY TO FIND A *NEW* TYPE OF SPECIAL BEAUTY.
BUT IT HAD TO BE SOMETHING PLEASING TO ANYONE WHO SAW IT. TAKE THE MOVIE *WAR OF THE WORLDS*, FOR INSTANCE. EVEN WITH TEN TIMES THE MONEY, YOU CAN'T WATCH A MOVIE TEN TIMES AS INTERESTING.

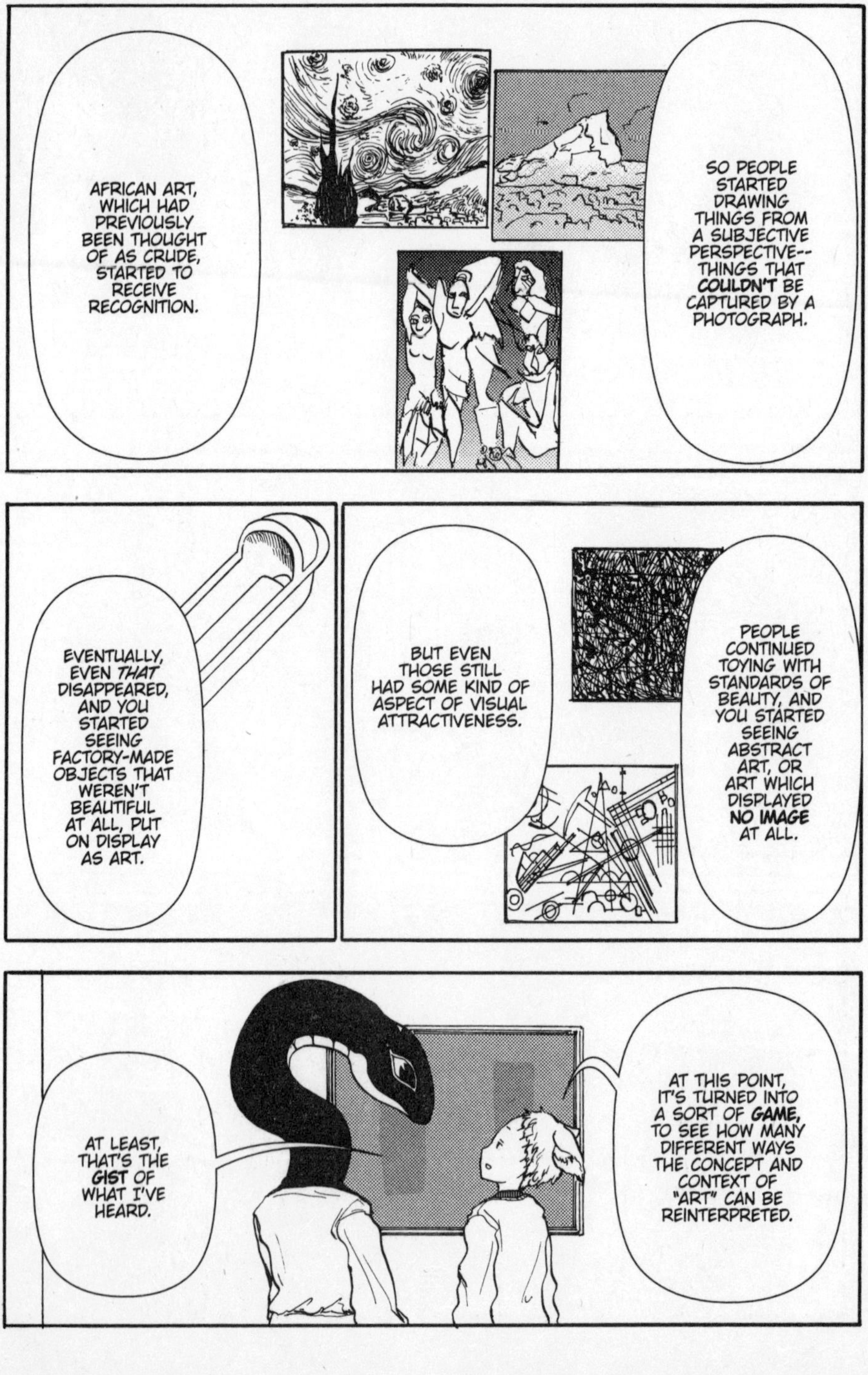
SO PEOPLE STARTED DRAWING THINGS FROM A SUBJECTIVE PERSPECTIVE--THINGS THAT **COULDN'T** BE CAPTURED BY A PHOTOGRAPH.
AFRICAN ART, WHICH HAD PREVIOUSLY BEEN THOUGHT OF AS CRUDE, STARTED TO RECEIVE RECOGNITION.
PEOPLE CONTINUED TOYING WITH STANDARDS OF BEAUTY, AND YOU STARTED SEEING ABSTRACT ART, OR ART WHICH DISPLAYED **NO IMAGE** AT ALL.
BUT EVEN THOSE STILL HAD SOME KIND OF ASPECT OF VISUAL ATTRACTIVENESS.
EVENTUALLY, EVEN *THAT* DISAPPEARED, AND YOU STARTED SEEING FACTORY-MADE OBJECTS THAT WEREN'T BEAUTIFUL AT ALL, PUT ON DISPLAY AS ART.
AT THIS POINT, IT'S TURNED INTO A SORT OF **GAME**, TO SEE HOW MANY DIFFERENT WAYS THE CONCEPT AND CONTEXT OF "ART" CAN BE REINTERPRETED.
AT LEAST, THAT'S THE **GIST** OF WHAT I'VE HEARD.

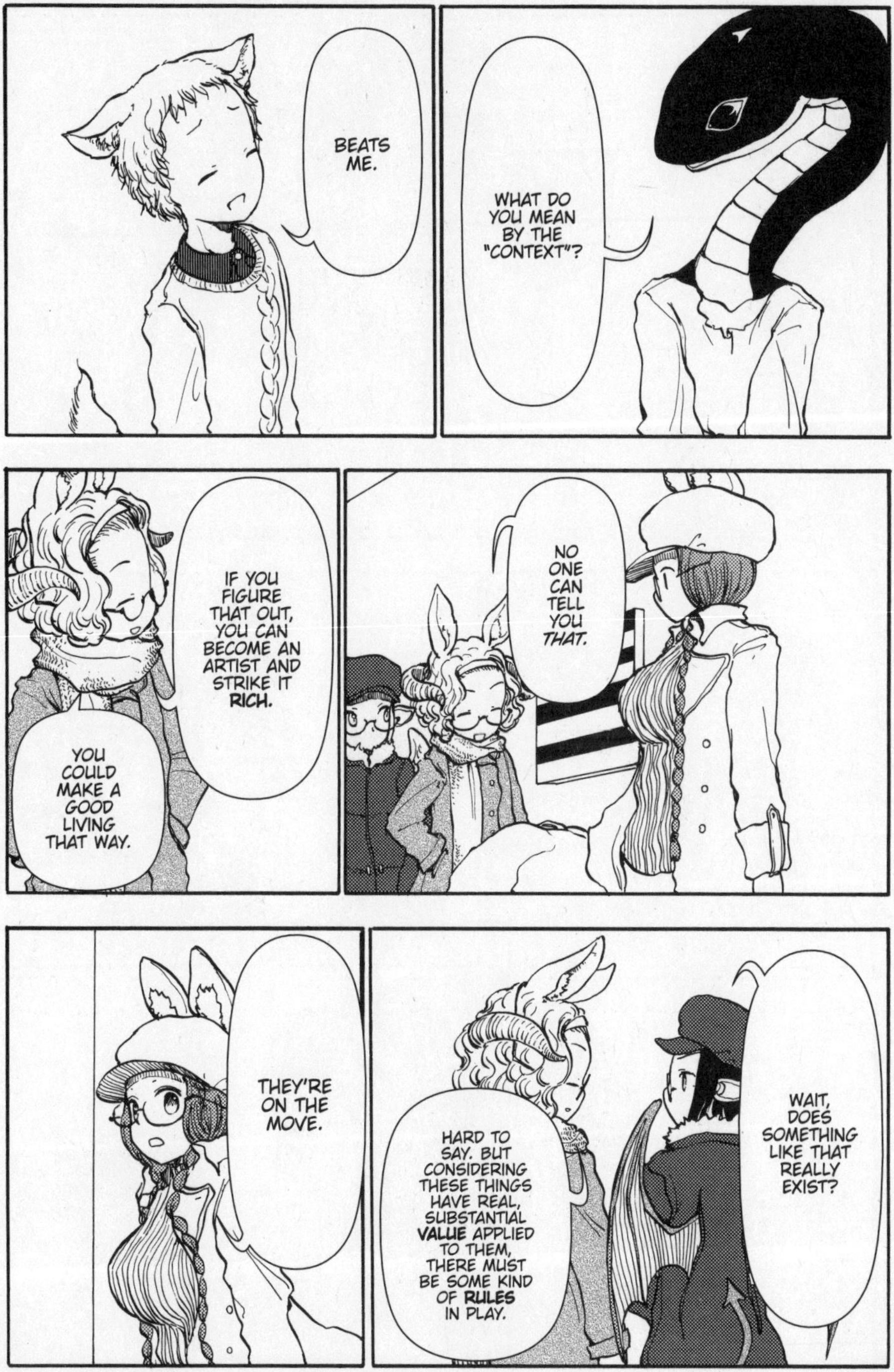
WHAT DO YOU MEAN BY THE "CONTEXT"?
BEATS ME.
NO ONE CAN TELL YOU *THAT.*
IF YOU FIGURE THAT OUT, YOU CAN BECOME AN ARTIST AND STRIKE IT **RICH.**
YOU COULD MAKE A GOOD LIVING THAT WAY.
WAIT, DOES SOMETHING LIKE THAT REALLY EXIST?
HARD TO SAY. BUT CONSIDERING THESE THINGS HAVE REAL, SUBSTANTIAL **VALUE** APPLIED TO THEM, THERE MUST BE SOME KIND OF **RULES** IN PLAY.
THEY'RE ON THE MOVE.

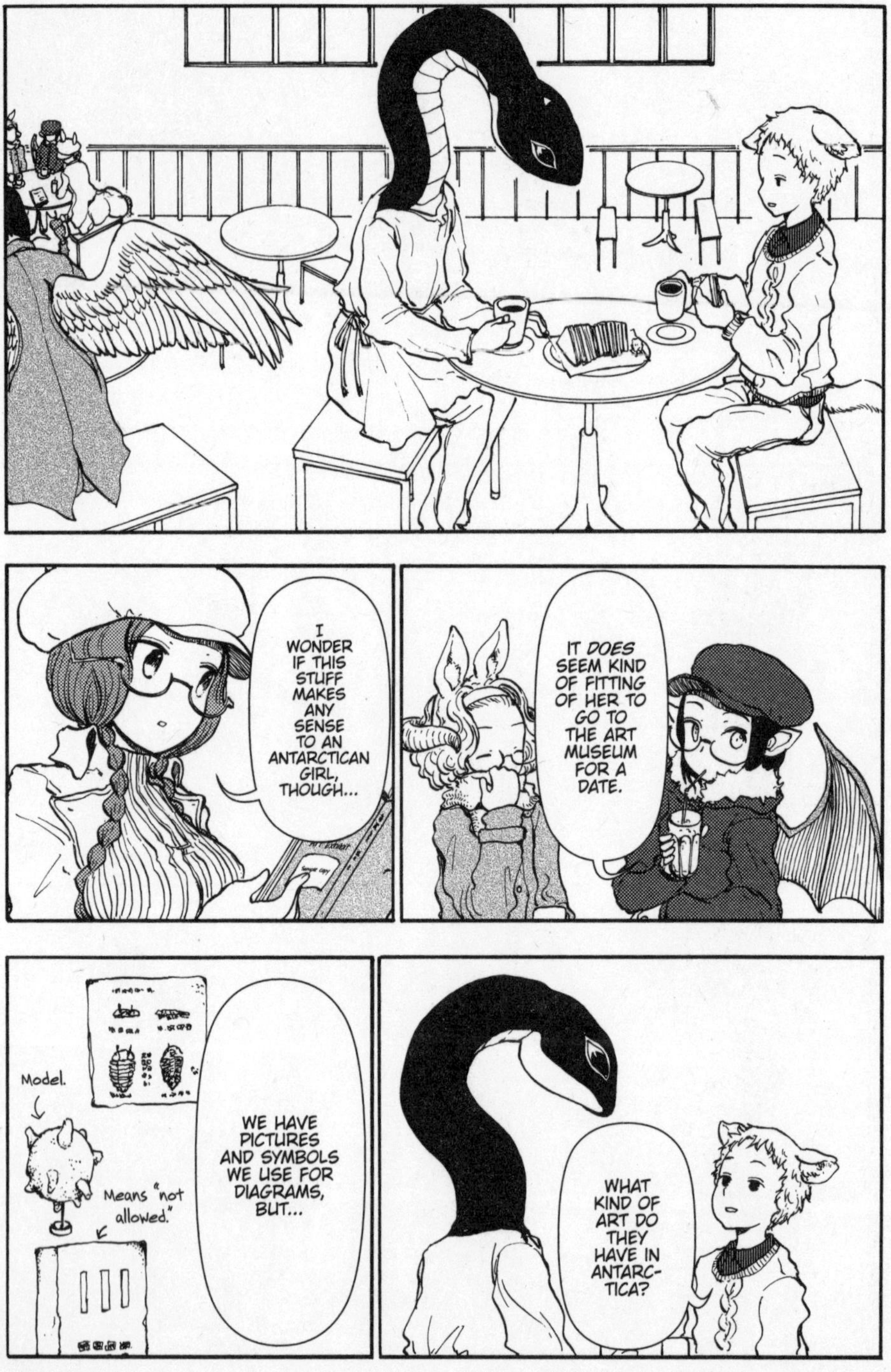
IT DOES SEEM KIND OF FITTING OF HER TO GO TO THE ART MUSEUM FOR A DATE.
I WONDER IF THIS STUFF MAKES ANY SENSE TO AN ANTARCTICAN GIRL, THOUGH...
WHAT KIND OF ART DO THEY HAVE IN ANTARC-TICA?
WE HAVE PICTURES AND SYMBOLS WE USE FOR DIAGRAMS, BUT...
Model.
Means "not allowed."

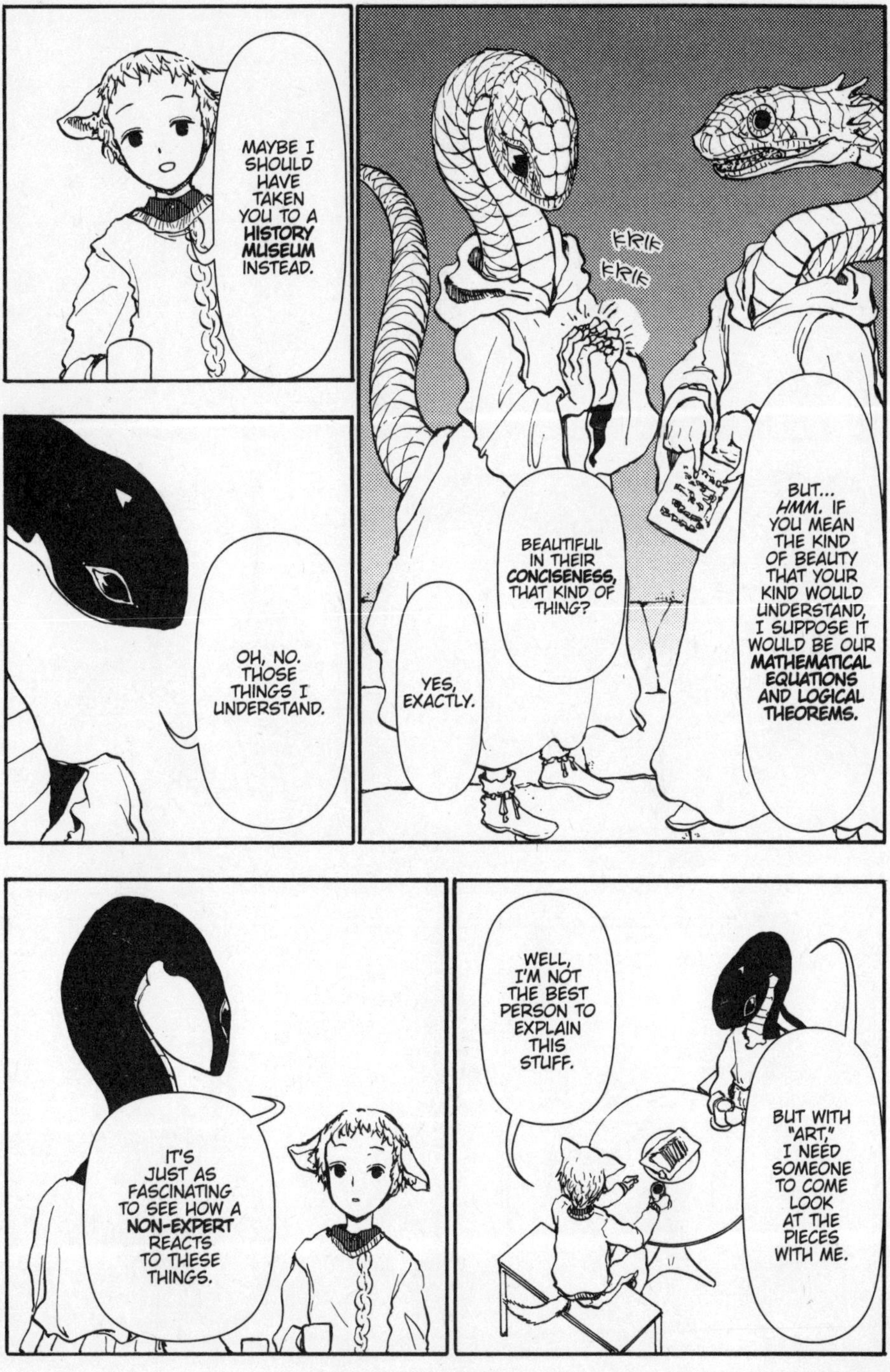
BUT... HMM. IF YOU MEAN THE KIND OF BEAUTY THAT YOUR KIND WOULD UNDERSTAND, I SUPPOSE IT WOULD BE OUR MATHEMATICAL EQUATIONS AND LOGICAL THEOREMS.
KRIK KRIK
BEAUTIFUL IN THEIR CONCISENESS, THAT KIND OF THING?
YES, EXACTLY.
MAYBE I SHOULD HAVE TAKEN YOU TO A HISTORY MUSEUM INSTEAD.
OH, NO. THOSE THINGS I UNDERSTAND.
WELL, I'M NOT THE BEST PERSON TO EXPLAIN THIS STUFF.
BUT WITH "ART," I NEED SOMEONE TO COME LOOK AT THE PIECES WITH ME.
IT'S JUST AS FASCINATING TO SEE HOW A NON-EXPERT REACTS TO THESE THINGS.

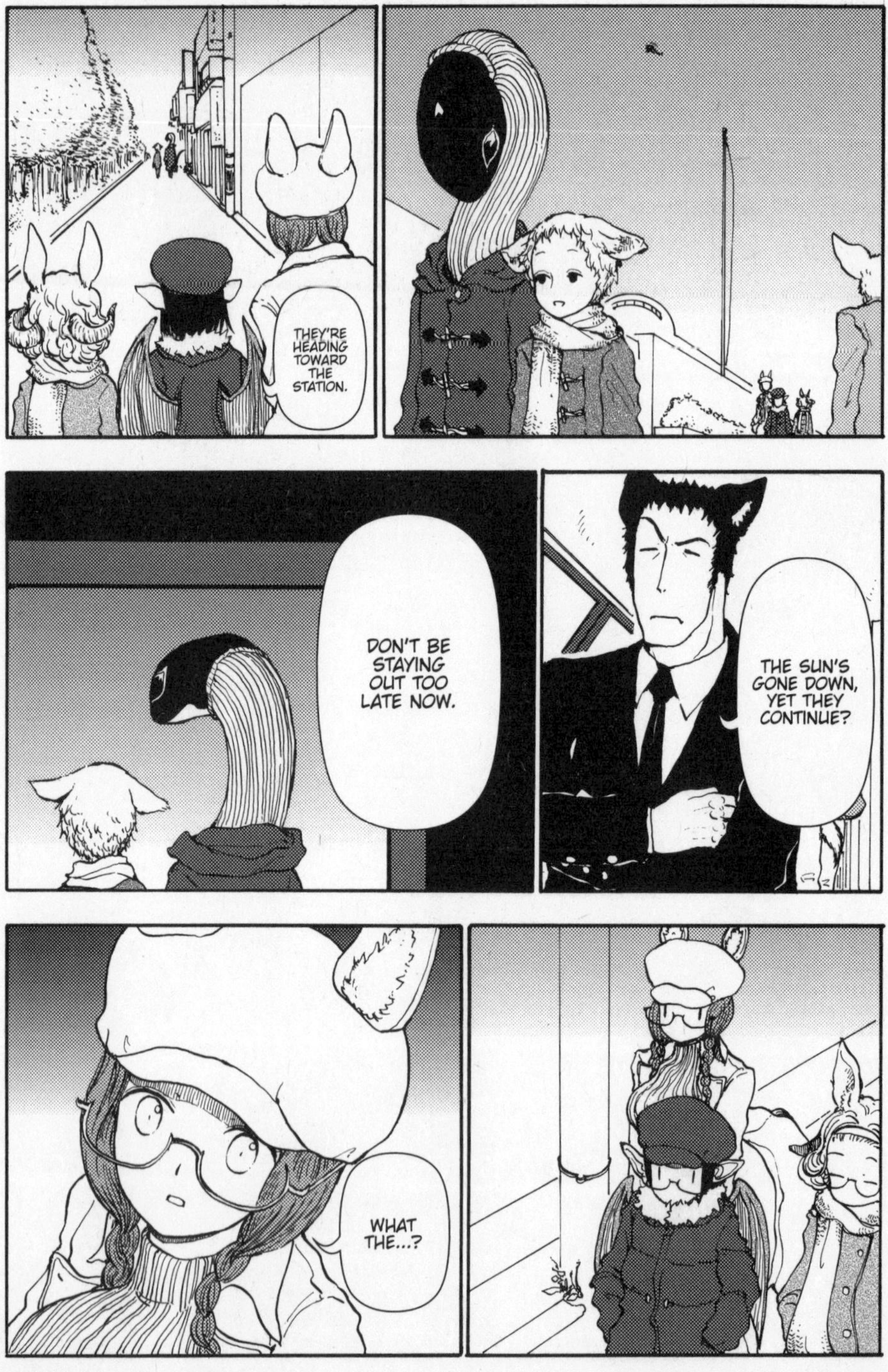
THEY'RE HEADING TOWARD THE STATION.
THE SUN'S GONE DOWN, YET THEY CONTINUE?
DON'T BE STAYING OUT TOO LATE NOW.
WHAT THE...?

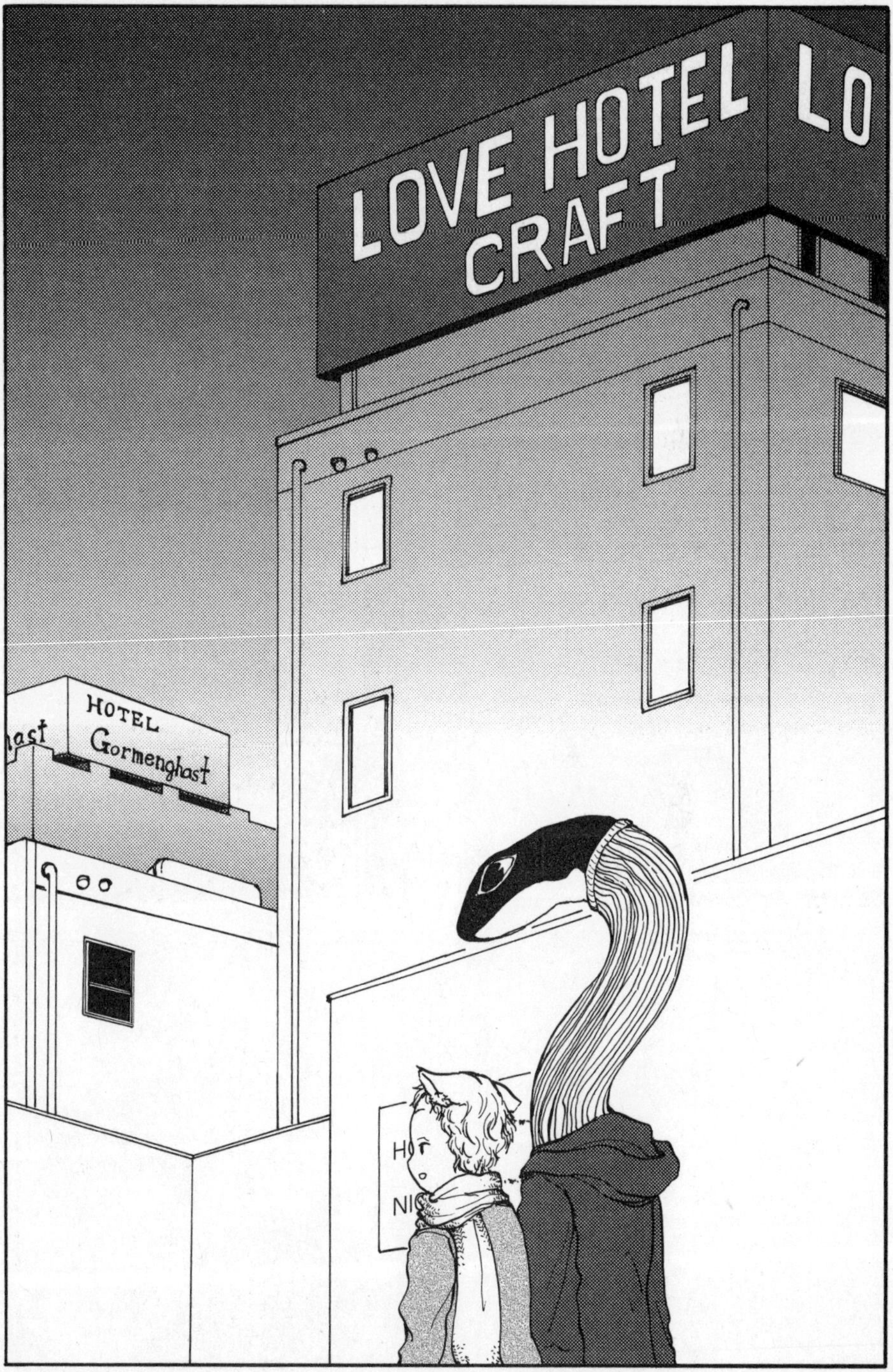
LOVE HOTEL
CRAFT
HOTEL
Gormenghast

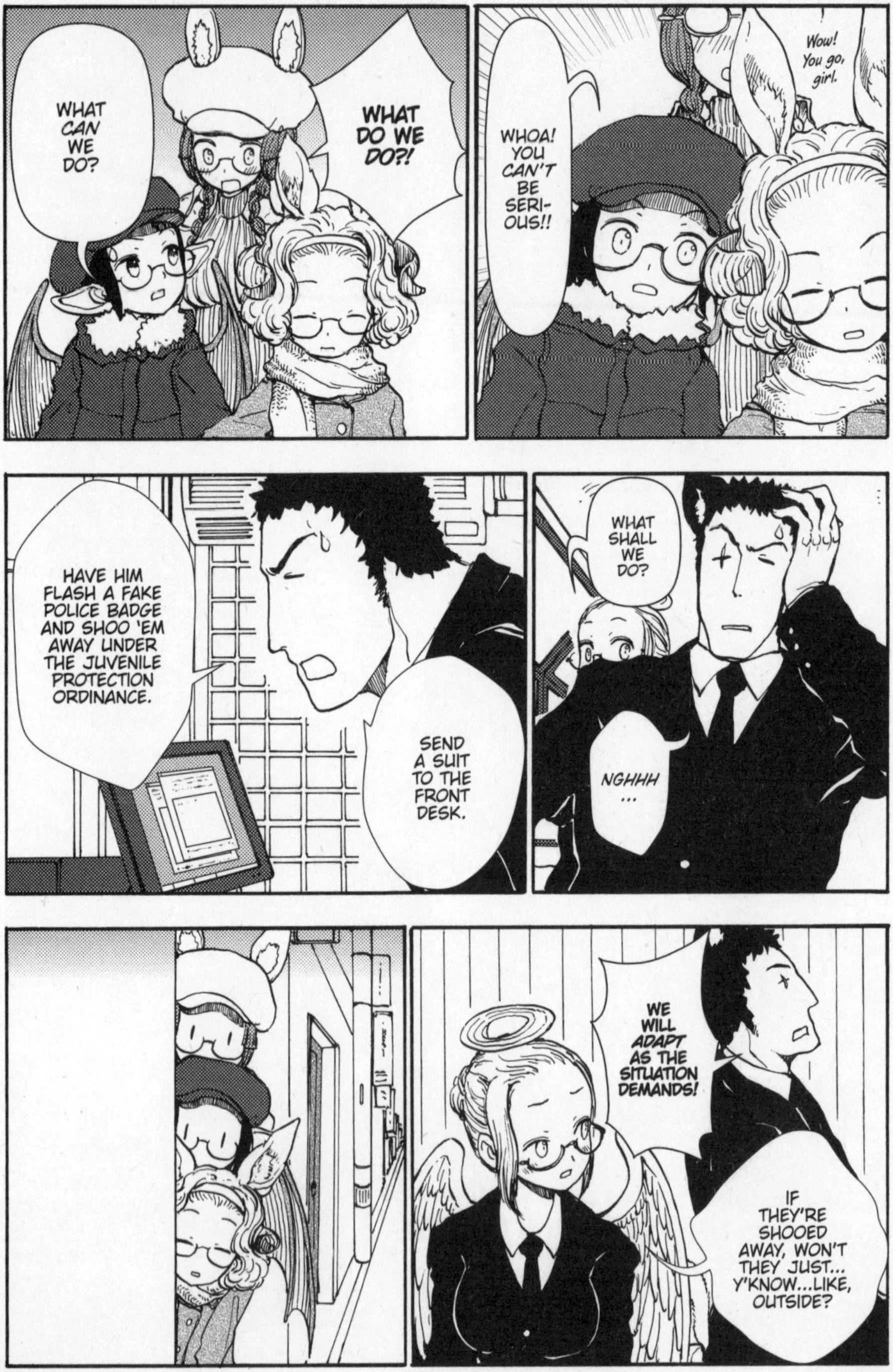
Wow! You go, girl.
WHOA! YOU CAN'T BE SERI-OUS!!
WHAT DO WE DO?!
WHAT CAN WE DO?
WHAT SHALL WE DO?
NGHHH ...
SEND A SUIT TO THE FRONT DESK.
HAVE HIM FLASH A FAKE POLICE BADGE AND SHOO 'EM AWAY UNDER THE JUVENILE PROTECTION ORDINANCE.
WE WILL ADAPT AS THE SITUATION DEMANDS!
IF THEY'RE SHOOED AWAY, WON'T THEY JUST... Y'KNOW...LIKE, OUTSIDE?

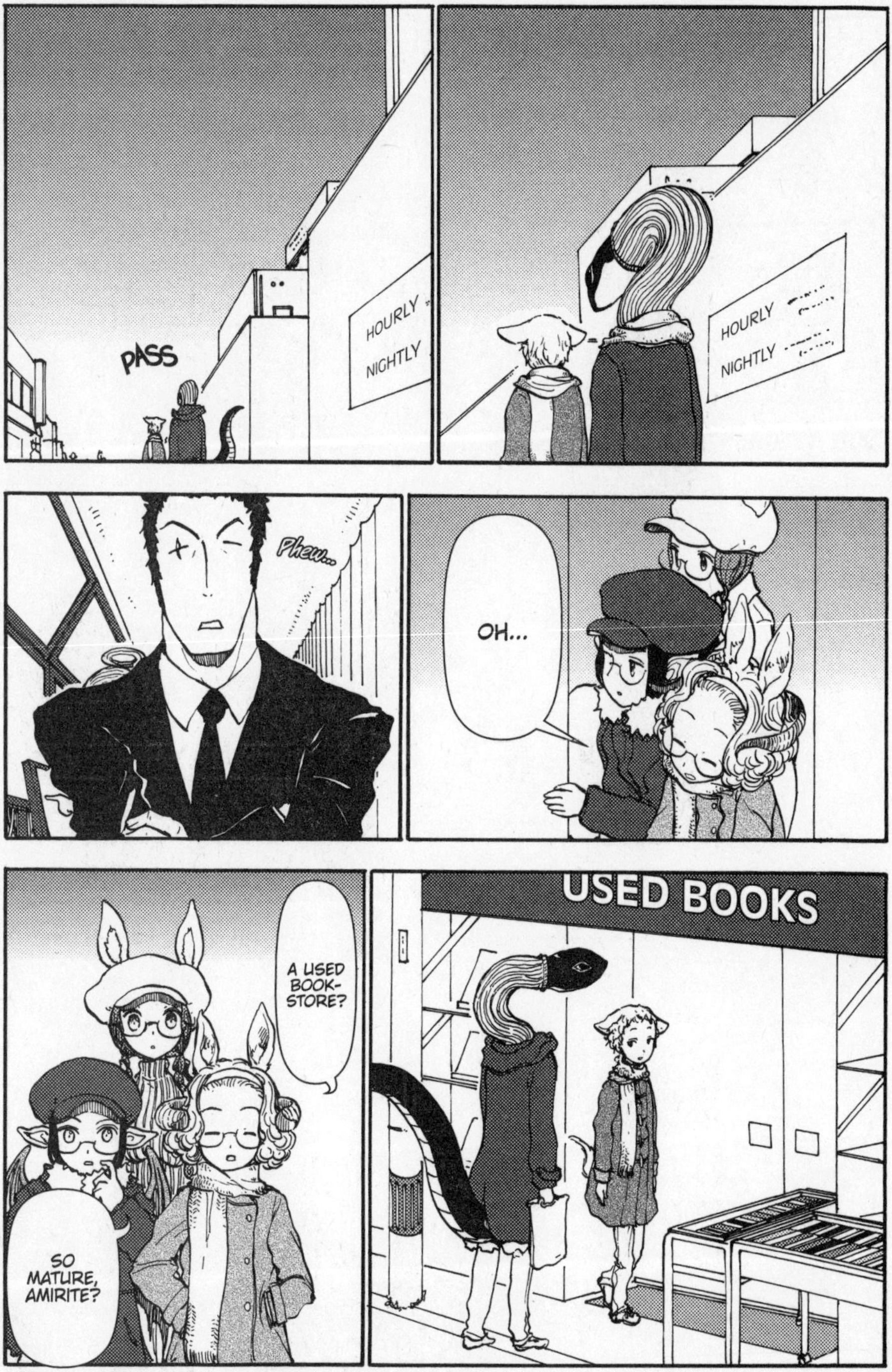
HOURLY
NIGHTLY
PASS
HOURLY
NIGHTLY
OH...
Phew...
USED BOOKS
A USED BOOK-STORE?
SO MATURE, AMIRITE?

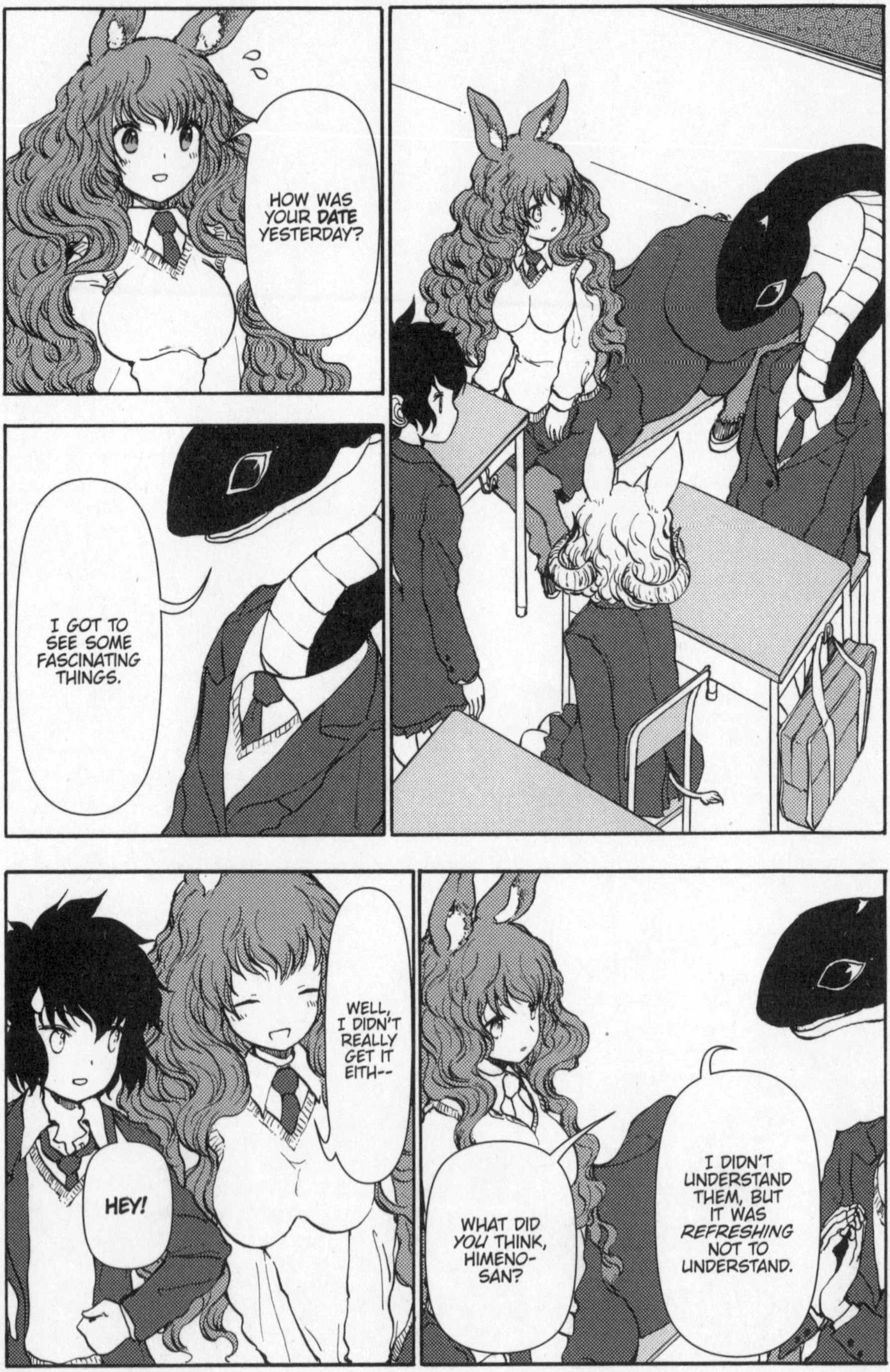
HOW WAS YOUR **DATE** YESTERDAY?
I GOT TO SEE SOME FASCINATING THINGS.
I DIDN'T UNDERSTAND THEM, BUT IT WAS *REFRESHING* NOT TO UNDERSTAND.
WHAT DID *YOU* THINK, HIMENO-SAN?
WELL, I DIDN'T REALLY GET IT EITH--
HEY!

A Centaur's Life

TRADITIONAL DRESS FROM AROUND THE WORLD (FRANCE)

AT THE LIBERATION FESTIVAL, CENTAURS DRESSED AS GUARDS OF THE FIRST FRENCH EMPIRE MARCH DOWN A LARGE STREET IN PARIS, BEGINNING AT WHAT WERE ONCE CENTAUR "STUD FARMS" AND ARRIVING AT THE FORMER BARRACKS. THE WESTERN CENTAURS, ONCE "BRED" AS SLAVES, HAVE NO HISTORY OF THEIR ANCIENT PAST. OLD TRACES OF CENTAURS BEAR NO CONNECTION TO THE CURRENT STATE, AND SERVE AS LITTLE MORE THAN ARCHAEOLOGICAL RELICS. THE HISTORY OF WESTERN CENTAURS AS *PEOPLE* BEGAN WITH THEIR EMANCIPATION FROM THE SHACKLES OF SLAVERY BY THAT HERO OF LEGEND, NAPOLEON. AND SO, TOO, BEGAN AN AGE OF GLORY. THE IMPERIAL ARMY, COMPOSED MAINLY OF LIBERATED CENTAURS, CONQUERED LANDS ACROSS EUROPE, AGGRESSIVELY WIELDING THEIR REPUTATION AS THE MIGHTIEST FORCE IN THE WORLD.

AFTER THE FALL OF THE FIRST EMPIRE CAME THE REVIVAL OF THE MONARCHY, WHICH DESPISED THE CENTAUR SOLDIERS, WHO WERE ALMOST INVARIABLY VEHEMENT BONAPARTISTS. THE MONARCHY WAS ULTIMATELY UNABLE TO STOP THE LIBERATION FESTIVAL, JUST AS THE FRENCH REPUBLIC THAT FOLLOWED WAS UNABLE TO STOP THE MARCH OF THE NAZIS WHO WOULD CAPTURE PARIS. ONE NEED LOOK NO FURTHER THAN THAT "MOST MISERABLE OF MONARCHS," KING LOUIS, TO SEE WHAT FATE AWAITED ANYONE WHO DARED TRY.

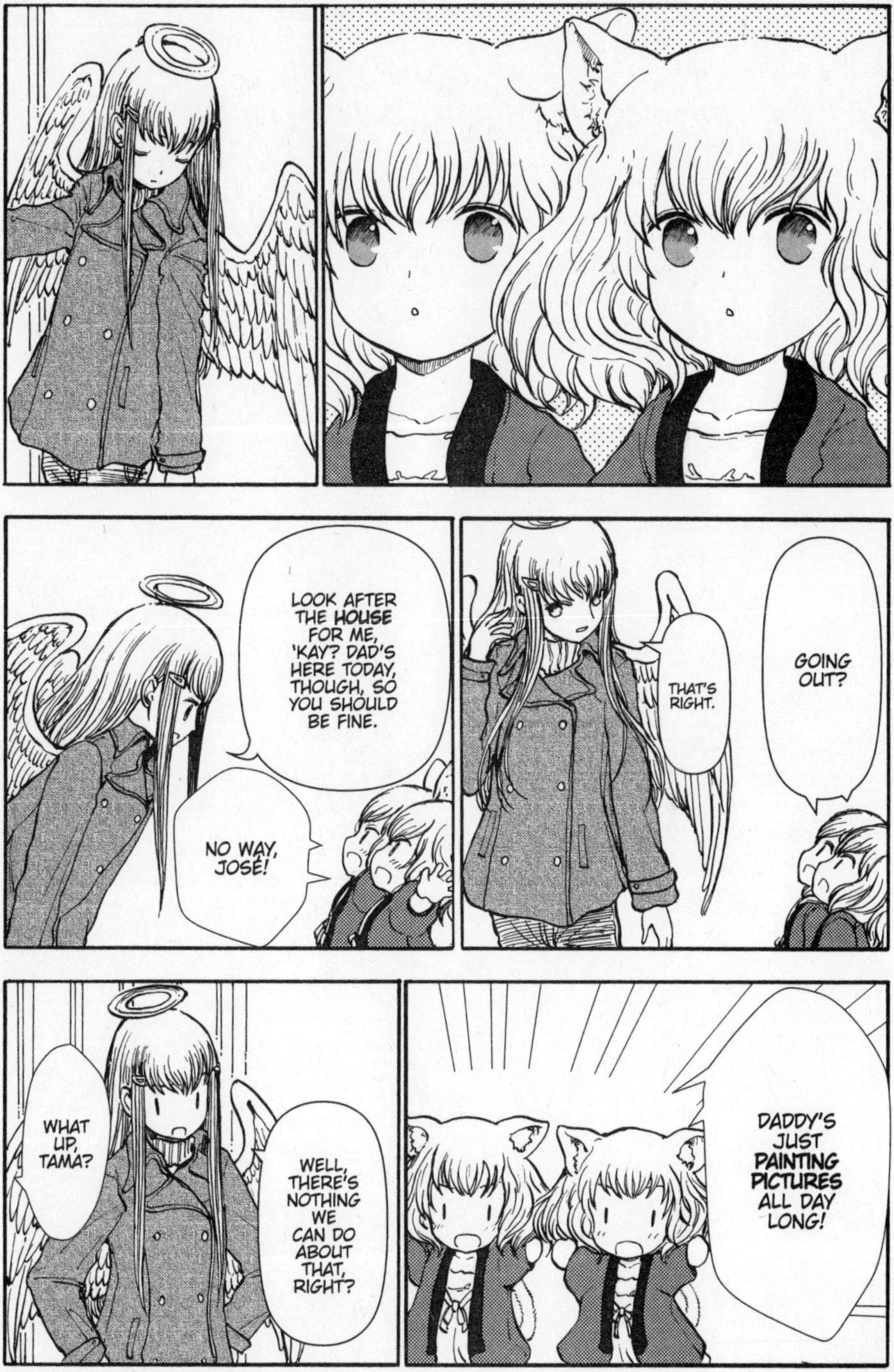
GOING OUT?
THAT'S RIGHT.
LOOK AFTER THE HOUSE FOR ME, 'KAY? DAD'S HERE TODAY, THOUGH, SO YOU SHOULD BE FINE.
NO WAY, JOSÉ!
DADDY'S JUST PAINTING PICTURES ALL DAY LONG!
WELL, THERE'S NOTHING WE CAN DO ABOUT THAT, RIGHT?
WHAT UP, TAMA?

CHAPTER 46

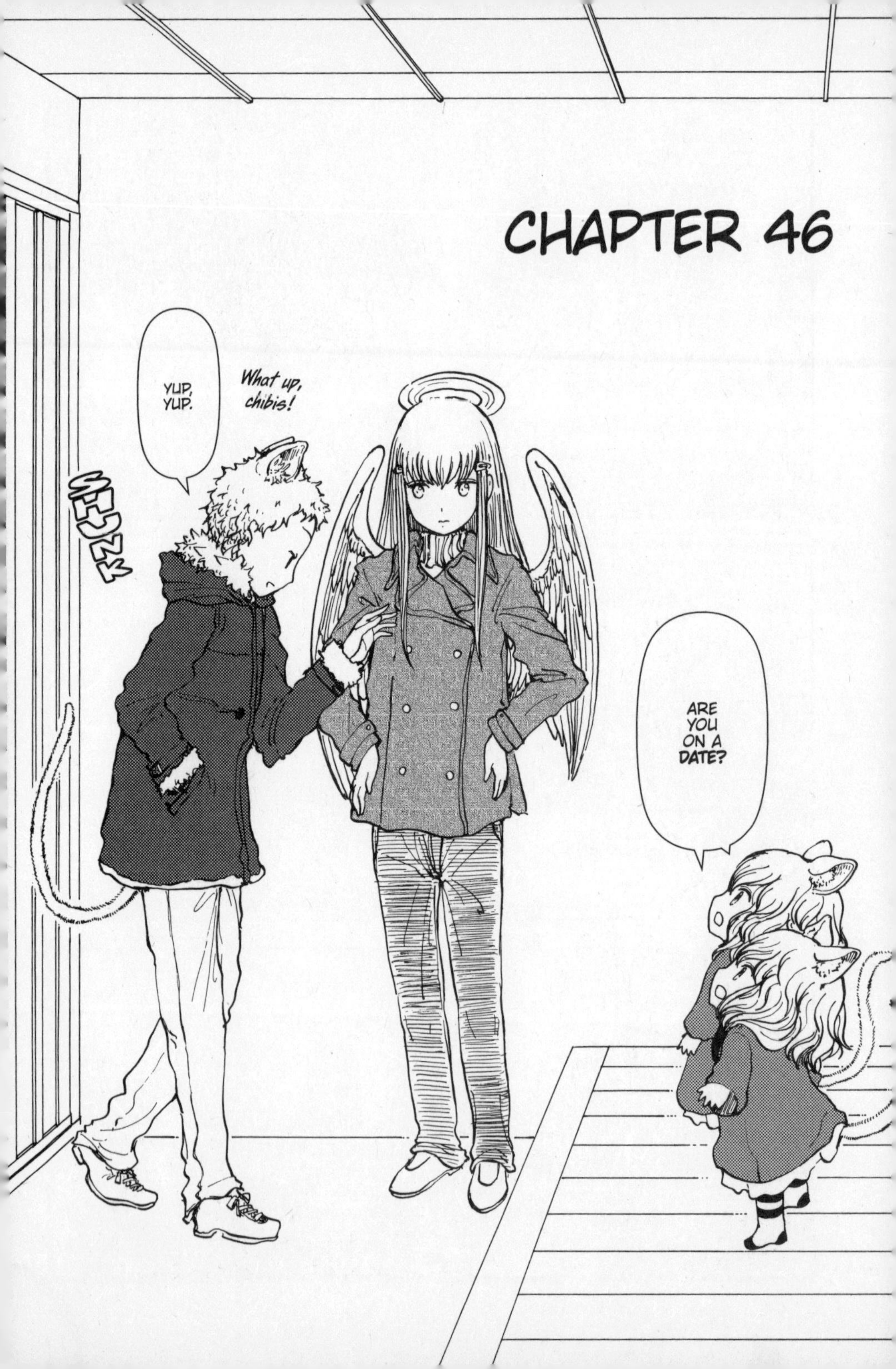
ARE YOU ON A DATE?
What up, chibis!
YUP, YUP.
SHUNK

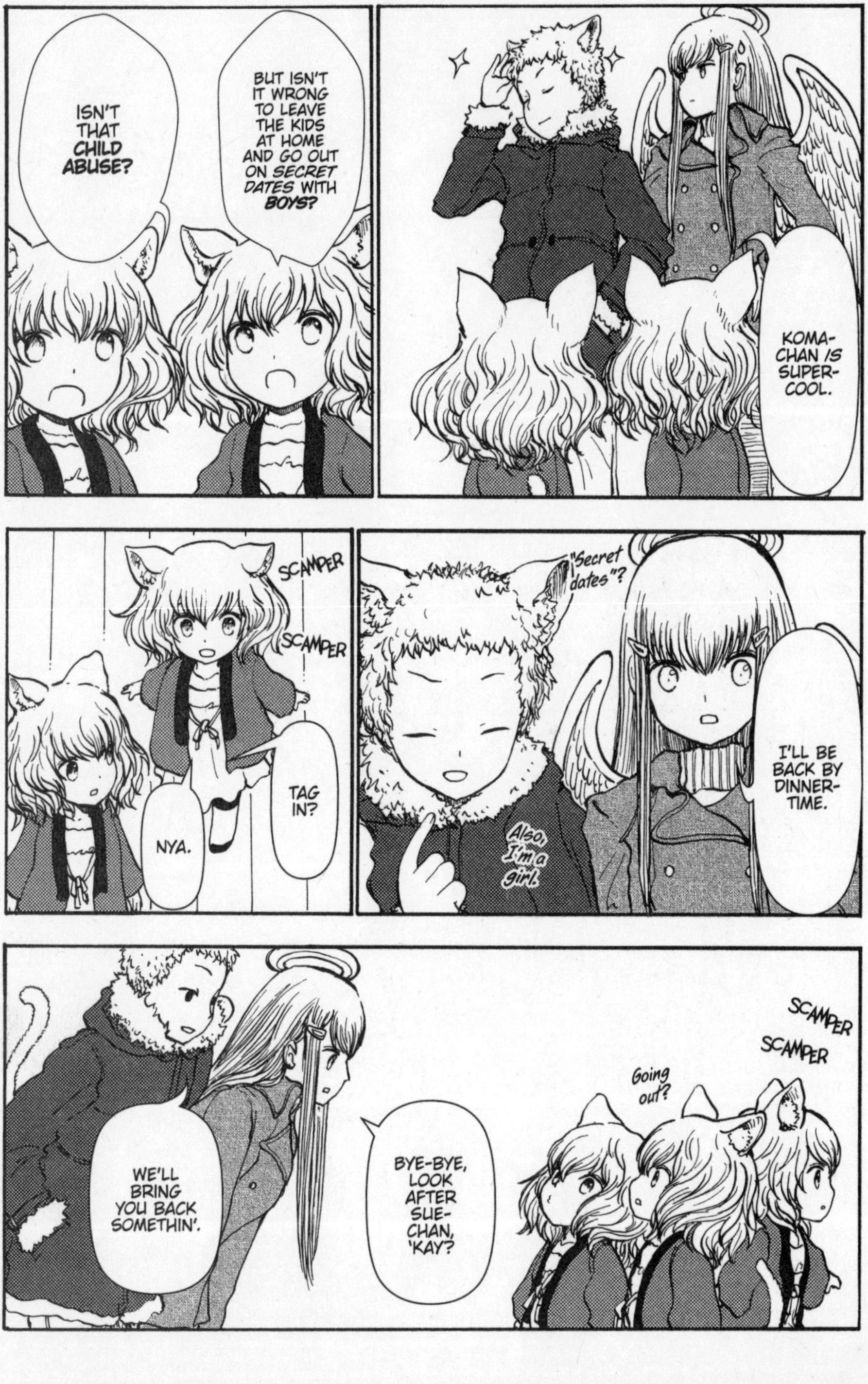
KOMA-CHAN IS SUPER-COOL.
BUT ISN'T IT WRONG TO LEAVE THE KIDS AT HOME AND GO OUT ON SECRET DATES WITH BOYS?
ISN'T THAT CHILD ABUSE?
I'LL BE BACK BY DINNER-TIME.
"Secret dates"?
Also, I'm a girl.
SCAMPER
SCAMPER
TAG IN?
NYA.
SCAMPER
SCAMPER
Going out?
BYE-BYE, LOOK AFTER SUE-CHAN, 'KAY?
WE'LL BRING YOU BACK SOMETHIN'.

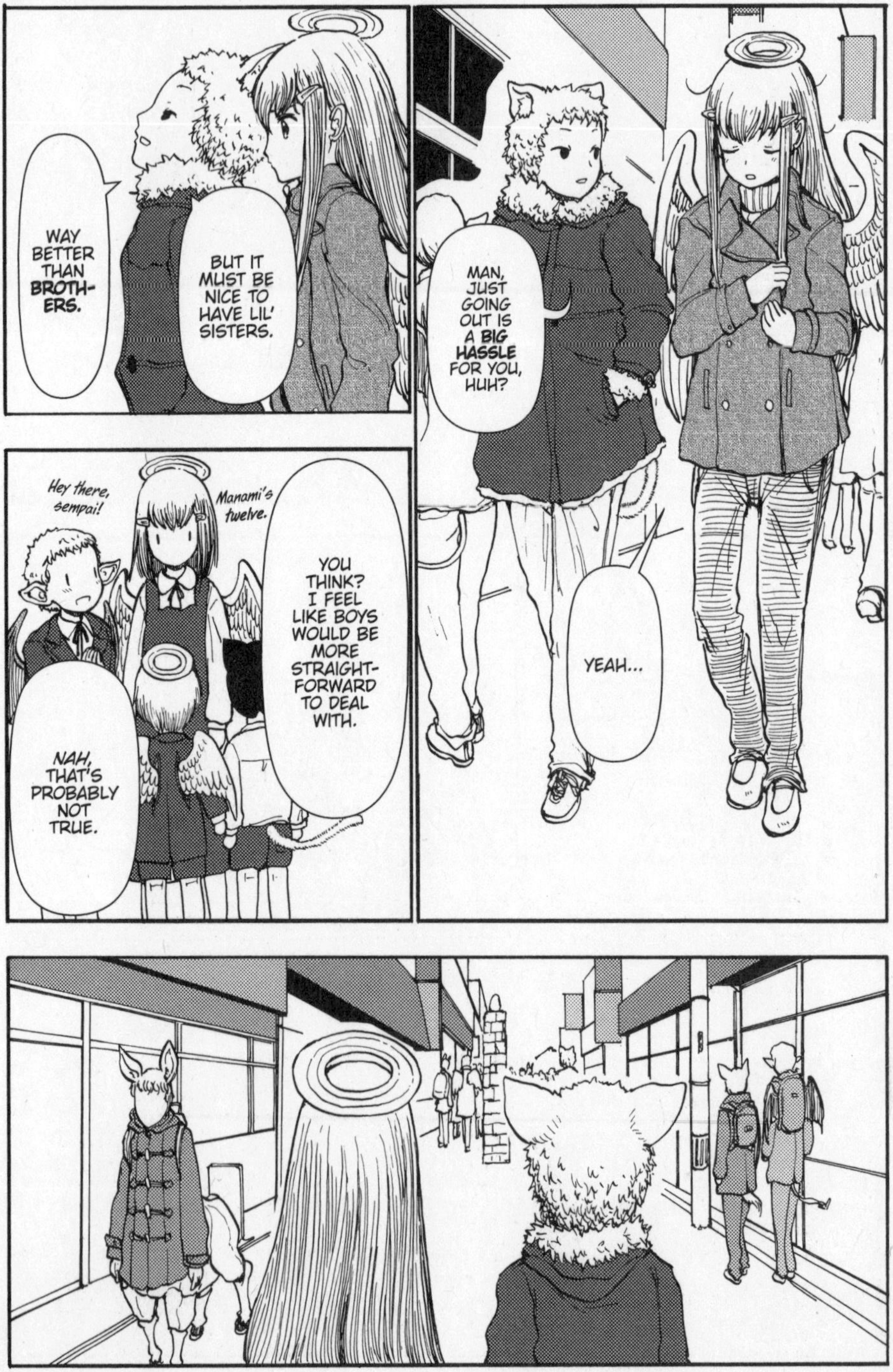
MAN, JUST GOING OUT IS A **BIG HASSLE** FOR YOU, HUH?
YEAH...
BUT IT MUST BE NICE TO HAVE LIL' SISTERS.
WAY BETTER THAN **BROTHERS.**
Manami's twelve.
YOU THINK? I FEEL LIKE BOYS WOULD BE MORE STRAIGHTFORWARD TO DEAL WITH.
Hey there, sempai!
NAH, THAT'S PROBABLY NOT TRUE.

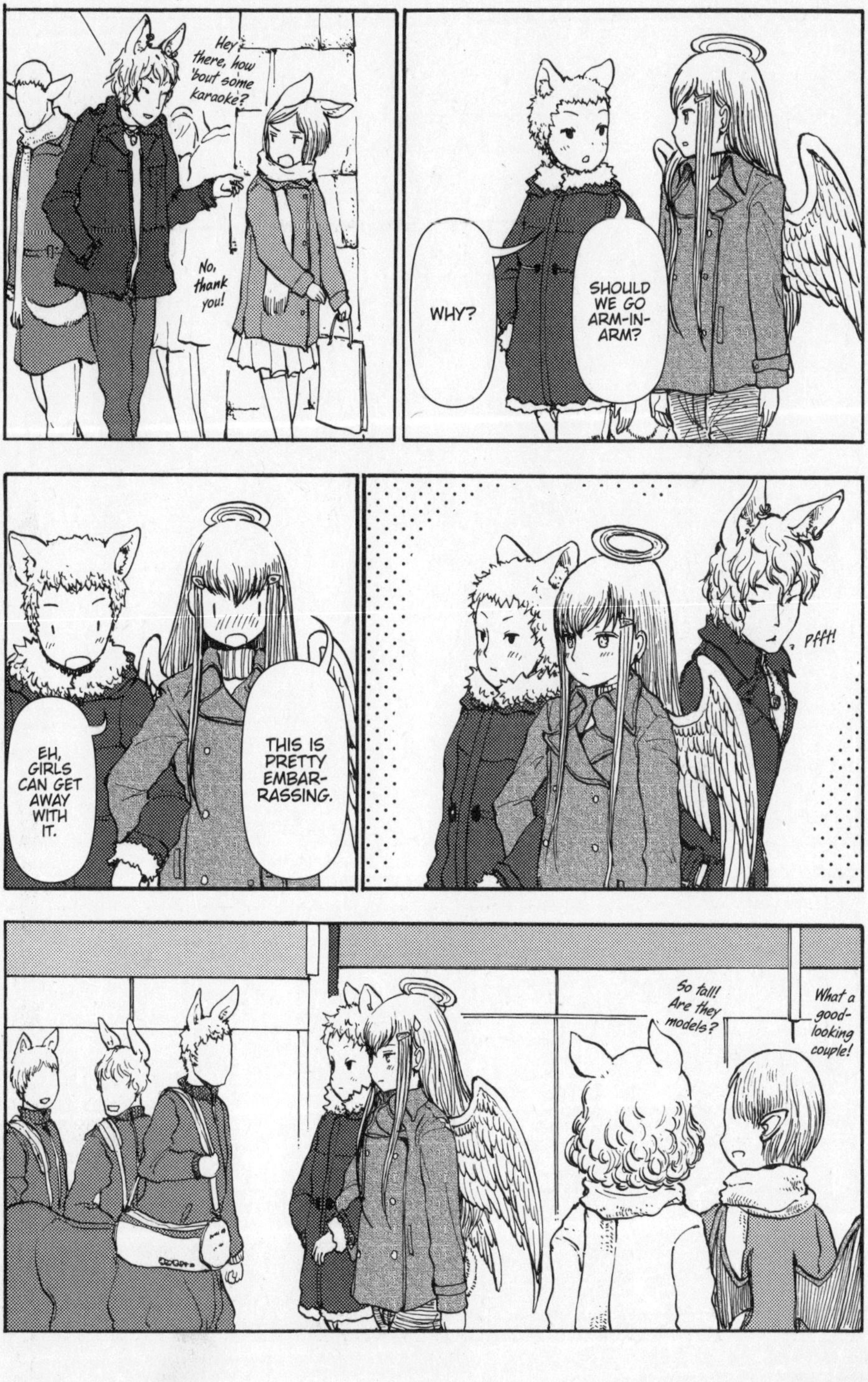
SHOULD WE GO ARM-IN-ARM?
WHY?
Hey there, how 'bout some karaoke?
No, thank you!
Pfft!
THIS IS PRETTY EMBARRASSING.
EH, GIRLS CAN GET AWAY WITH IT.
What a good-looking couple!
So tall! Are they models?

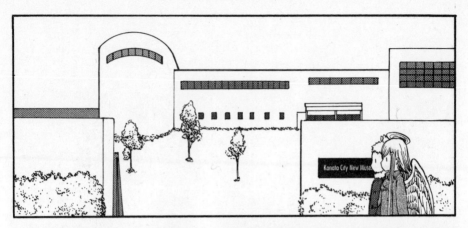

Kanata City New Muse

Children
Adults
Students
Military
Senior

WITH STUFF LIKE THIS, YOU SPEND MORE TIME READING **THE ANALYSIS** THAN LOOKING AT THE ACTUAL PIECE.

OTHERWISE YOU WON'T *UNDERSTAND* THEM.

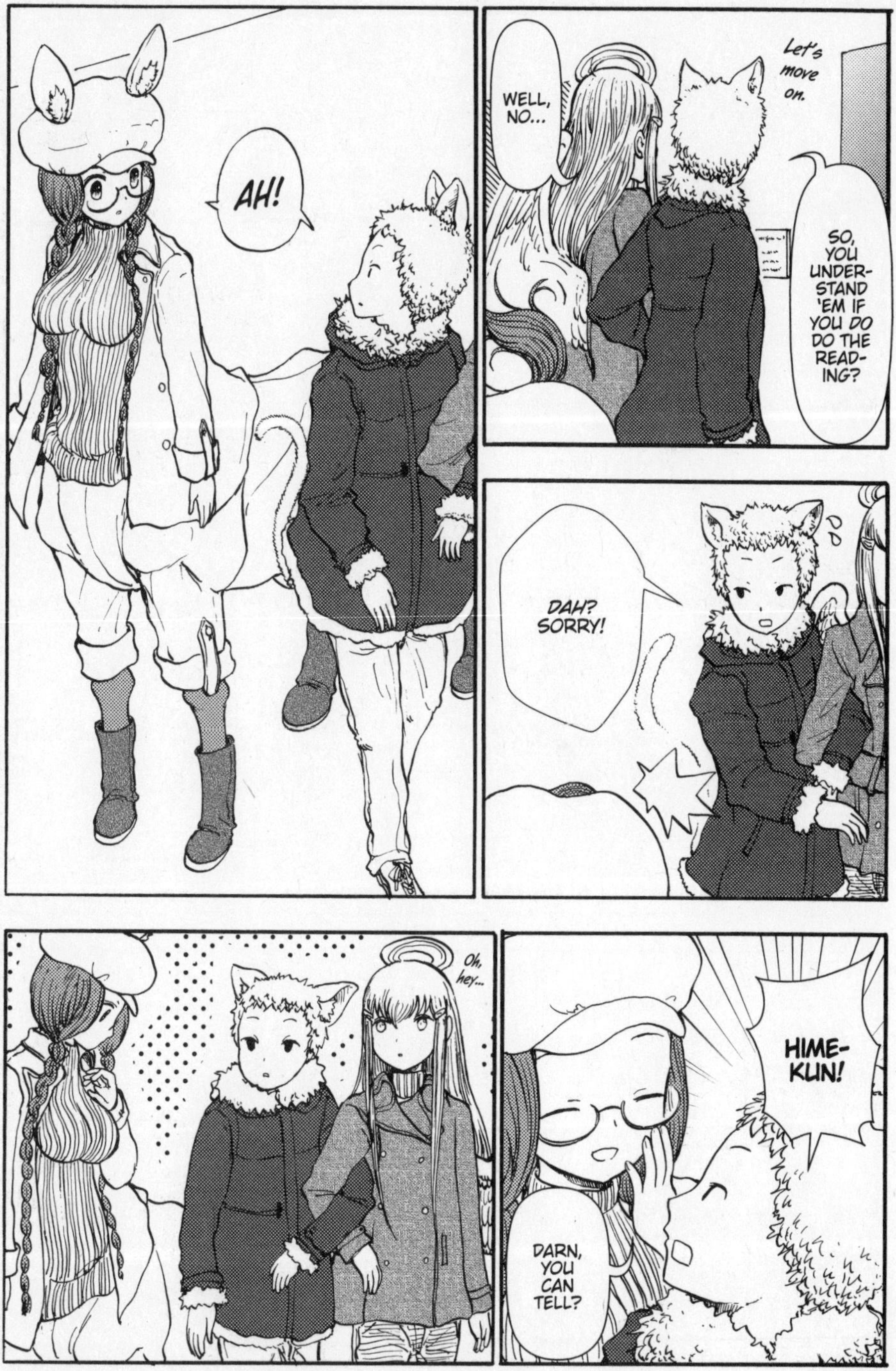
SO, YOU UNDER-STAND 'EM IF YOU DO DO THE READ-ING?
WELL, NO...
Let's move on.
DAH? SORRY!
AH!
HIME-KUN!
DARN, YOU CAN TELL?
Oh, hey...

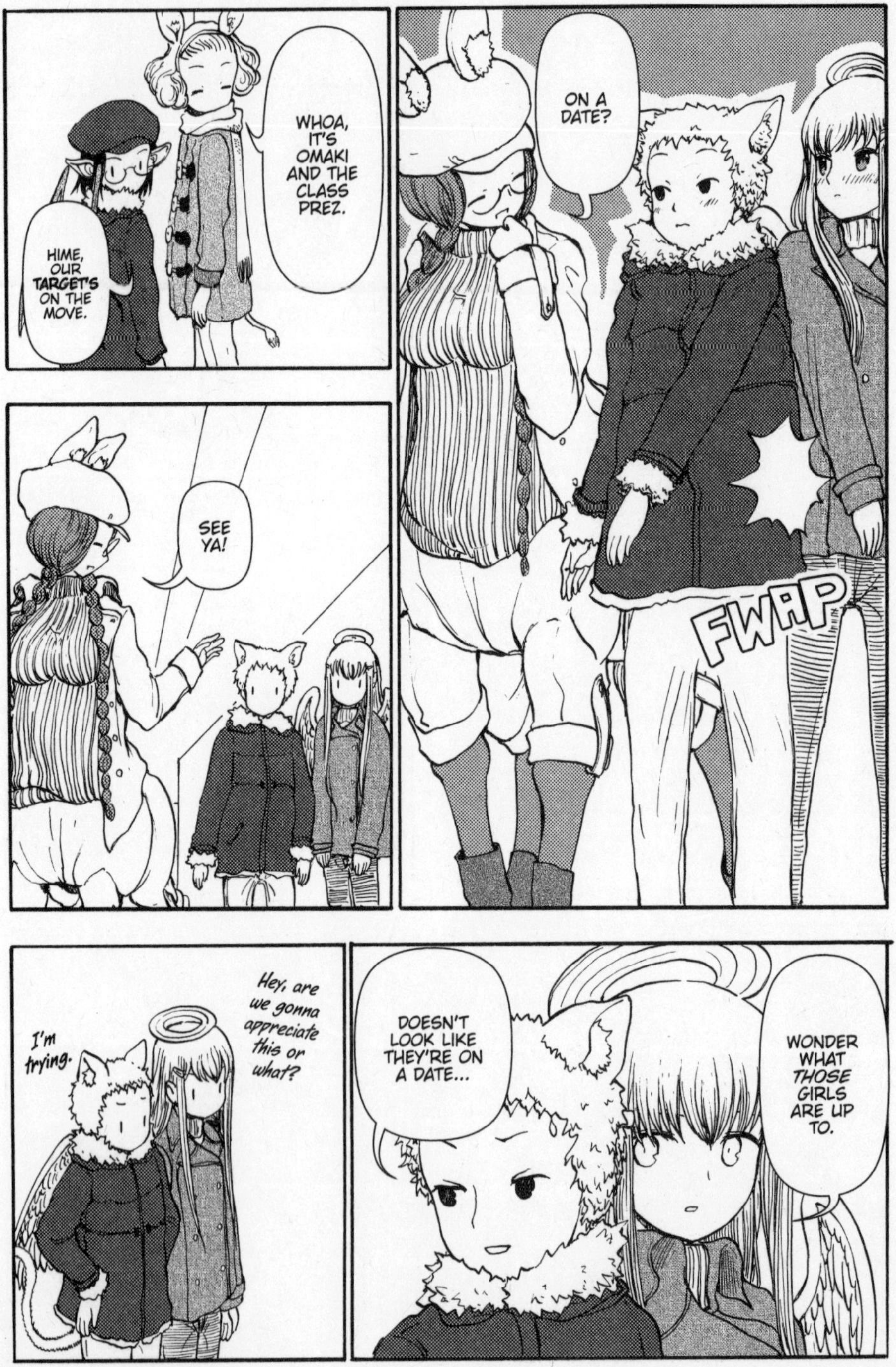
ON A DATE?
FWAP
WHOA, IT'S OMAKI AND THE CLASS PREZ.
HIME, OUR TARGET'S ON THE MOVE.
SEE YA!
WONDER WHAT THOSE GIRLS ARE UP TO.
DOESN'T LOOK LIKE THEY'RE ON A DATE...
Hey, are we gonna appreciate this or what?
I'm trying.

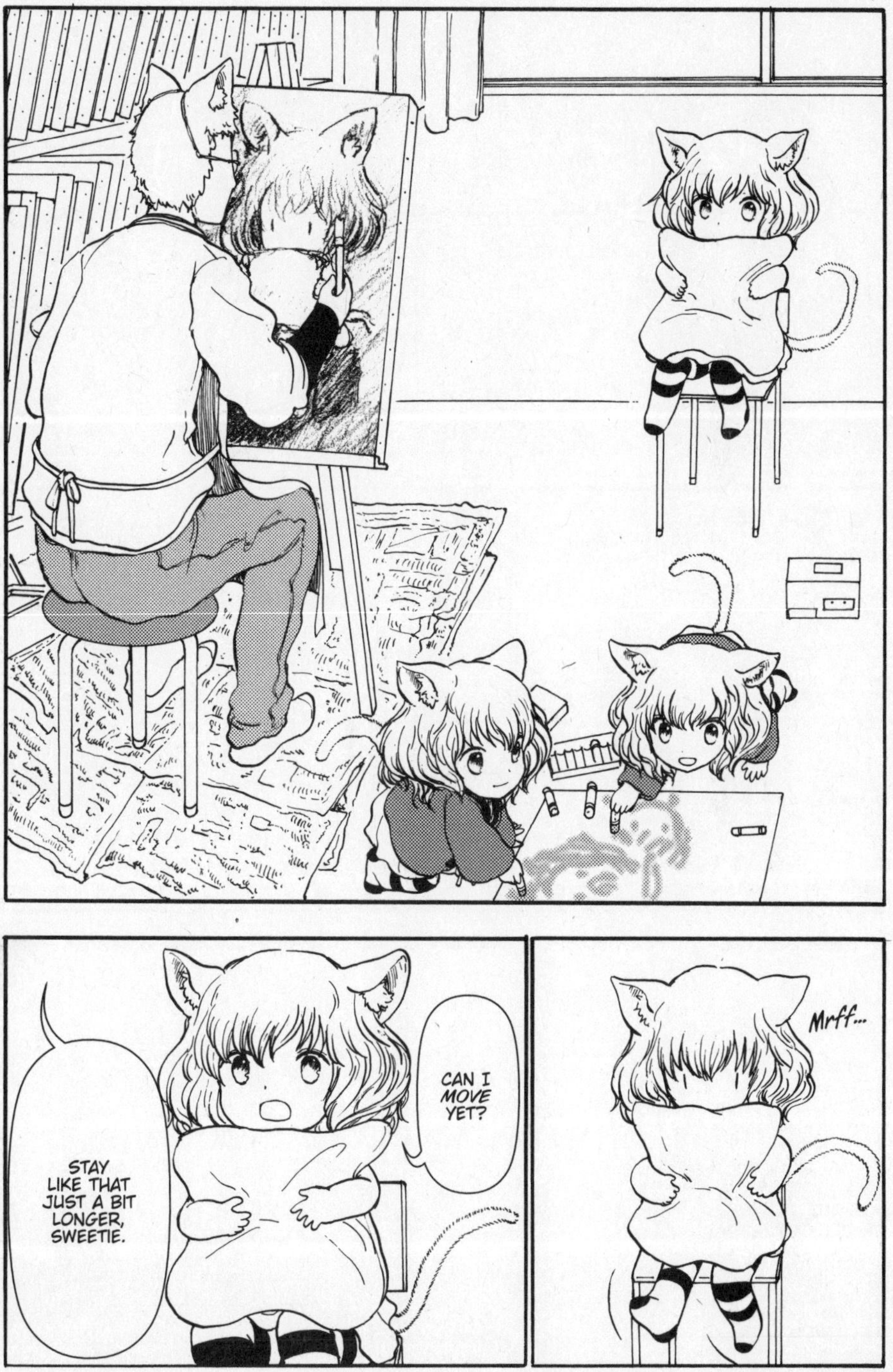
Mrff...
CAN I MOVE YET?
STAY LIKE THAT JUST A BIT LONGER, SWEETIE.

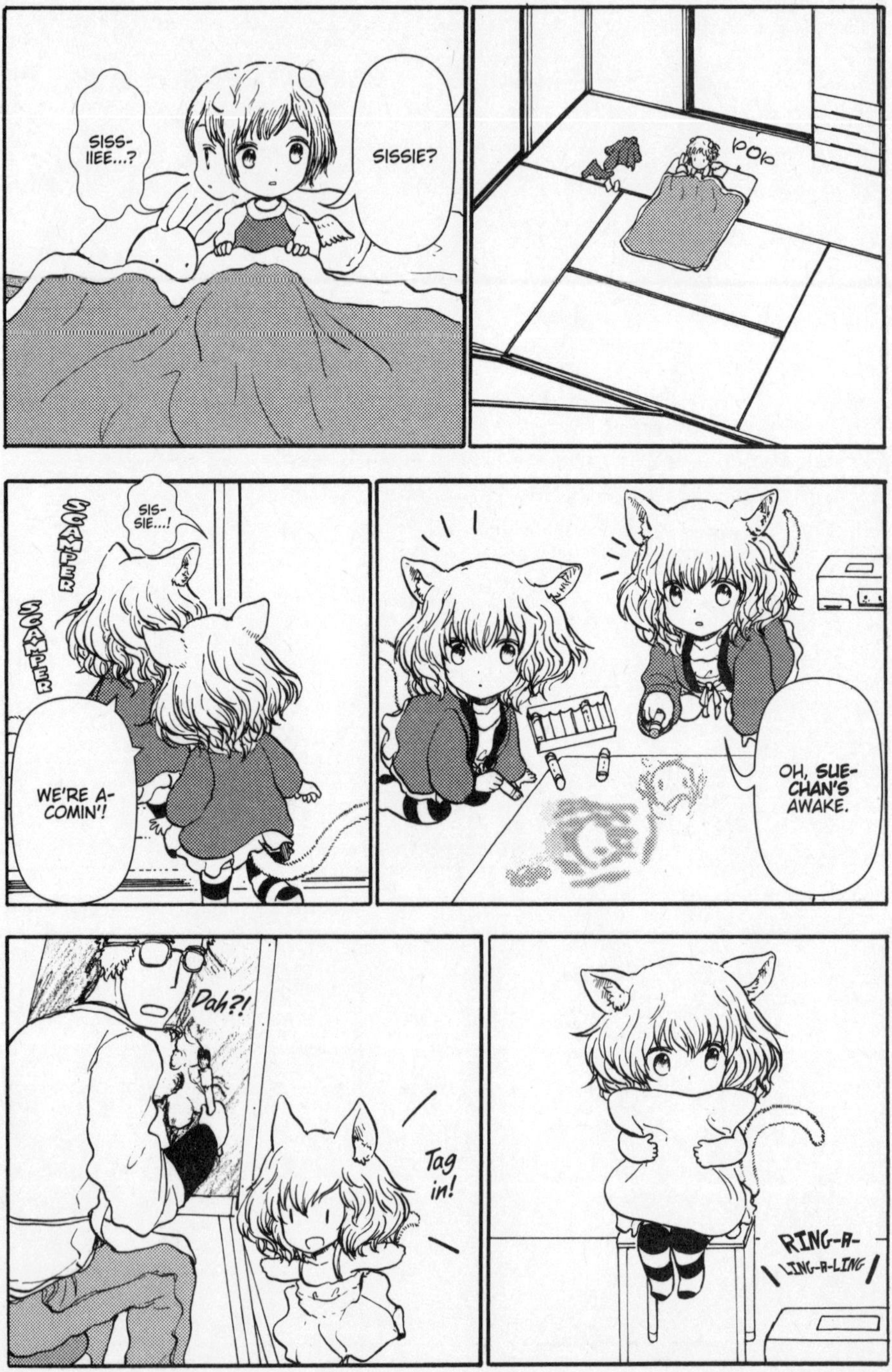
POP
SISSIE?
SISS-IIEE...?
OH, SUE-CHAN'S AWAKE.
SIS-SIE...!
SCAMPER SCAMPER
WE'RE A-COMIN'!
RING-A-LING-A-LING
Dah?!
Tag in!

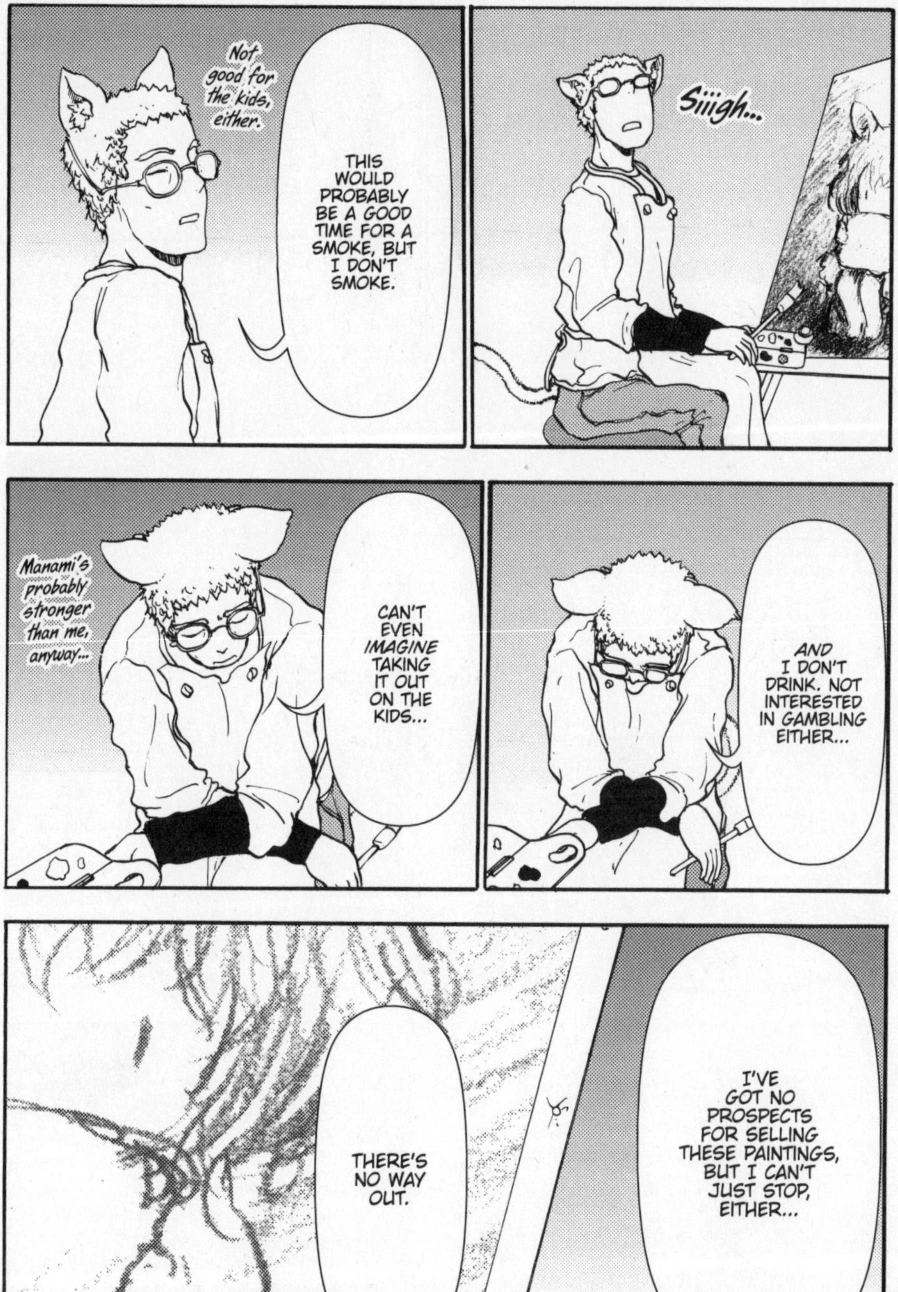
Siiigh...
THIS WOULD PROBABLY BE A GOOD TIME FOR A SMOKE, BUT I DON'T SMOKE.
Not good for the kids, either.
AND I DON'T DRINK. NOT INTERESTED IN GAMBLING EITHER...
CAN'T EVEN *IMAGINE* TAKING IT OUT ON THE KIDS...
Manami's probably stronger than me, anyway...
I'VE GOT NO PROSPECTS FOR SELLING THESE PAINTINGS, BUT I CAN'T JUST STOP, EITHER...
THERE'S NO WAY OUT.

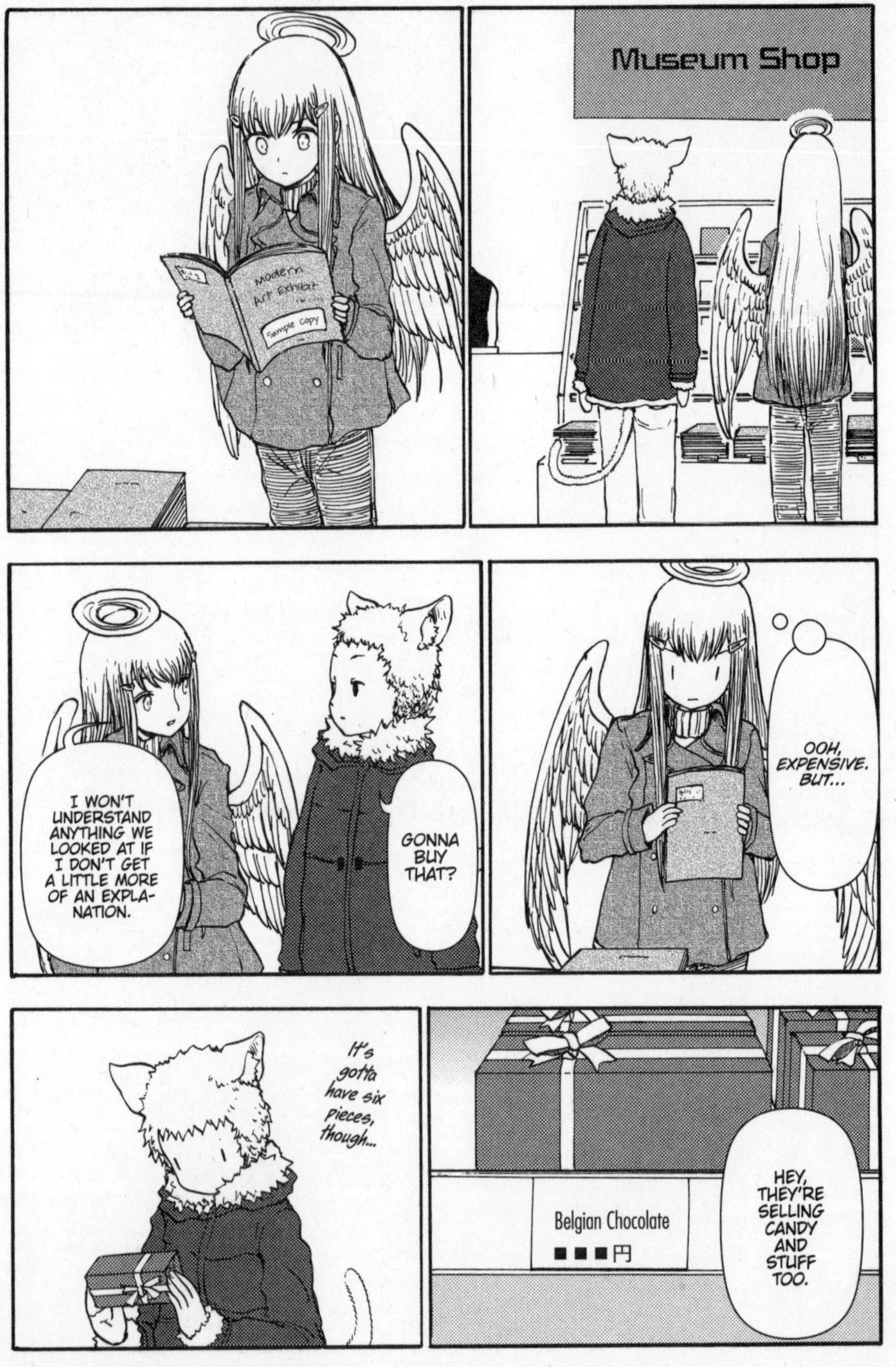
Museum Shop
Modern Art Exhibit
Sample copy
OOH, EXPENSIVE. BUT...
GONNA BUY THAT?
I WON'T UNDERSTAND ANYTHING WE LOOKED AT IF I DON'T GET A LITTLE MORE OF AN EXPLANATION.
Belgian Chocolate
■■■円
HEY, THEY'RE SELLING CANDY AND STUFF TOO.
It's gotta have six pieces, though...

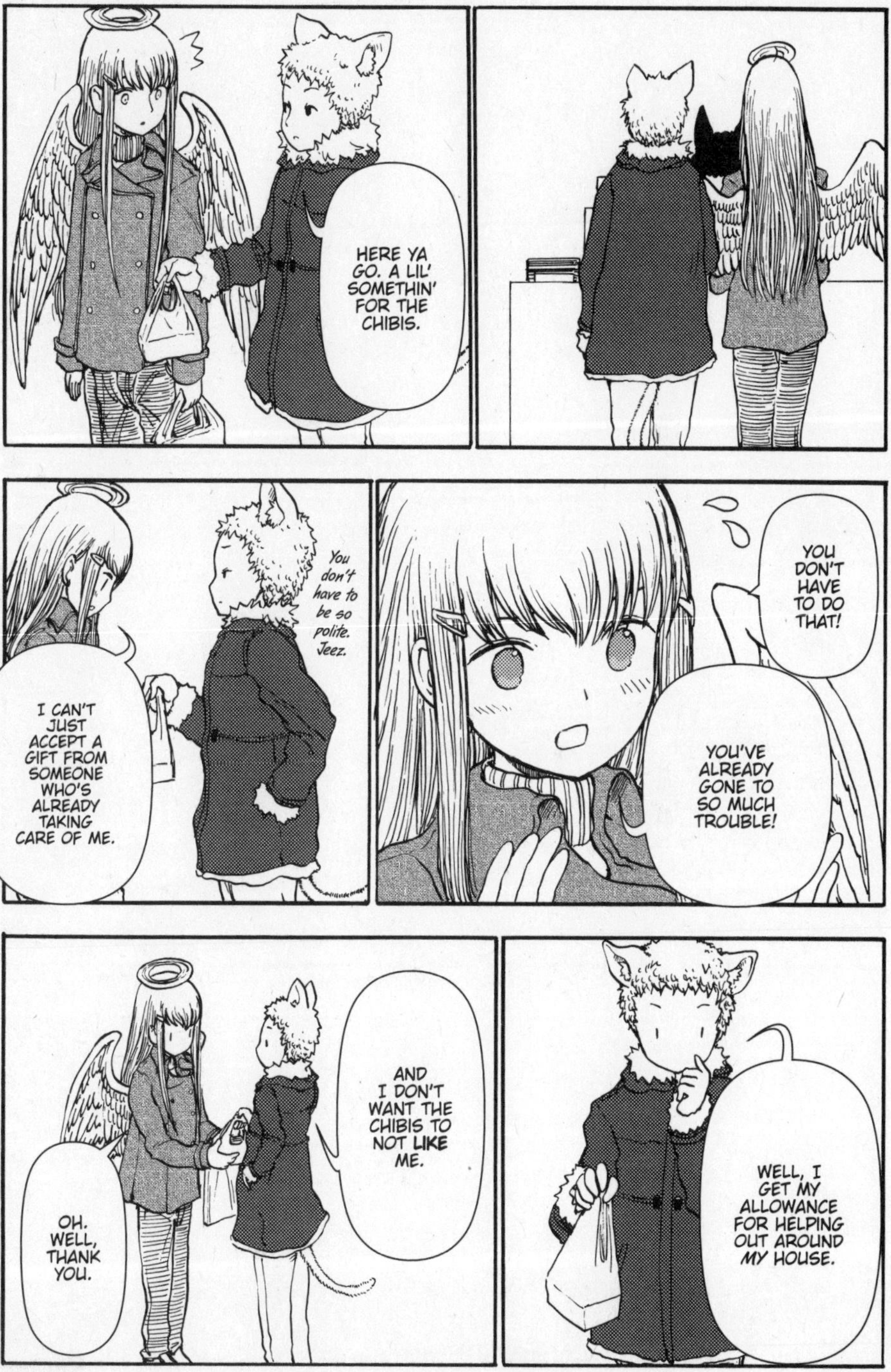
HERE YA GO. A LIL' SOMETHIN' FOR THE CHIBIS.
YOU DON'T HAVE TO DO THAT!
YOU'VE ALREADY GONE TO SO MUCH TROUBLE!
You don't have to be so polite. Jeez.
I CAN'T JUST ACCEPT A GIFT FROM SOMEONE WHO'S ALREADY TAKING CARE OF ME.
WELL, I GET MY ALLOWANCE FOR HELPING OUT AROUND MY HOUSE.
AND I DON'T WANT THE CHIBIS TO NOT LIKE ME.
OH. WELL, THANK YOU.

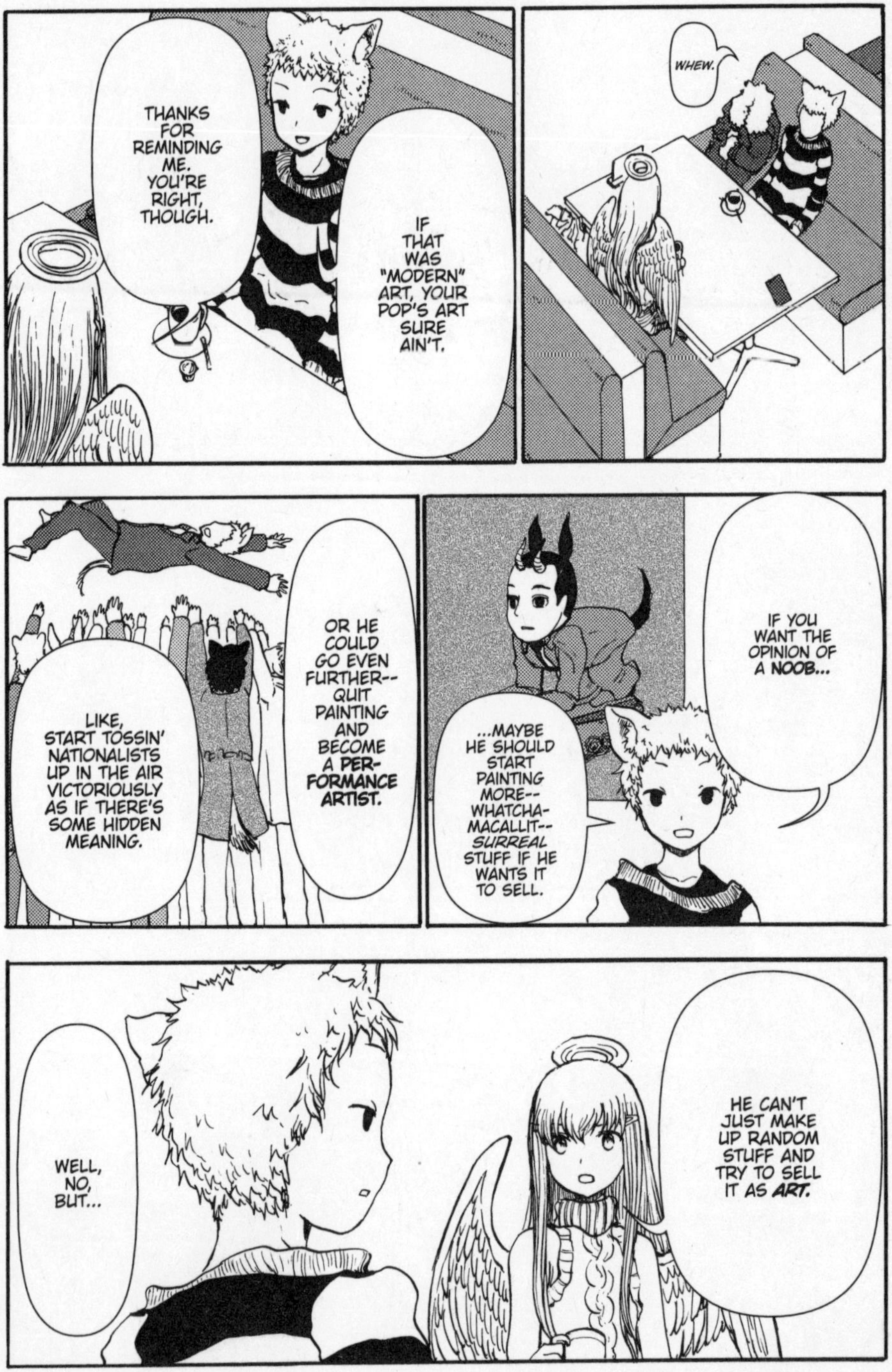
WHEW.
IF THAT WAS "MODERN" ART, YOUR POP'S ART SURE AIN'T.
THANKS FOR REMINDING ME. YOU'RE RIGHT, THOUGH.
IF YOU WANT THE OPINION OF A NOOB...
...MAYBE HE SHOULD START PAINTING MORE--WHATCHAMACALLIT--SURREAL STUFF IF HE WANTS IT TO SELL.
OR HE COULD GO EVEN FURTHER--QUIT PAINTING AND BECOME A PERFORMANCE ARTIST.
LIKE, START TOSSIN' NATIONALISTS UP IN THE AIR VICTORIOUSLY AS IF THERE'S SOME HIDDEN MEANING.
HE CAN'T JUST MAKE UP RANDOM STUFF AND TRY TO SELL IT AS ART.
WELL, NO, BUT...

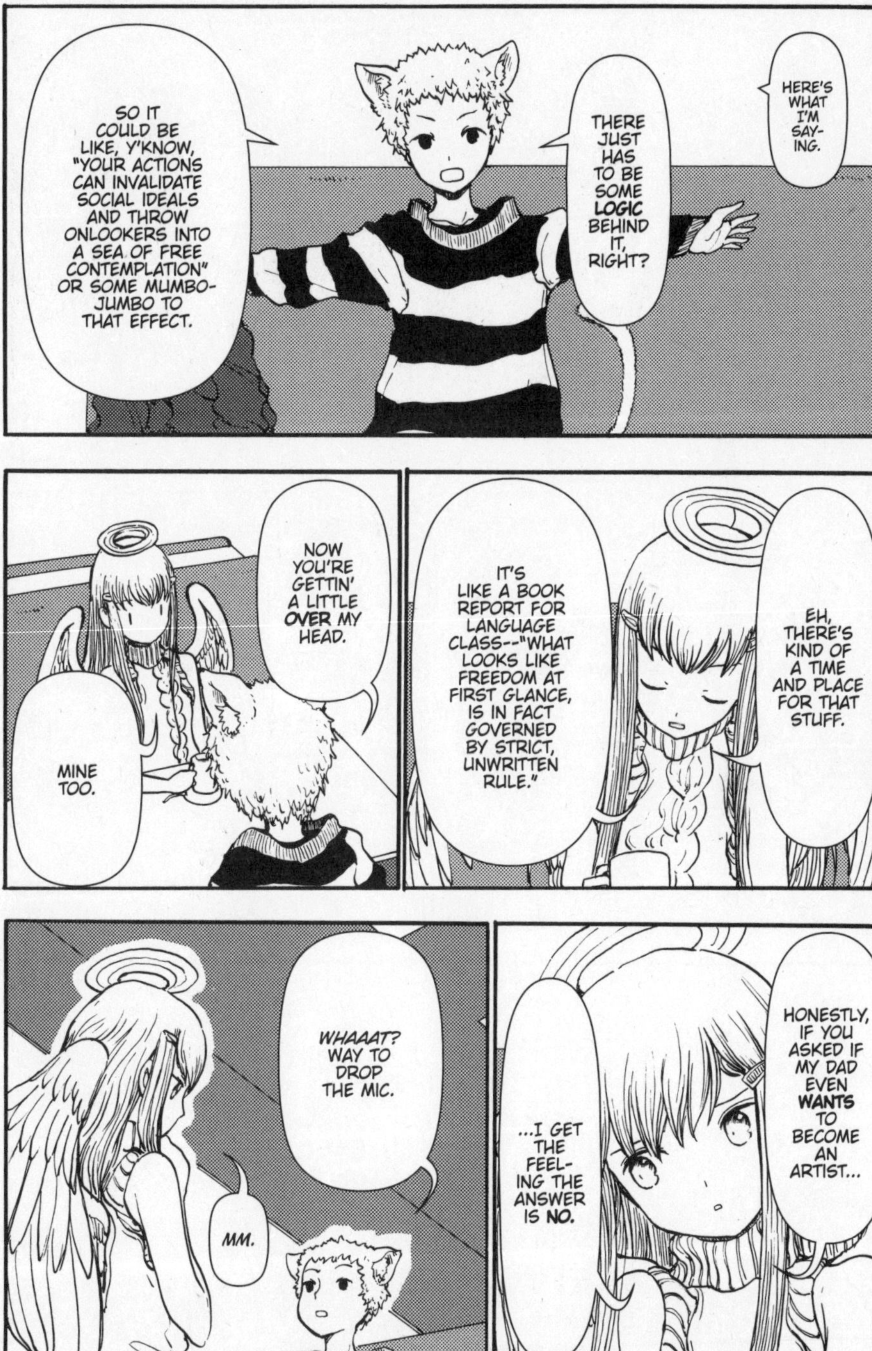
HERE'S WHAT I'M SAY-ING.
THERE JUST HAS TO BE SOME **LOGIC** BEHIND IT, RIGHT?
SO IT COULD BE LIKE, Y'KNOW, "YOUR ACTIONS CAN INVALIDATE SOCIAL IDEALS AND THROW ONLOOKERS INTO A SEA OF FREE CONTEMPLATION" OR SOME MUMBO-JUMBO TO THAT EFFECT.
EH, THERE'S KIND OF A TIME AND PLACE FOR THAT STUFF.
IT'S LIKE A BOOK REPORT FOR LANGUAGE CLASS--"WHAT LOOKS LIKE FREEDOM AT FIRST GLANCE, IS IN FACT GOVERNED BY STRICT, UNWRITTEN RULE."
NOW YOU'RE GETTIN' A LITTLE **OVER** MY HEAD.
MINE TOO.
HONESTLY, IF YOU ASKED IF MY DAD EVEN **WANTS** TO BECOME AN ARTIST...
...I GET THE FEEL-ING THE ANSWER IS **NO**.
WHAAAT? WAY TO DROP THE MIC.
MM.

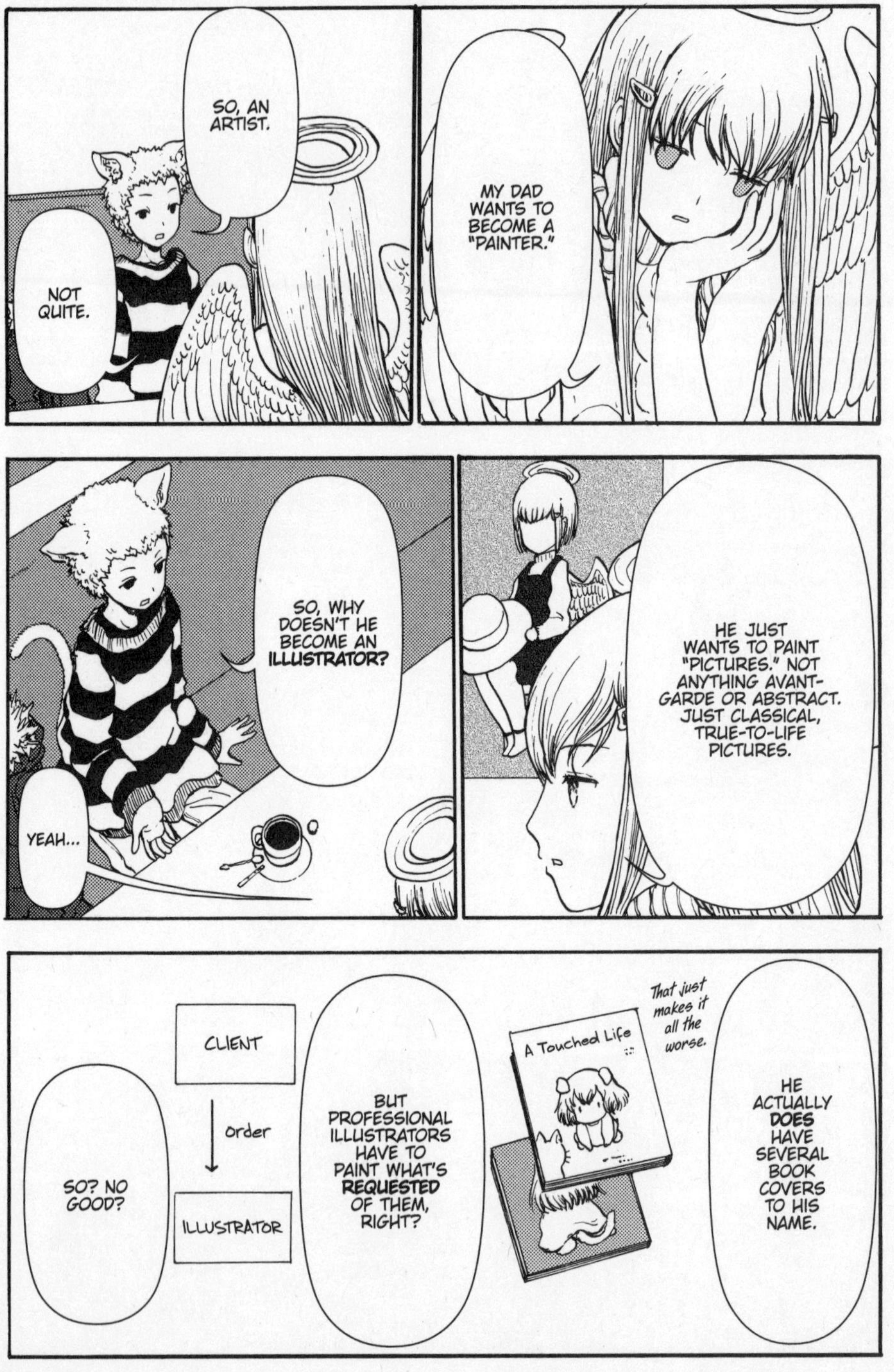

MY DAD WANTS TO BECOME A "PAINTER."
SO, AN ARTIST.
NOT QUITE.
HE JUST WANTS TO PAINT "PICTURES." NOT ANYTHING AVANT-GARDE OR ABSTRACT. JUST CLASSICAL, TRUE-TO-LIFE PICTURES.
SO, WHY DOESN'T HE BECOME AN **ILLUSTRATOR?**
YEAH...
HE ACTUALLY **DOES** HAVE SEVERAL BOOK COVERS TO HIS NAME.
That just makes it all the worse.
A Touched Life
BUT PROFESSIONAL ILLUSTRATORS HAVE TO PAINT WHAT'S **REQUESTED** OF THEM, RIGHT?
CLIENT
order
ILLUSTRATOR
SO? NO GOOD?

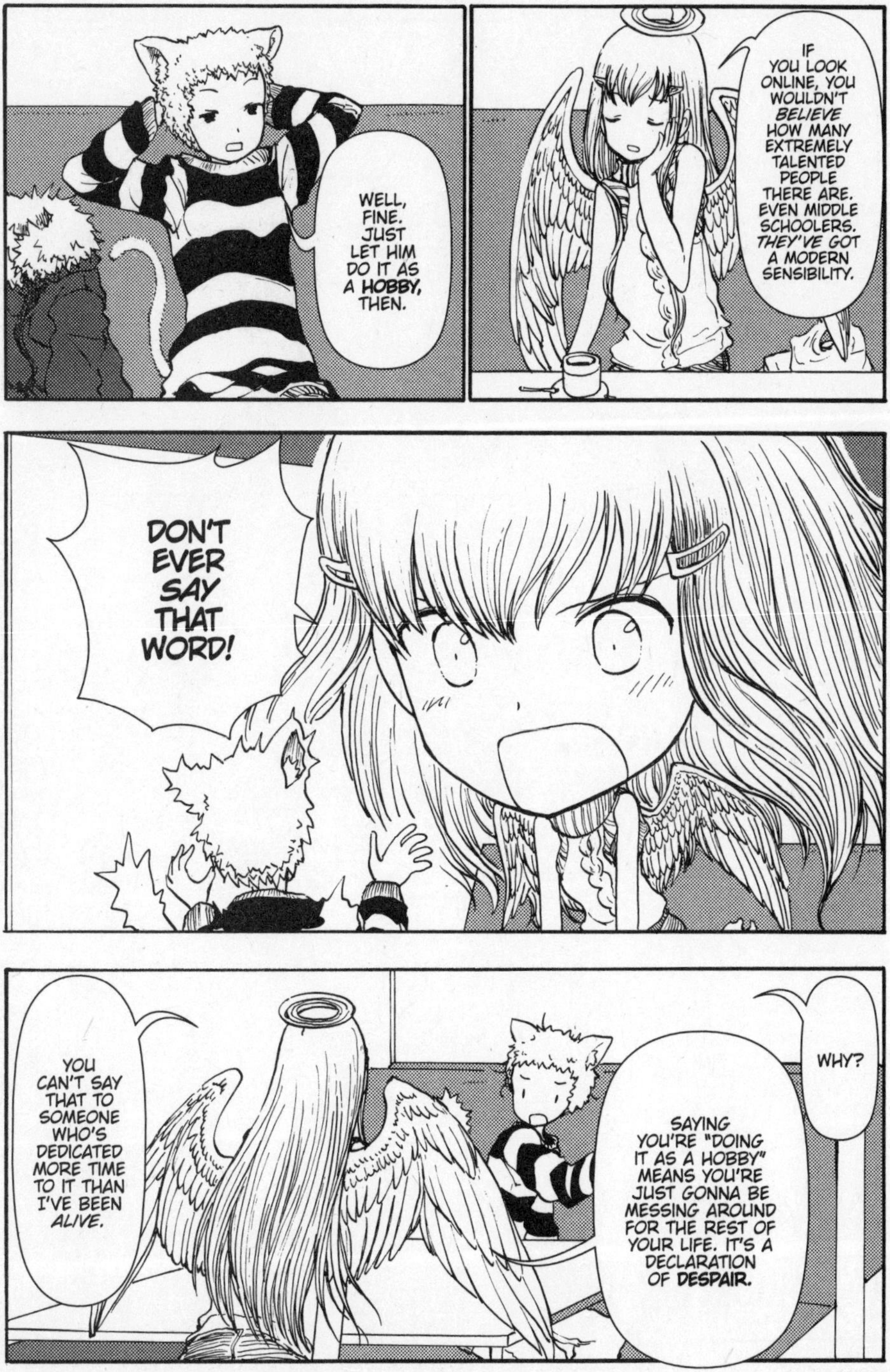
IF YOU LOOK ONLINE, YOU WOULDN'T *BELIEVE* HOW MANY EXTREMELY TALENTED PEOPLE THERE ARE. EVEN MIDDLE SCHOOLERS. *THEY'VE* GOT A MODERN SENSIBILITY.
WELL, FINE. JUST LET HIM DO IT AS A **HOBBY,** THEN.
DON'T EVER SAY THAT WORD!
WHY?
SAYING YOU'RE "DOING IT AS A HOBBY" MEANS YOU'RE JUST GONNA BE MESSING AROUND FOR THE REST OF YOUR LIFE. IT'S A DECLARATION OF **DESPAIR.**
YOU CAN'T SAY THAT TO SOMEONE WHO'S DEDICATED MORE TIME TO IT THAN I'VE BEEN *ALIVE.*

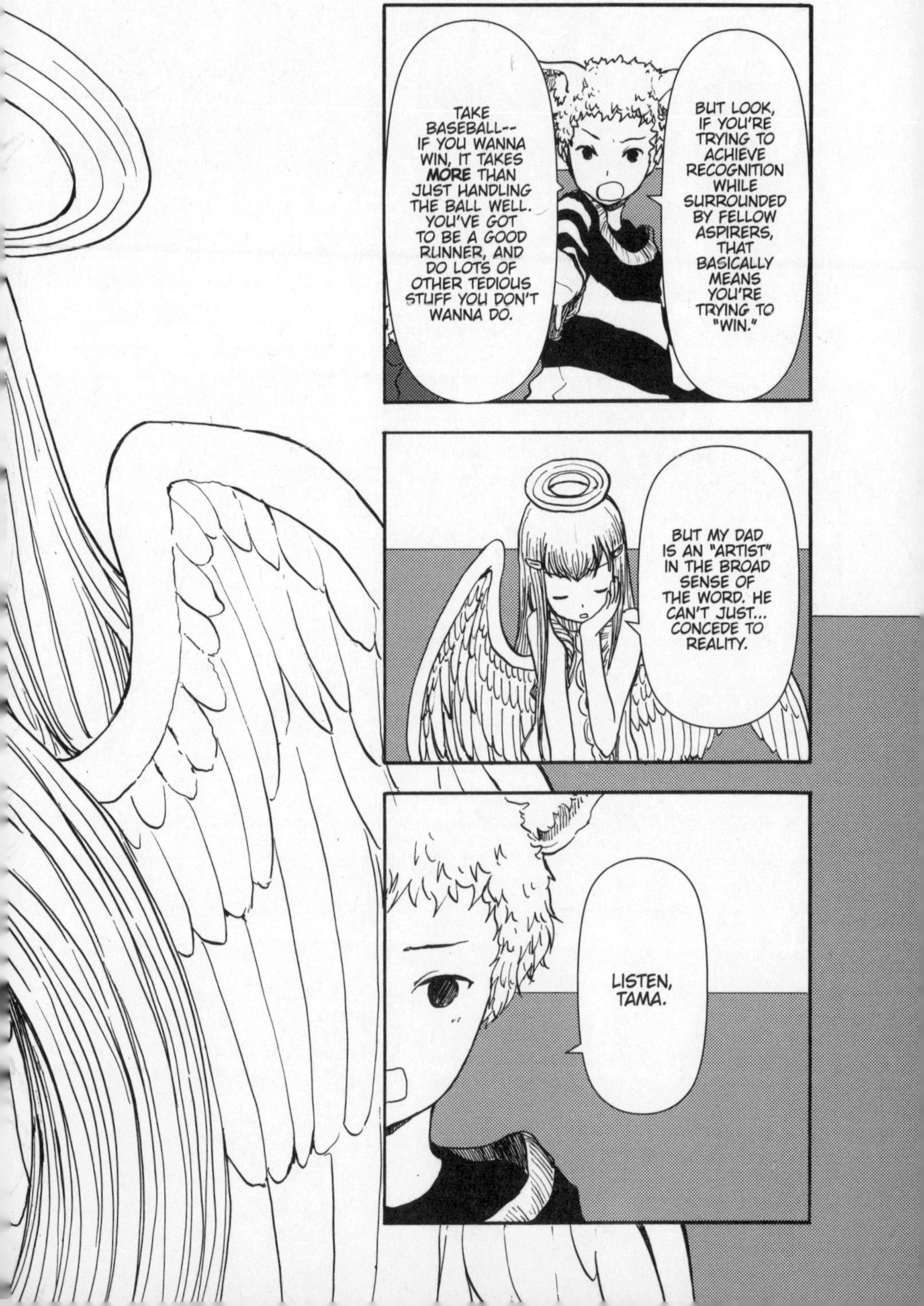
BUT LOOK, IF YOU'RE TRYING TO ACHIEVE RECOGNITION WHILE SURROUNDED BY FELLOW ASPIRERS, THAT BASICALLY MEANS YOU'RE TRYING TO "WIN."
TAKE BASEBALL-- IF YOU WANNA WIN, IT TAKES **MORE** THAN JUST HANDLING THE BALL WELL. YOU'VE GOT TO BE A GOOD RUNNER, AND DO LOTS OF OTHER TEDIOUS STUFF YOU DON'T WANNA DO.
BUT MY DAD IS AN "ARTIST" IN THE BROAD SENSE OF THE WORD. HE CAN'T JUST... CONCEDE TO REALITY.
LISTEN, TAMA.

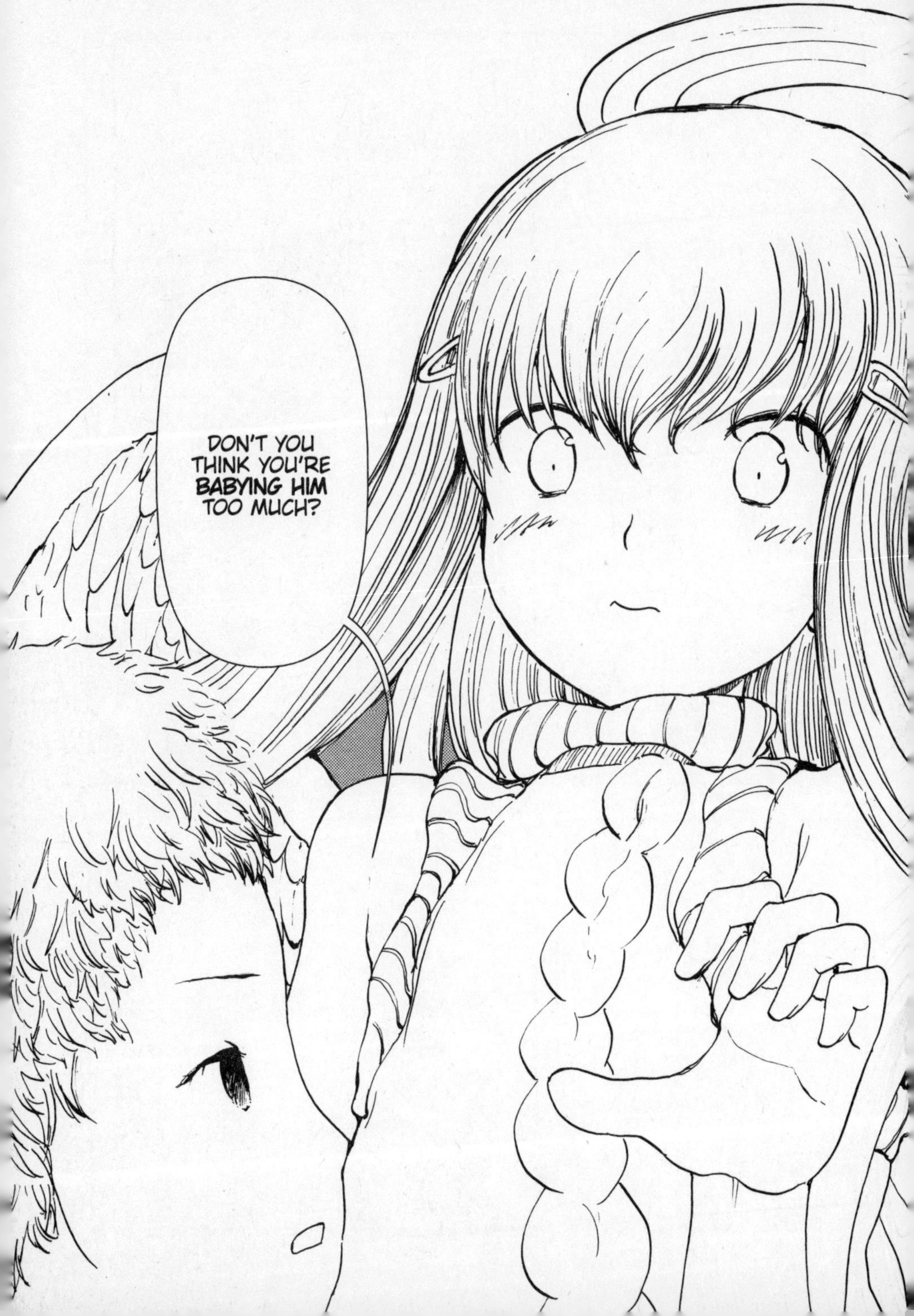
DON'T YOU THINK YOU'RE BABYING HIM TOO MUCH?

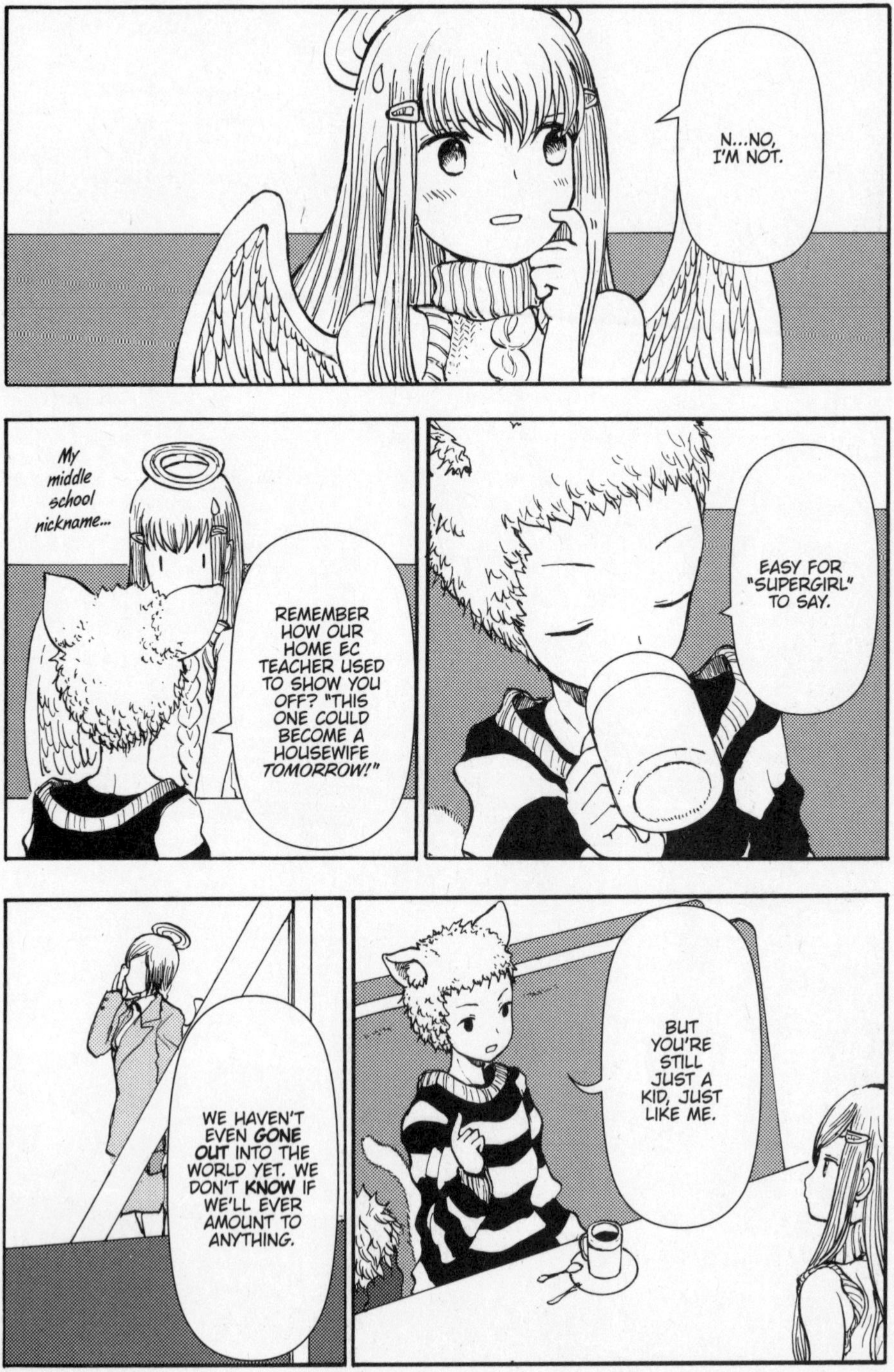
N...NO, I'M NOT.
EASY FOR "SUPERGIRL" TO SAY.
My middle school nickname...
REMEMBER HOW OUR HOME EC TEACHER USED TO SHOW YOU OFF? "THIS ONE COULD BECOME A HOUSEWIFE TOMORROW!"
BUT YOU'RE STILL JUST A KID, JUST LIKE ME.
WE HAVEN'T EVEN GONE OUT INTO THE WORLD YET. WE DON'T KNOW IF WE'LL EVER AMOUNT TO ANYTHING.

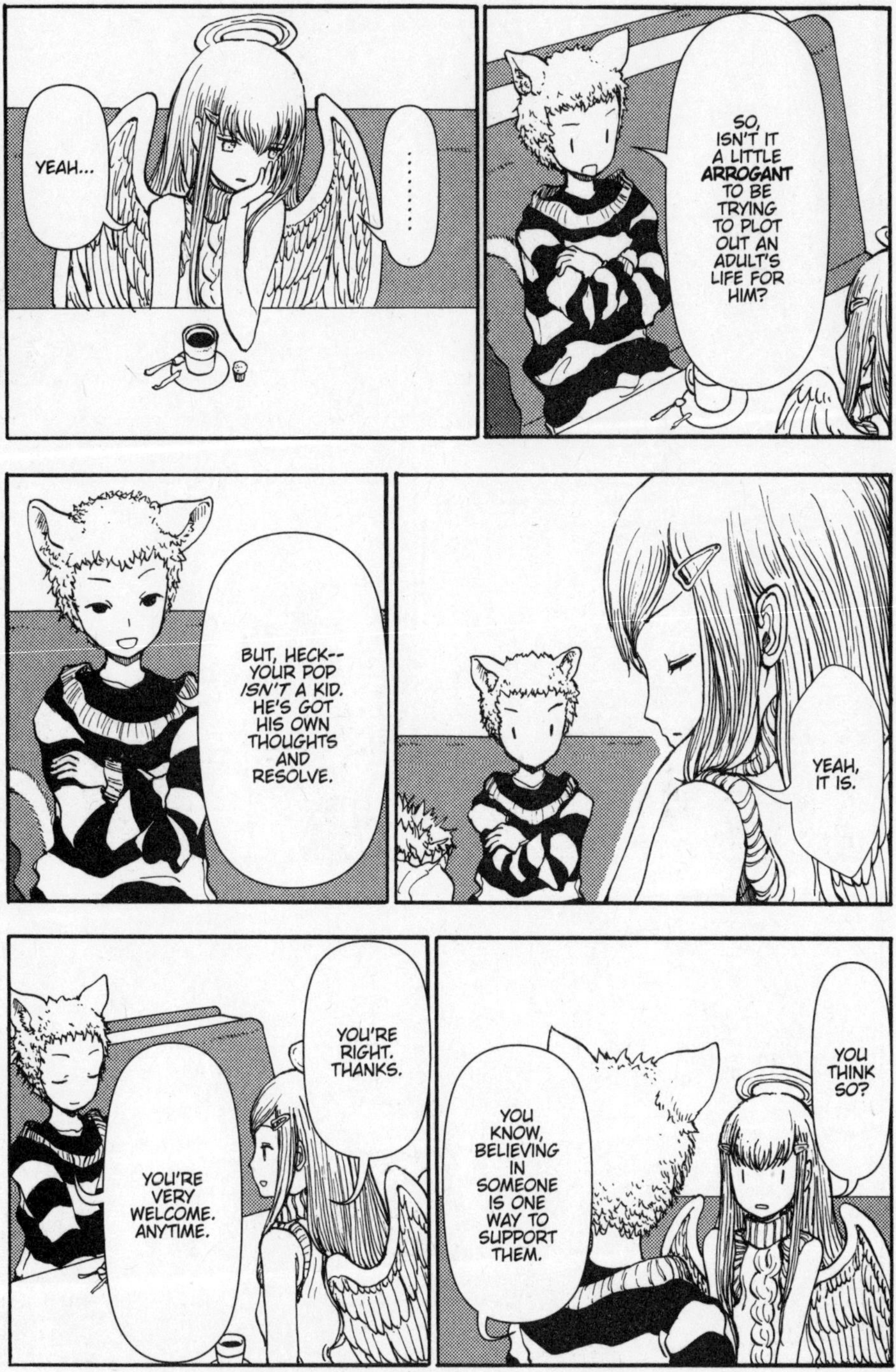
SO, ISN'T IT A LITTLE **ARROGANT** TO BE TRYING TO PLOT OUT AN ADULT'S LIFE FOR HIM?
......
YEAH...
YEAH, IT IS.
BUT, HECK-- YOUR POP *ISN'T* A KID. HE'S GOT HIS OWN THOUGHTS AND RESOLVE.
YOU THINK SO?
YOU KNOW, BELIEVING IN SOMEONE IS ONE WAY TO SUPPORT THEM.
YOU'RE RIGHT. THANKS.
YOU'RE VERY WELCOME. ANYTIME.

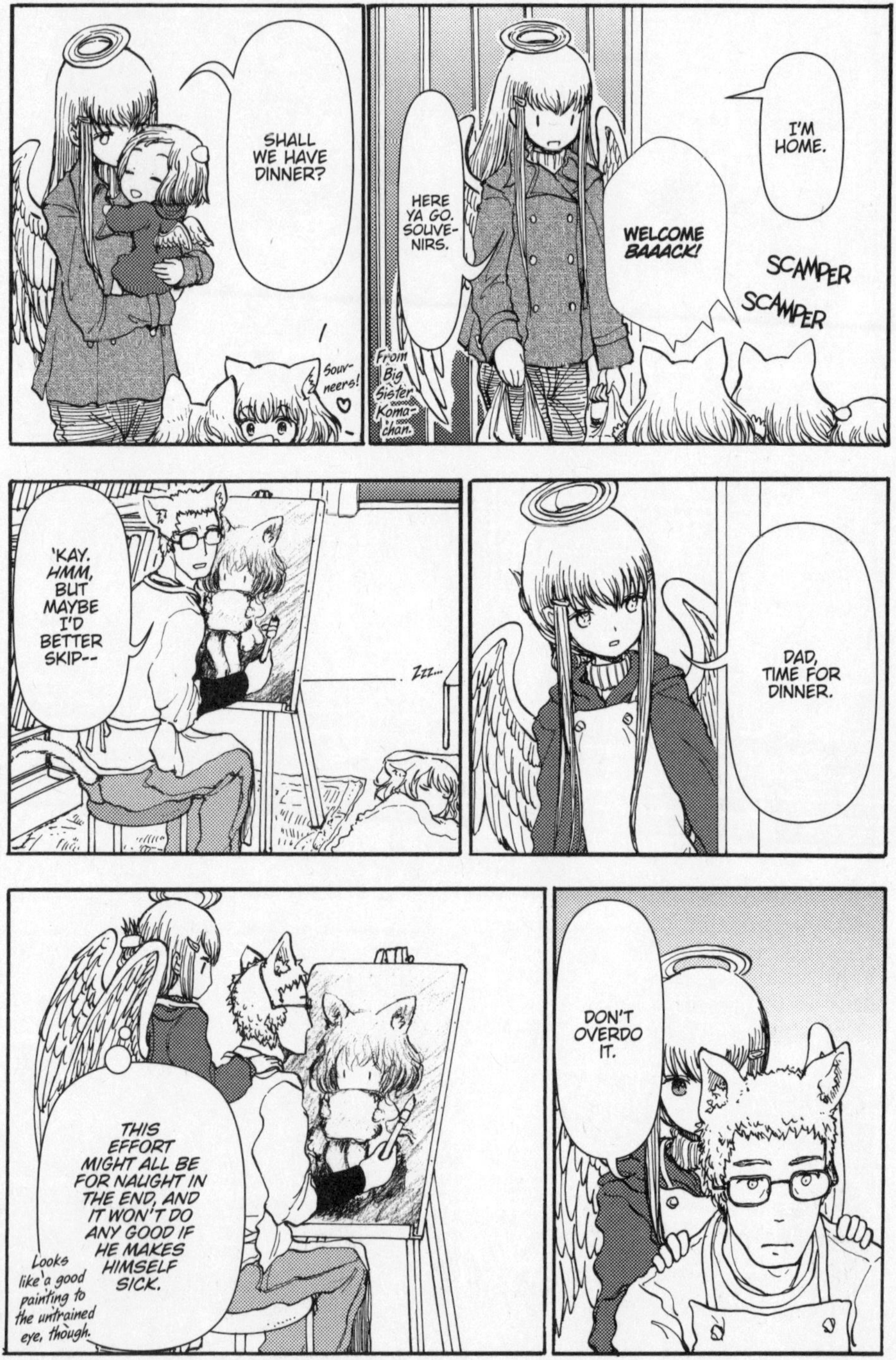
I'M HOME.
WELCOME BAAACK!
SCAMPER
SCAMPER
HERE YA GO. SOUVENIRS.
From Big Sister Koma-chan.
SHALL WE HAVE DINNER?
Souvneers! ♥
DAD, TIME FOR DINNER.
'KAY. HMM, BUT MAYBE I'D BETTER SKIP--
Zzz...
DON'T OVERDO IT.
THIS EFFORT MIGHT ALL BE FOR NAUGHT IN THE END, AND IT WON'T DO ANY GOOD IF HE MAKES HIMSELF SICK.
Looks like a good painting to the untrained eye, though.

A Centaur's Life

TRADITIONAL DRESS FROM AROUND THE WORLD (MONGOLIA)

AT THE *NAADAM* FESTIVAL HELD THROUGHOUT THE NATION OF MONGOLIA, THREE GAMES ARE TRADITIONALLY HELD: WRESTLING, HORSE RACING, AND ARCHERY. ALL THREE SERVED AS DRIVING FORCES BEHIND THE RISE OF THE UNPRECEDENTED MONGOLIAN EMPIRE ESTABLISHED BY THE LEGENDARY CONQUEROR GENGHIS KHAN. THE NEIGHBORING RED, CLASS-BASED NATION, LONG HELD AT THE MERCY OF THE MONGOLS, WOULD EVENTUALLY DECLARE MONGOLIA A SATELLITE NATION, BOLDLY IMPOSING UPON THE LAND'S TRADITIONS IN AN ATTEMPT TO CUT THEM OFF FROM THEIR PAST. MONGOLS WERE FORBIDDEN FROM LEARNING THEIR OWN HISTORY OR PAYING REVERENCE TO THEIR HISTORICAL HEROES. HOWEVER, INEVITABLE SOCIAL UPHEAVAL LED TO THE COLLAPSE OF THE CLASS-BASED SOCIETY, AND THE MONGOLIAN PEOPLE AND THEIR HISTORY WERE REVIVED.

THUS, THE BEAUTIFUL FORM OF THE MONGOLIAN ARCHER ADORNED IN TRADITIONAL GARB, SKILLFULLY LETTING LOOSE AN ARROW, IS A SIGHT STILL SEEN TODAY.

CHAPTER 47

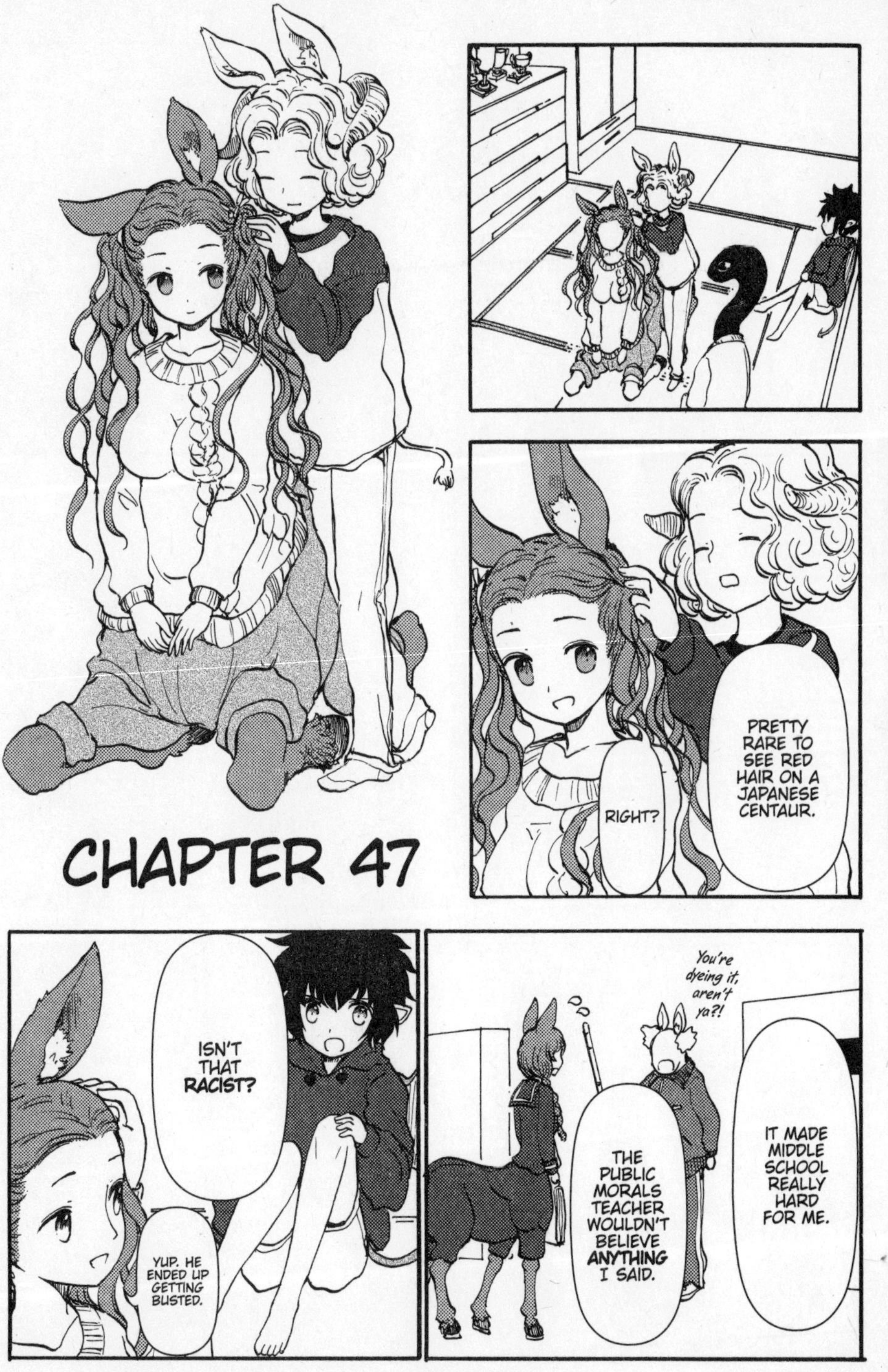
PRETTY RARE TO SEE RED HAIR ON A JAPANESE CENTAUR.
RIGHT?
CHAPTER 47
You're dyeing it, aren't ya?!
IT MADE MIDDLE SCHOOL REALLY HARD FOR ME.
THE PUBLIC MORALS TEACHER WOULDN'T BELIEVE ANYTHING I SAID.
ISN'T THAT RACIST?
YUP. HE ENDED UP GETTING BUSTED.

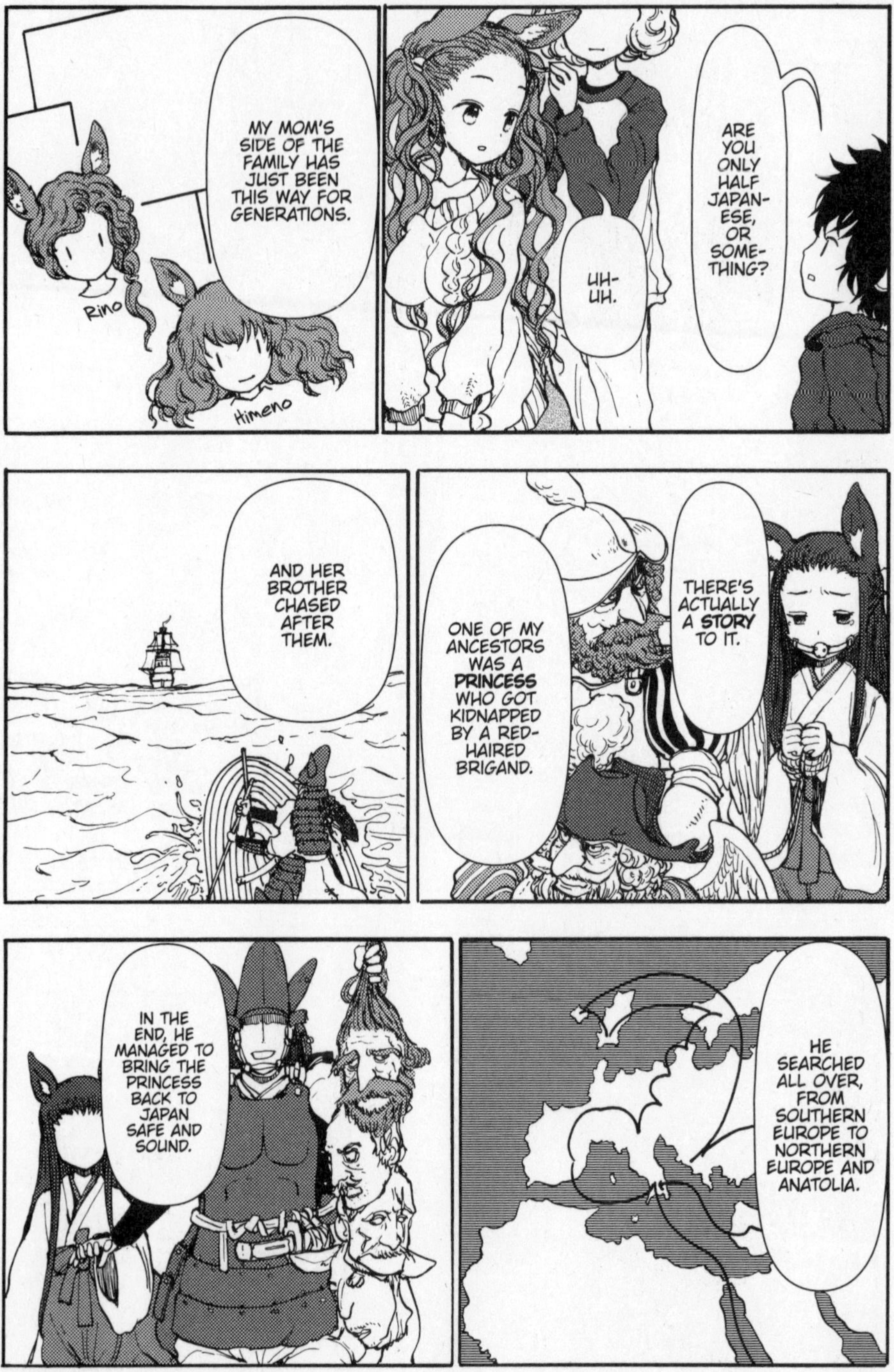
ARE YOU ONLY HALF JAPANESE, OR SOMETHING?
UH-UH.
MY MOM'S SIDE OF THE FAMILY HAS JUST BEEN THIS WAY FOR GENERATIONS.
Rino
Himeno
THERE'S ACTUALLY A **STORY** TO IT.
ONE OF MY ANCESTORS WAS A **PRINCESS** WHO GOT KIDNAPPED BY A RED-HAIRED BRIGAND.
AND HER BROTHER CHASED AFTER THEM.
HE SEARCHED ALL OVER, FROM SOUTHERN EUROPE TO NORTHERN EUROPE AND ANATOLIA.
IN THE END, HE MANAGED TO BRING THE PRINCESS BACK TO JAPAN SAFE AND SOUND.

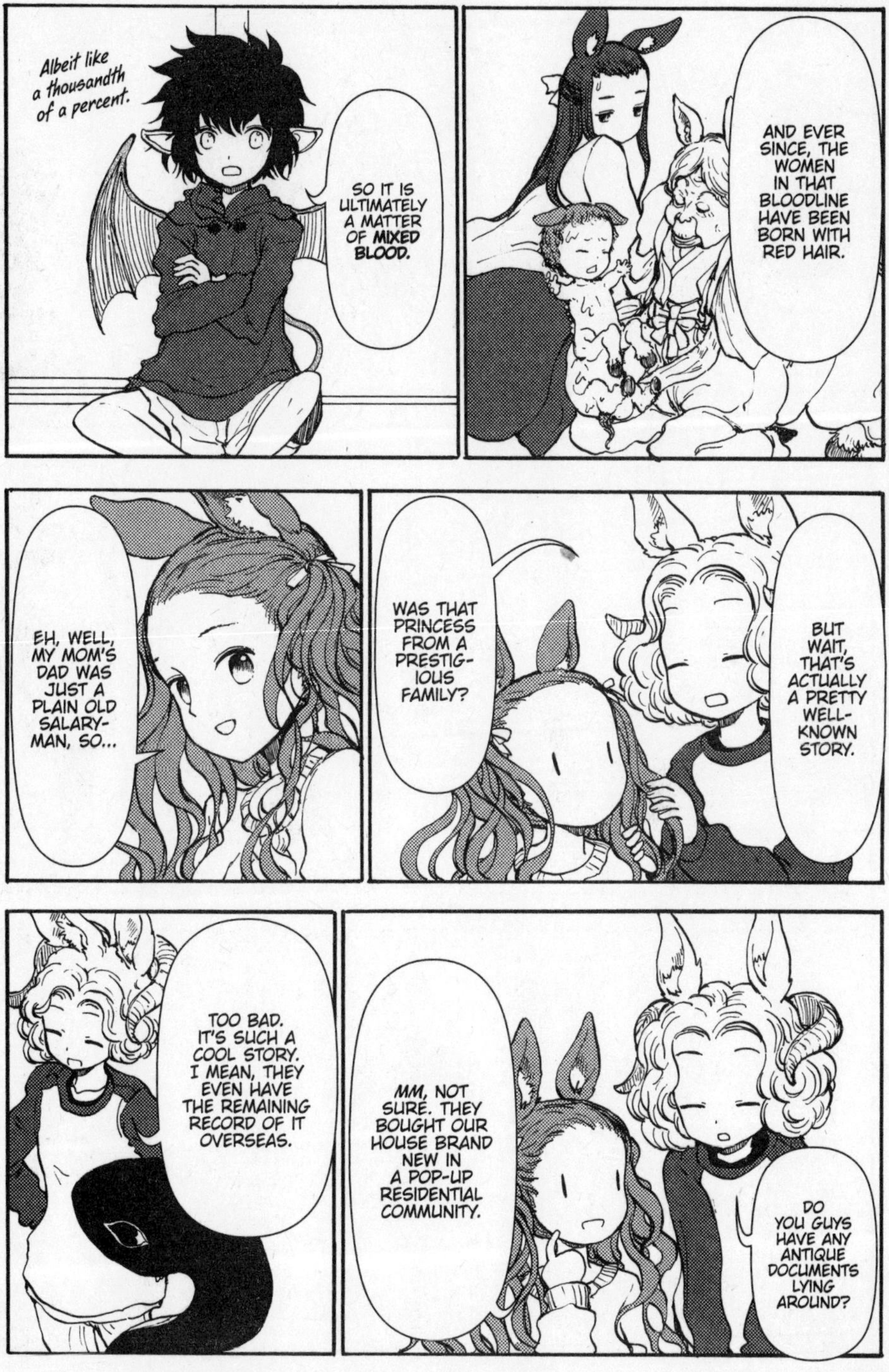
AND EVER SINCE, THE WOMEN IN THAT BLOODLINE HAVE BEEN BORN WITH RED HAIR.
SO IT IS ULTIMATELY A MATTER OF **MIXED BLOOD.**
Albeit like a thousandth of a percent.
BUT WAIT, THAT'S ACTUALLY A PRETTY WELL-KNOWN STORY.
WAS THAT PRINCESS FROM A PRESTIGIOUS FAMILY?
EH, WELL, MY MOM'S DAD WAS JUST A PLAIN OLD SALARYMAN, SO...
DO YOU GUYS HAVE ANY ANTIQUE DOCUMENTS LYING AROUND?
MM, NOT SURE. THEY BOUGHT OUR HOUSE BRAND NEW IN A POP-UP RESIDENTIAL COMMUNITY.
TOO BAD. IT'S SUCH A COOL STORY. I MEAN, THEY EVEN HAVE THE REMAINING RECORD OF IT OVERSEAS.

CREAK

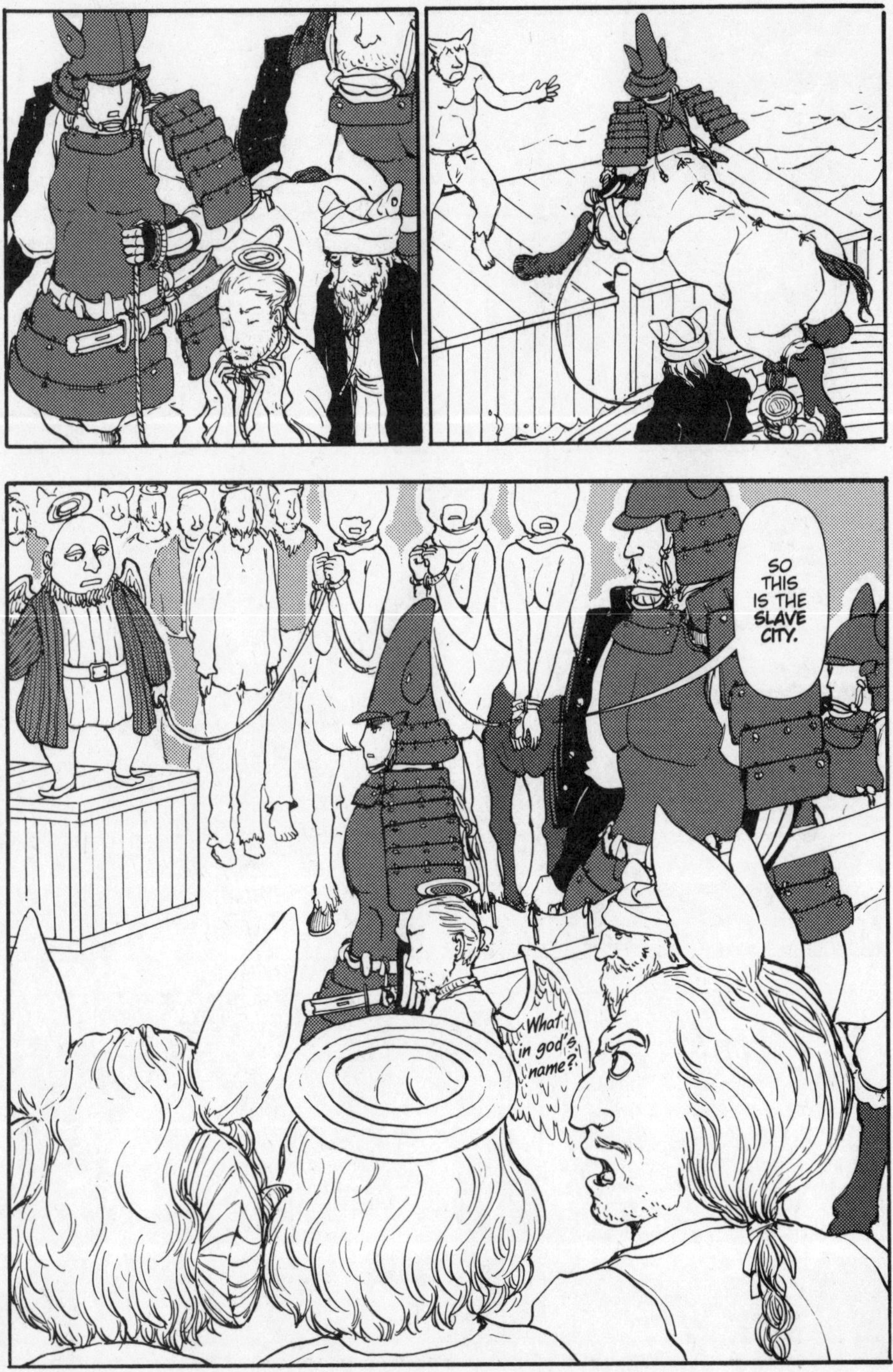
SO THIS IS THE SLAVE CITY.
What in god's name?

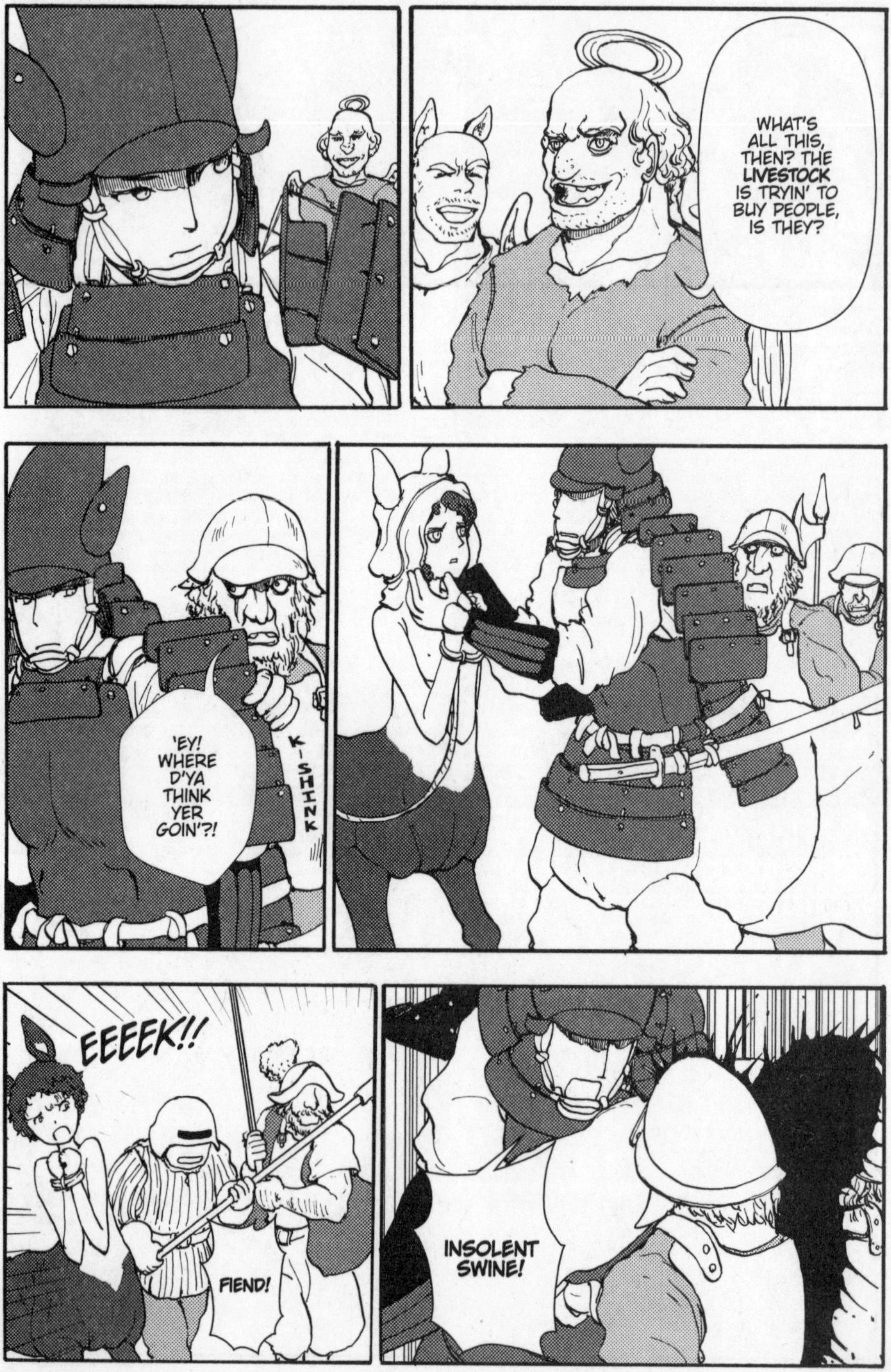
WHAT'S ALL THIS, THEN? THE **LIVESTOCK** IS TRYIN' TO BUY PEOPLE, IS THEY?
'EY! WHERE D'YA THINK YER GOIN'?!
KISHINK
INSOLENT SWINE!
EEEEK!!
FIEND!

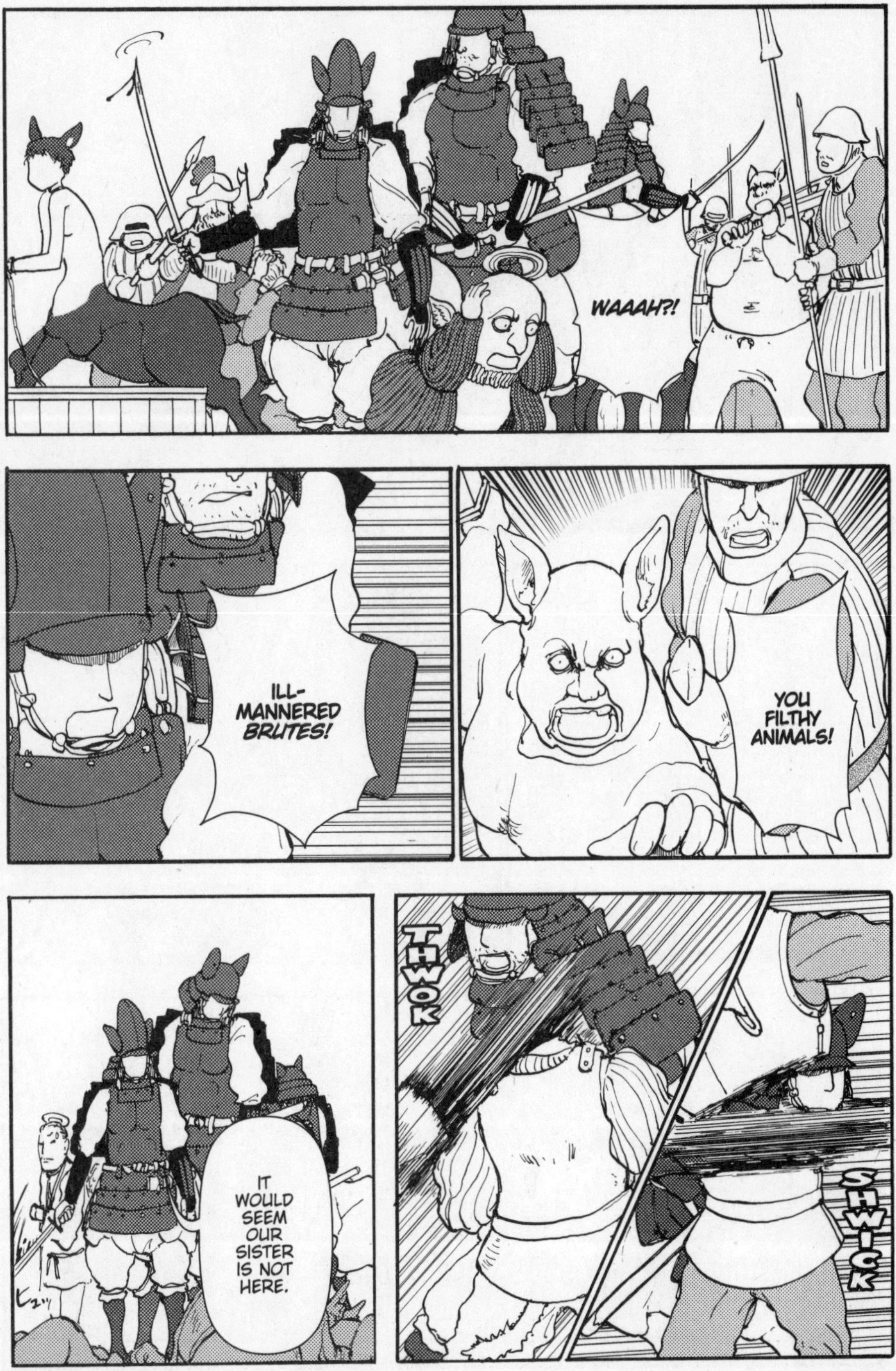
WAAAH?!
YOU FILTHY ANIMALS!
ILL-MANNERED BRUTES!
THWOK
SHWICK
IT WOULD SEEM OUR SISTER IS NOT HERE.

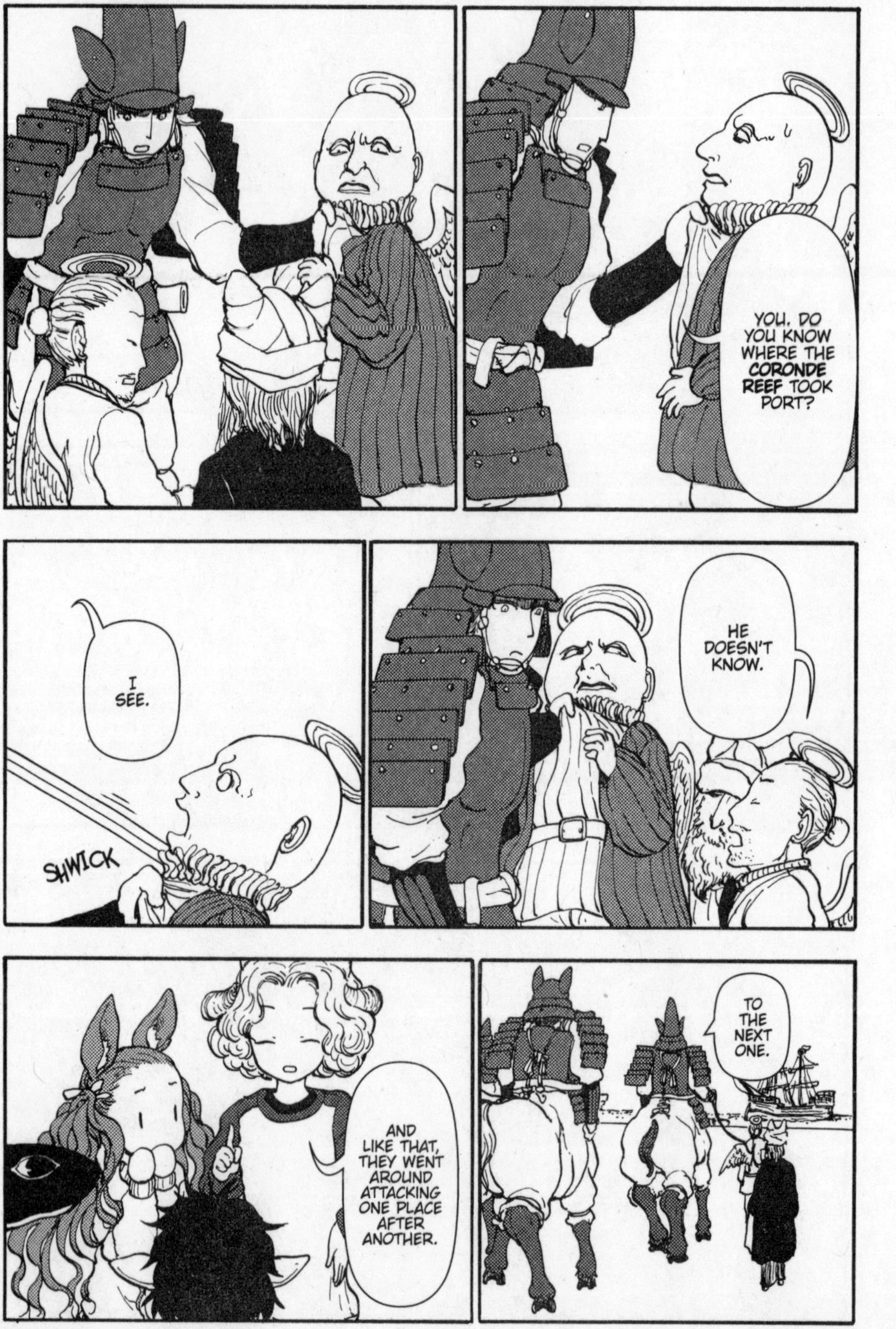
YOU. DO YOU KNOW WHERE THE **CORONDE REEF** TOOK PORT?
HE DOESN'T KNOW.
I SEE.
SHWICK
TO THE NEXT ONE.
AND LIKE THAT, THEY WENT AROUND ATTACKING ONE PLACE AFTER ANOTHER.

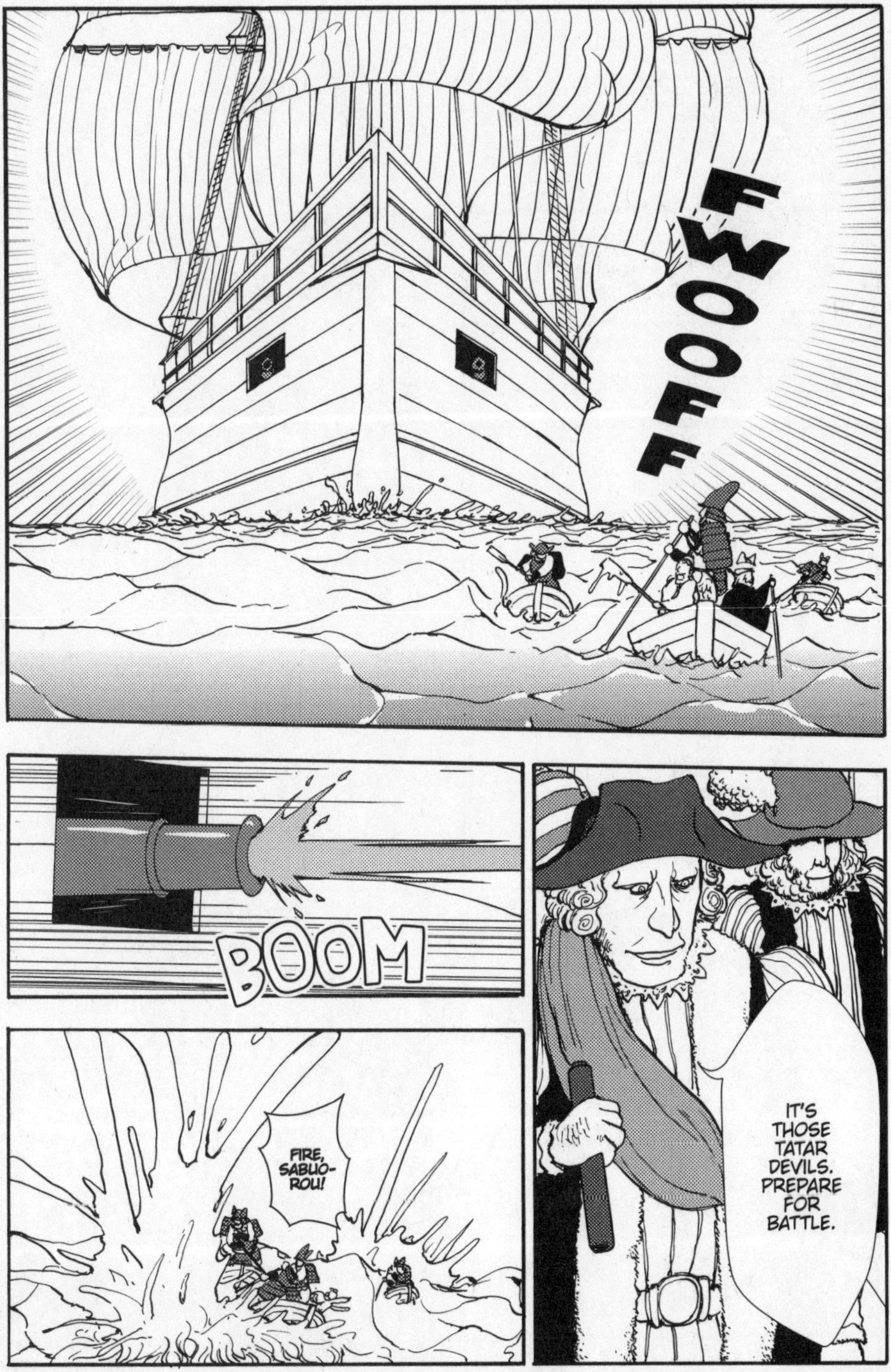
FWOOFF
IT'S THOSE TATAR DEVILS. PREPARE FOR BATTLE.
BOOM
FIRE, SABUO-ROU!

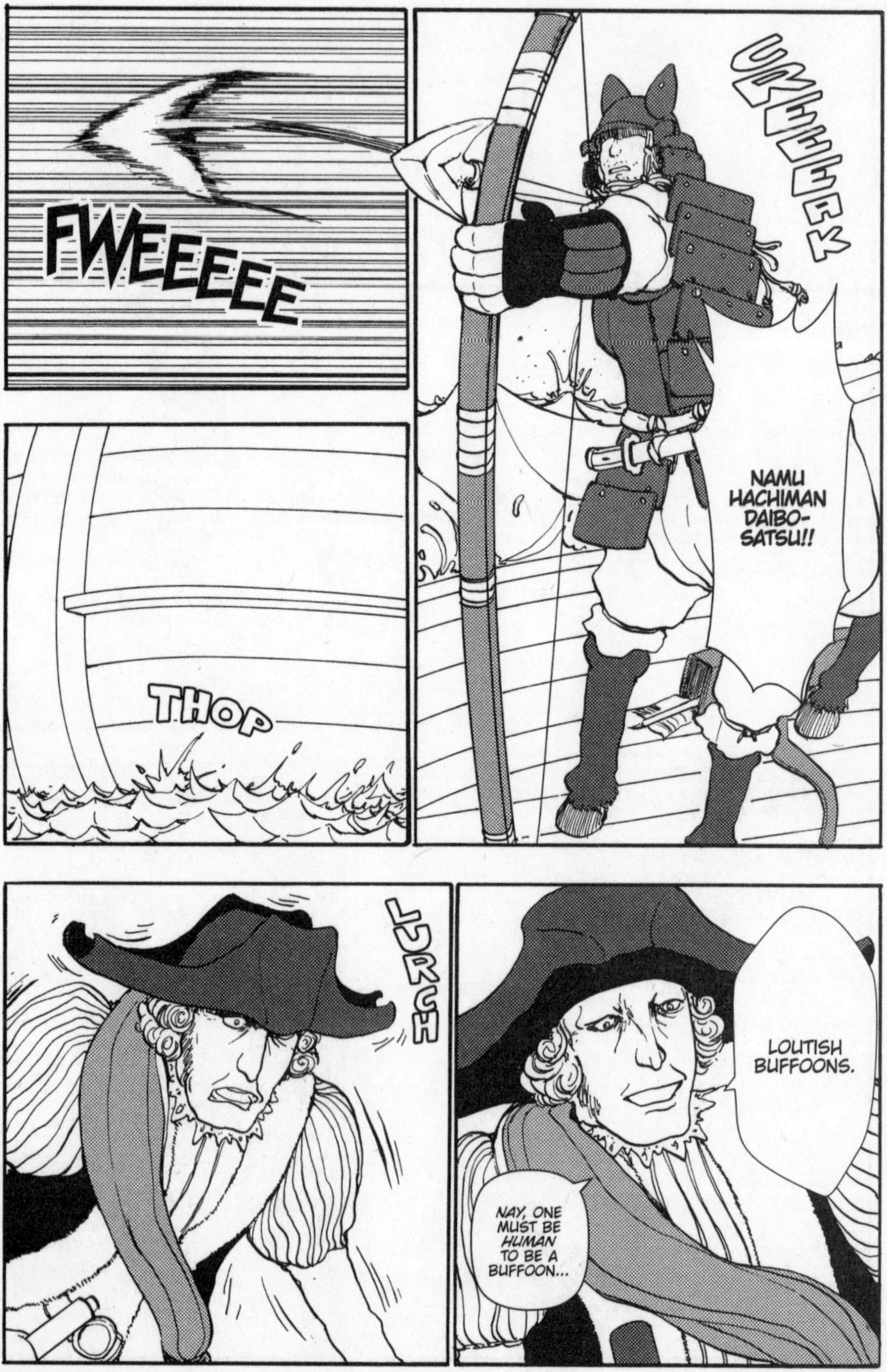
UREEEAK
NAMU HACHIMAN DAIBO-SATSU!!
FWEEEEEE
THOP
LOUTISH BUFFOONS.
NAY, ONE MUST BE *HUMAN* TO BE A BUFFOON...
LURCH

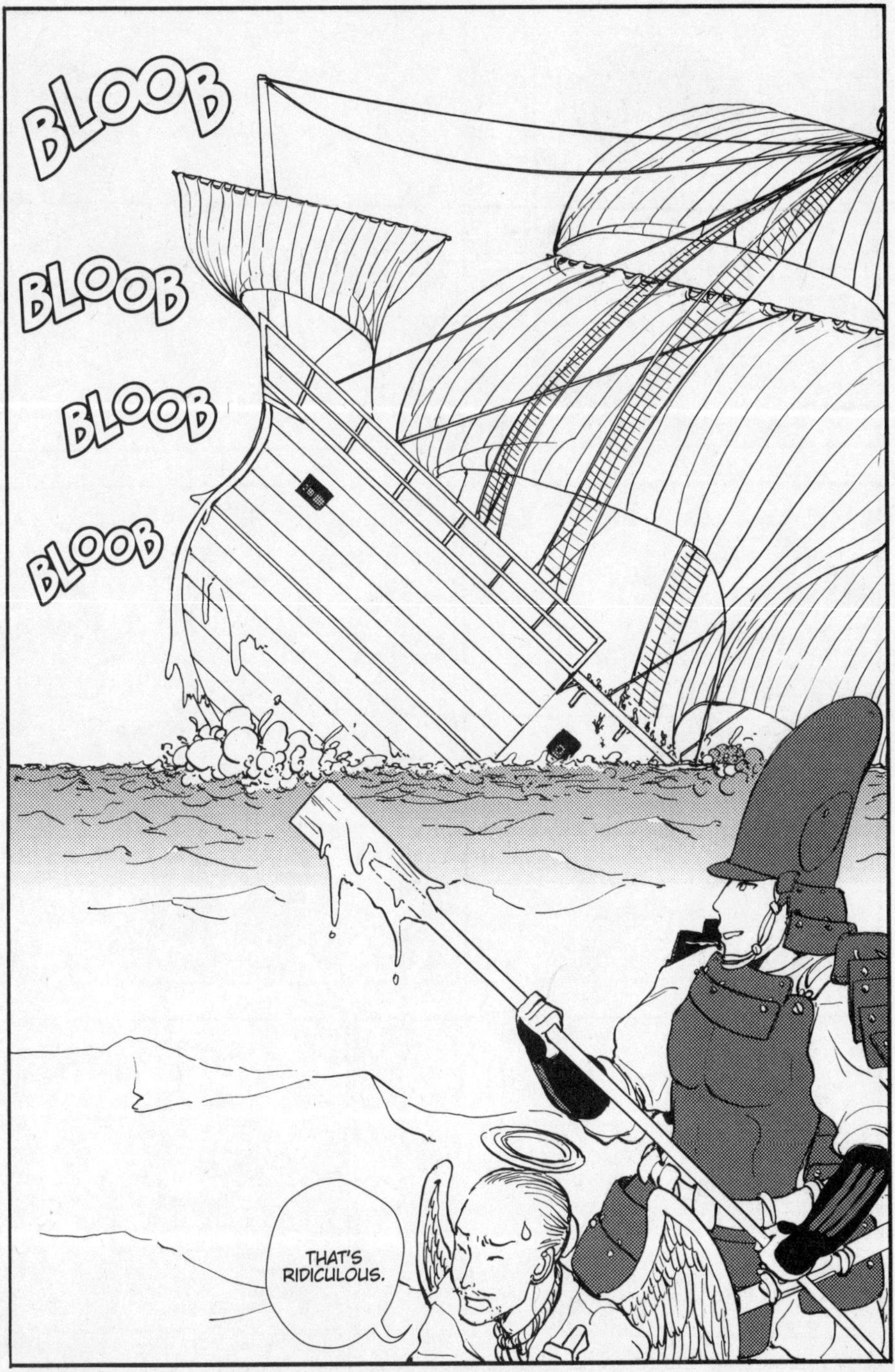
BLOOB
BLOOB
BLOOB
BLOOB
THAT'S RIDICULOUS.

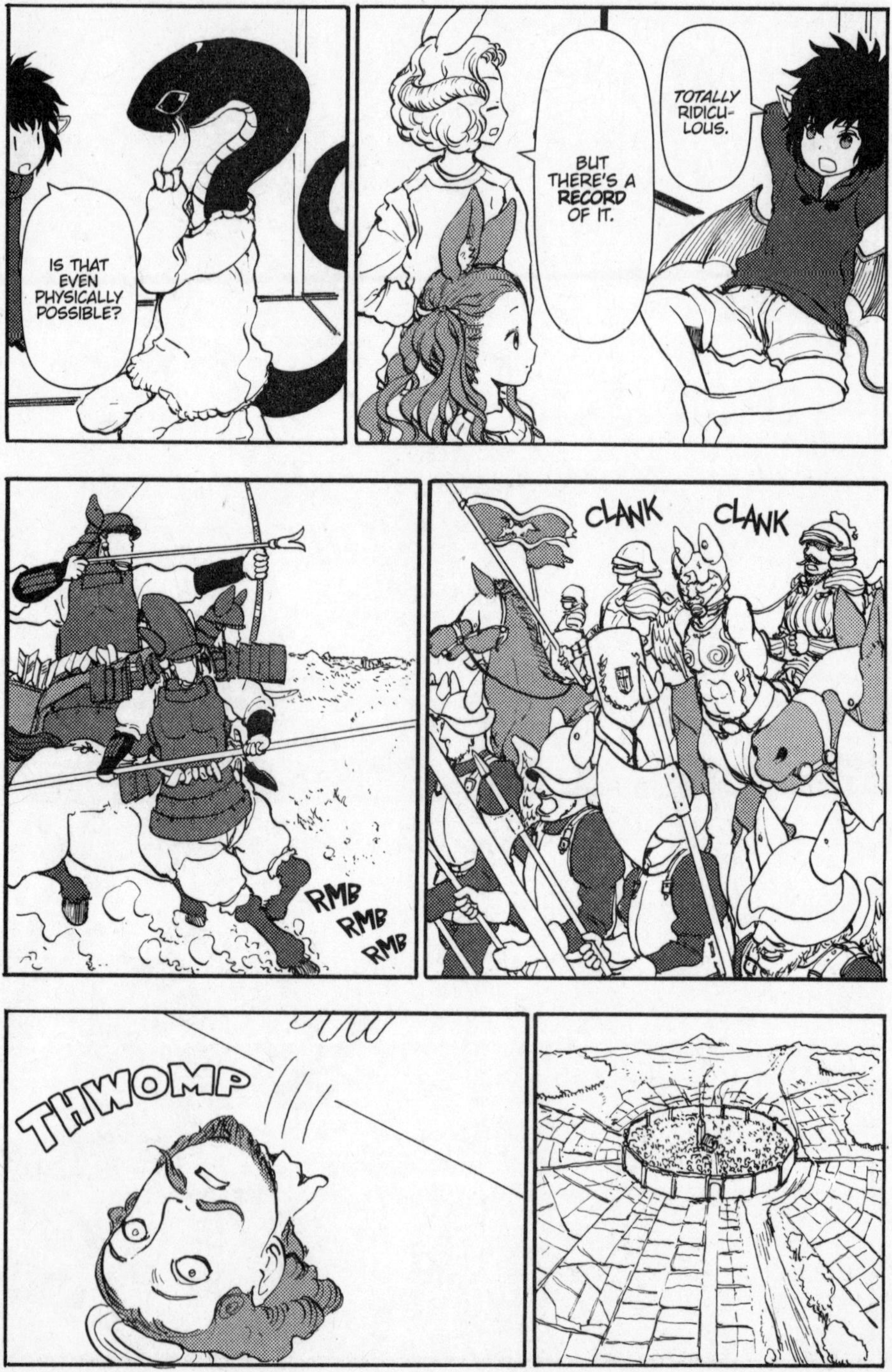
TOTALLY RIDICU-LOUS.
BUT THERE'S A RECORD OF IT.
IS THAT EVEN PHYSICALLY POSSIBLE?
CLANK
CLANK
RMB
RMB
RMB
THWOMP

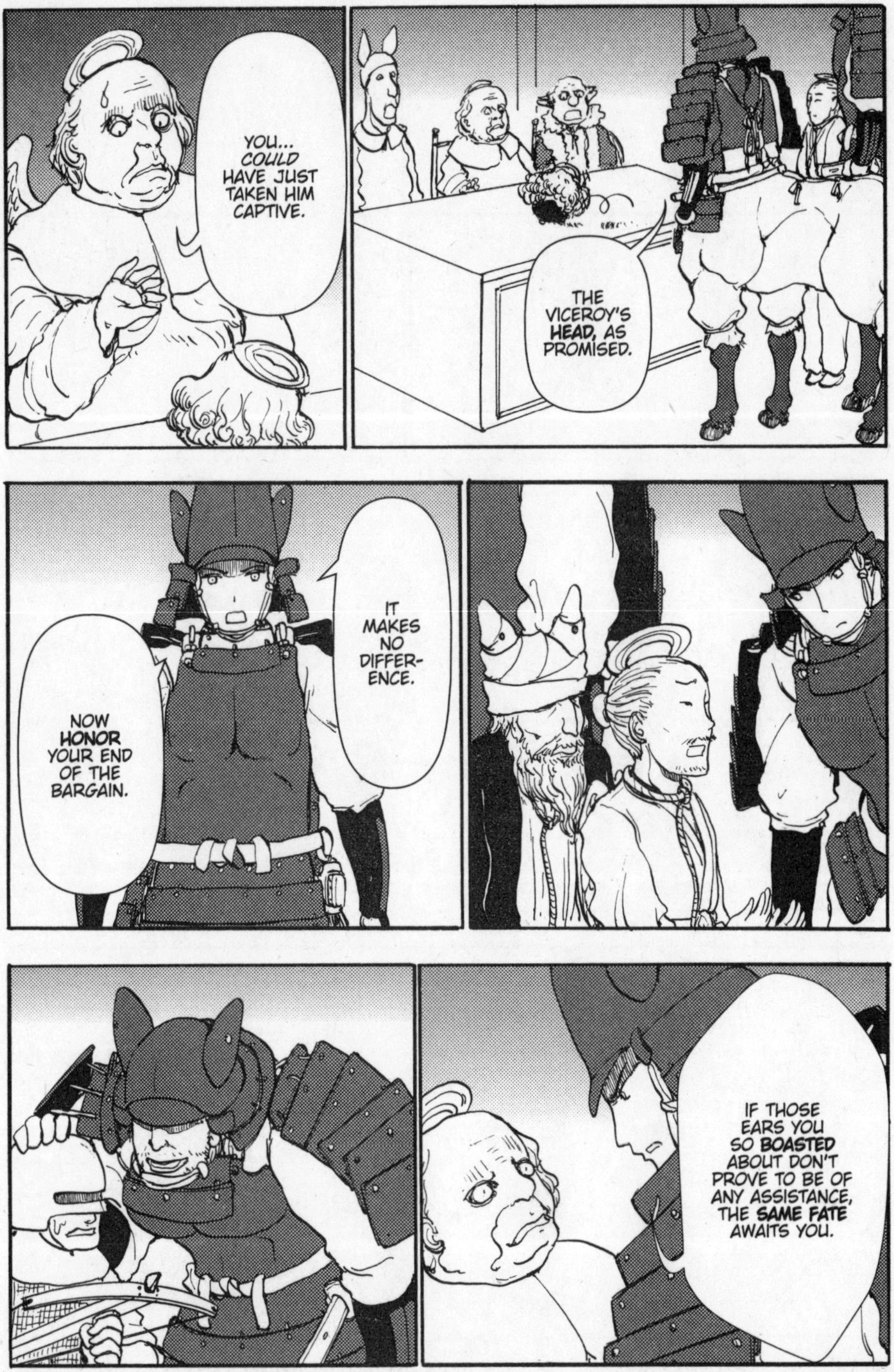
THE VICEROY'S HEAD, AS PROMISED.
YOU... COULD HAVE JUST TAKEN HIM CAPTIVE.
IT MAKES NO DIFFERENCE.
NOW HONOR YOUR END OF THE BARGAIN.
IF THOSE EARS YOU SO BOASTED ABOUT DON'T PROVE TO BE OF ANY ASSISTANCE, THE SAME FATE AWAITS YOU.

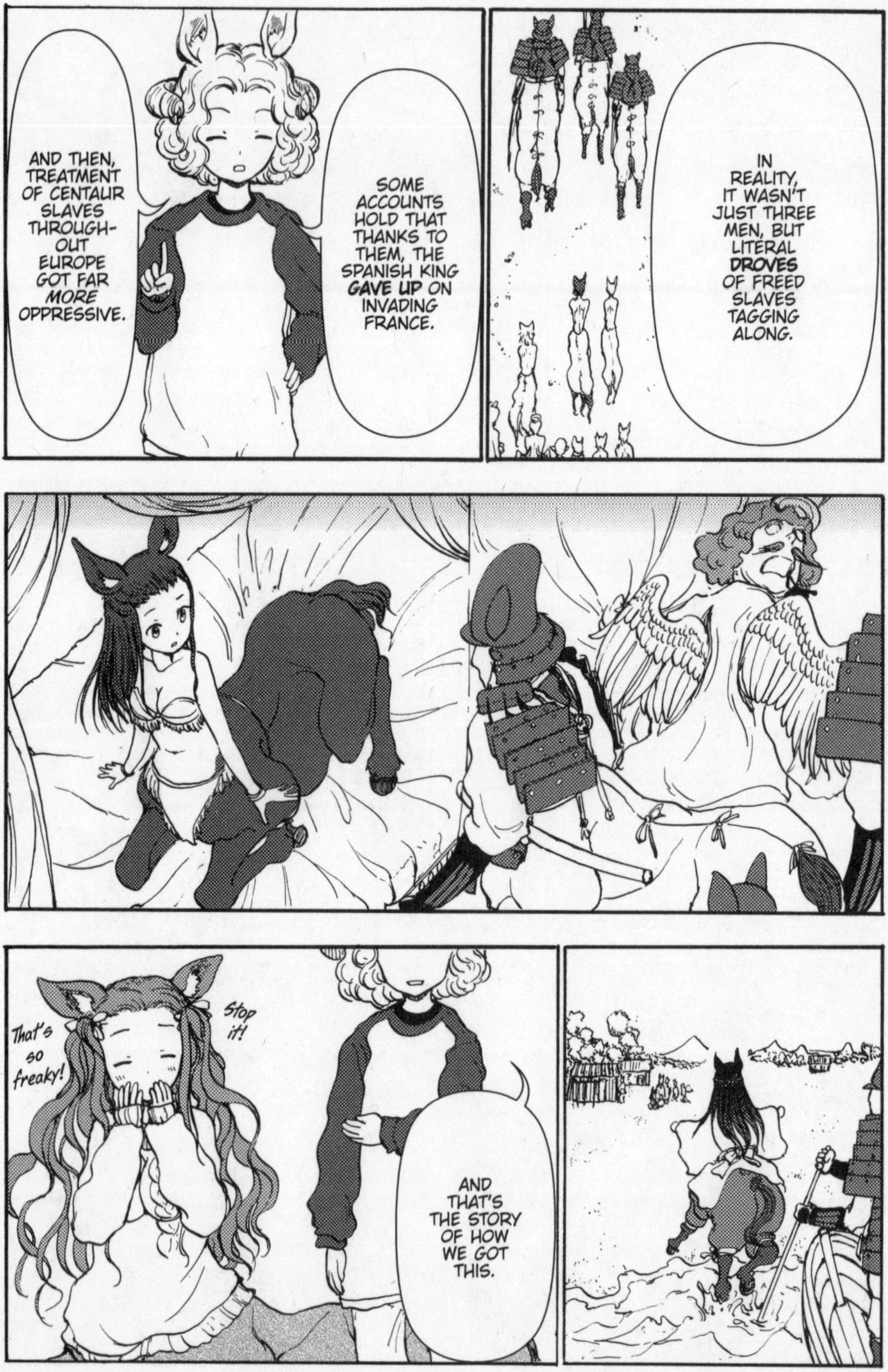
IN REALITY, IT WASN'T JUST THREE MEN, BUT LITERAL **DROVES** OF FREED SLAVES TAGGING ALONG.
SOME ACCOUNTS HOLD THAT THANKS TO THEM, THE SPANISH KING **GAVE UP** ON INVADING FRANCE.
AND THEN, TREATMENT OF CENTAUR SLAVES THROUGH-OUT EUROPE GOT FAR *MORE* OPPRESSIVE.
AND THAT'S THE STORY OF HOW WE GOT THIS.
Stop it!
That's so freaky!

A CentaUr's Life

TRADITIONAL DRESS FROM AROUND THE WORLD (KENYA)

WHILE THE METROPOLITAN CENTERS OF KENYA BEAR A STRONG EUROPEAN INFLUENCE, OTHER REGIONS STILL SERVE AS HOME TO NUMEROUS TRIBES, EACH WITH THEIR OWN UNIQUE TRADITIONS. IN THE TRADITIONAL FEMALE DRESS OF THE MAASAI TRIBE, WHICH HAS BEEN POPULARIZED IN CONTEMPORARY BOYS' FICTION, THE ORNATE NECKPIECES ADORNED WITH BEADS AND COWRIE SHELLS ARE PARTICULARLY EYE-CATCHING. THE BEADS IN THESE NECKPIECES ORIGINALLY CAME BY WAY OF THE MIDDLE EAST AND EUROPE, AND ARE ARRANGED INTO INTRICATE, COLORFUL DESIGNS--RED REPRESENTS OX BLOOD, WHITE REPRESENTS COW'S MILK, AND BLUE REPRESENTS THE SKY. RED CLOTH WRAPS KNOWN AS *SHUKA* ALSO CONTRAST VIBRANTLY WITH THE EARTH. BUT THIS VIBRANCE IS NOT EXCLUSIVE TO THE WOMEN--THE MEN OF THE MAASAI TRIBE ARE ALSO INCREDIBLY FASHIONABLE.

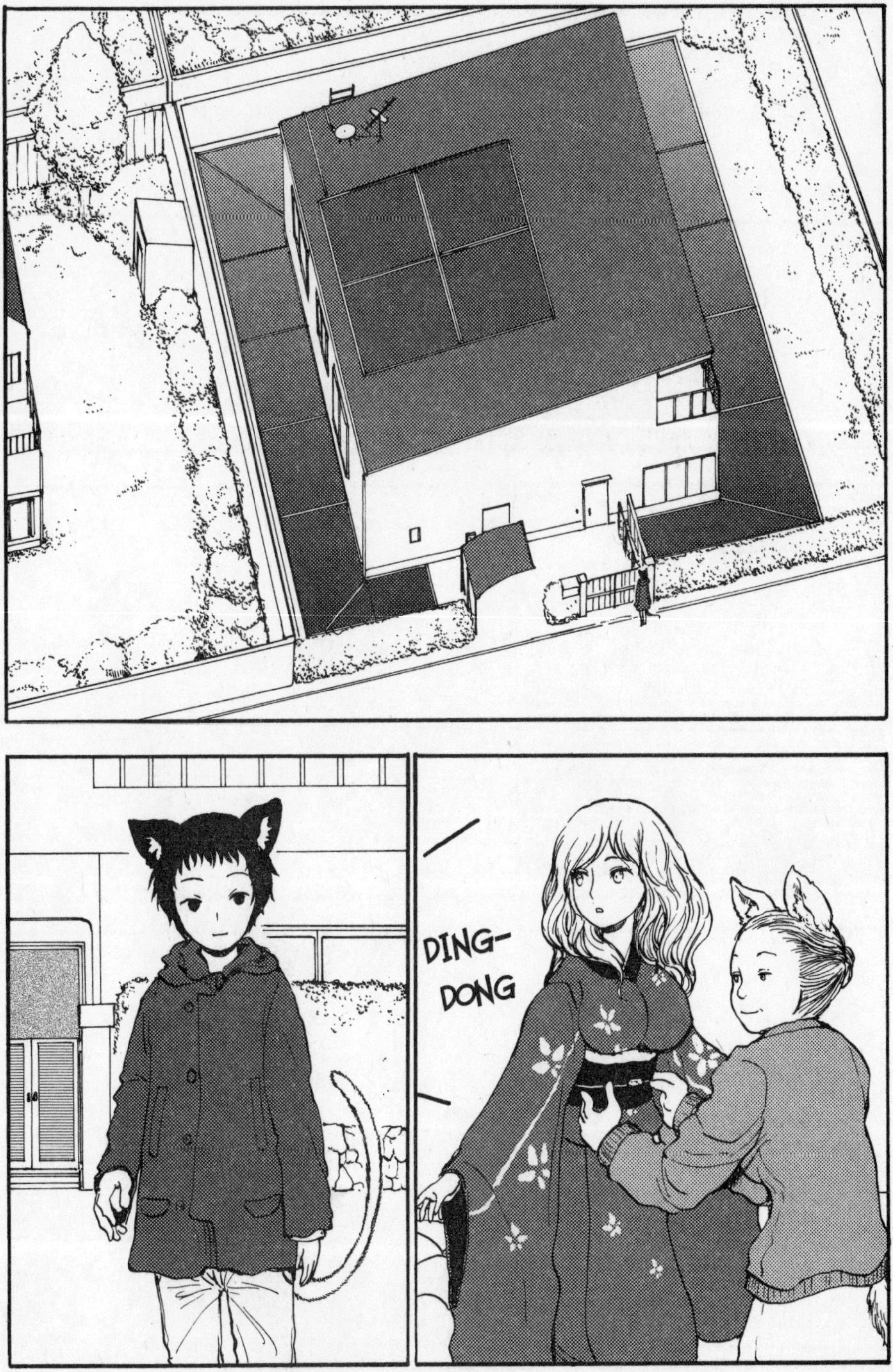
DING-
DONG

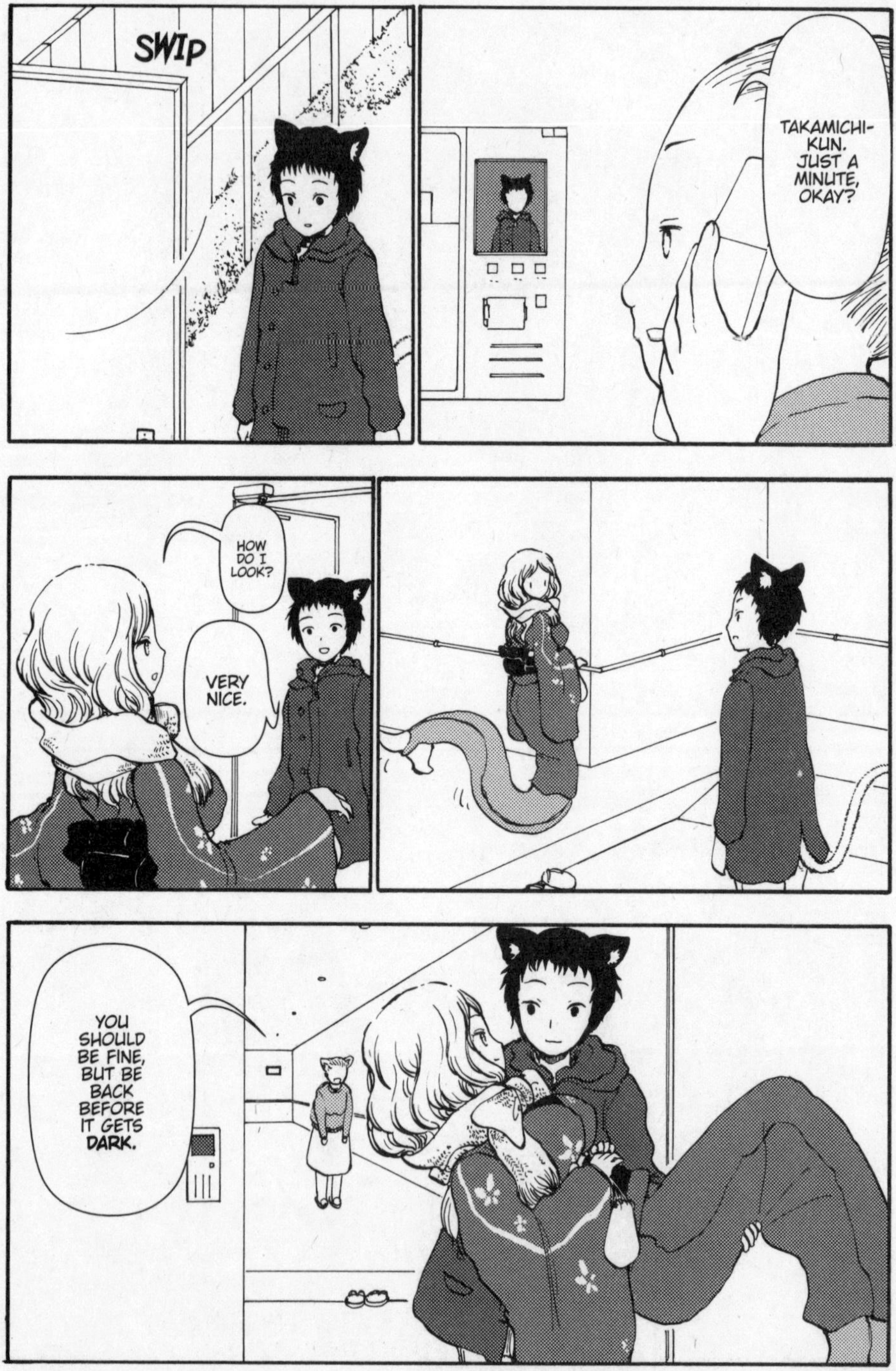
TAKAMICHI-KUN. JUST A MINUTE, OKAY?
SWIP
HOW DO I LOOK?
VERY NICE.
YOU SHOULD BE FINE, BUT BE BACK BEFORE IT GETS **DARK.**

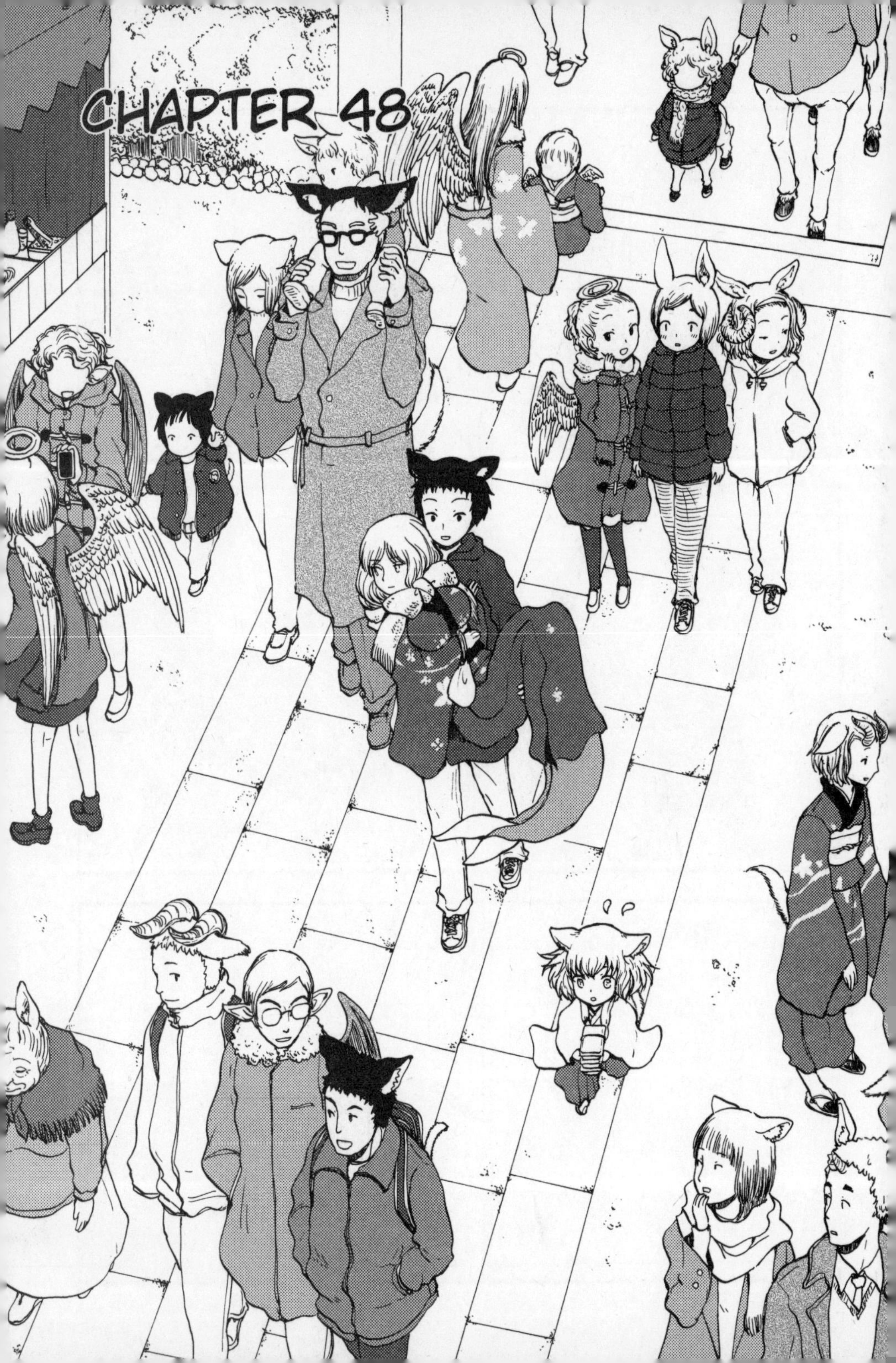
CHAPTER 48

Horseback
Archery
Exhibition

THWACK

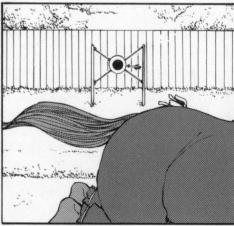

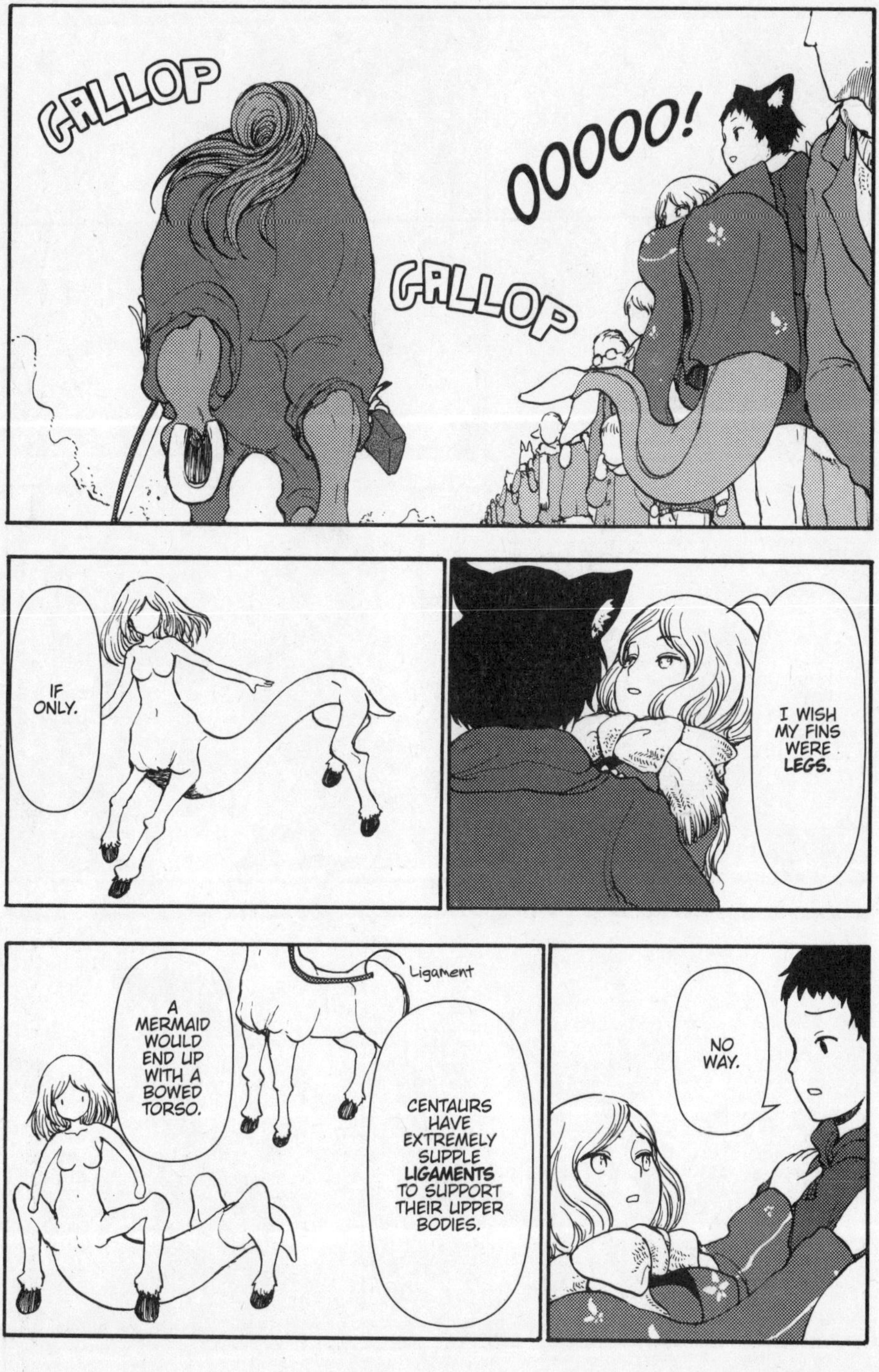
OOOOO!
GALLOP
GALLOP
I WISH MY FINS WERE **LEGS.**
IF ONLY.
NO WAY.
CENTAURS HAVE EXTREMELY SUPPLE **LIGAMENTS** TO SUPPORT THEIR UPPER BODIES.
Ligament
A MERMAID WOULD END UP WITH A BOWED TORSO.

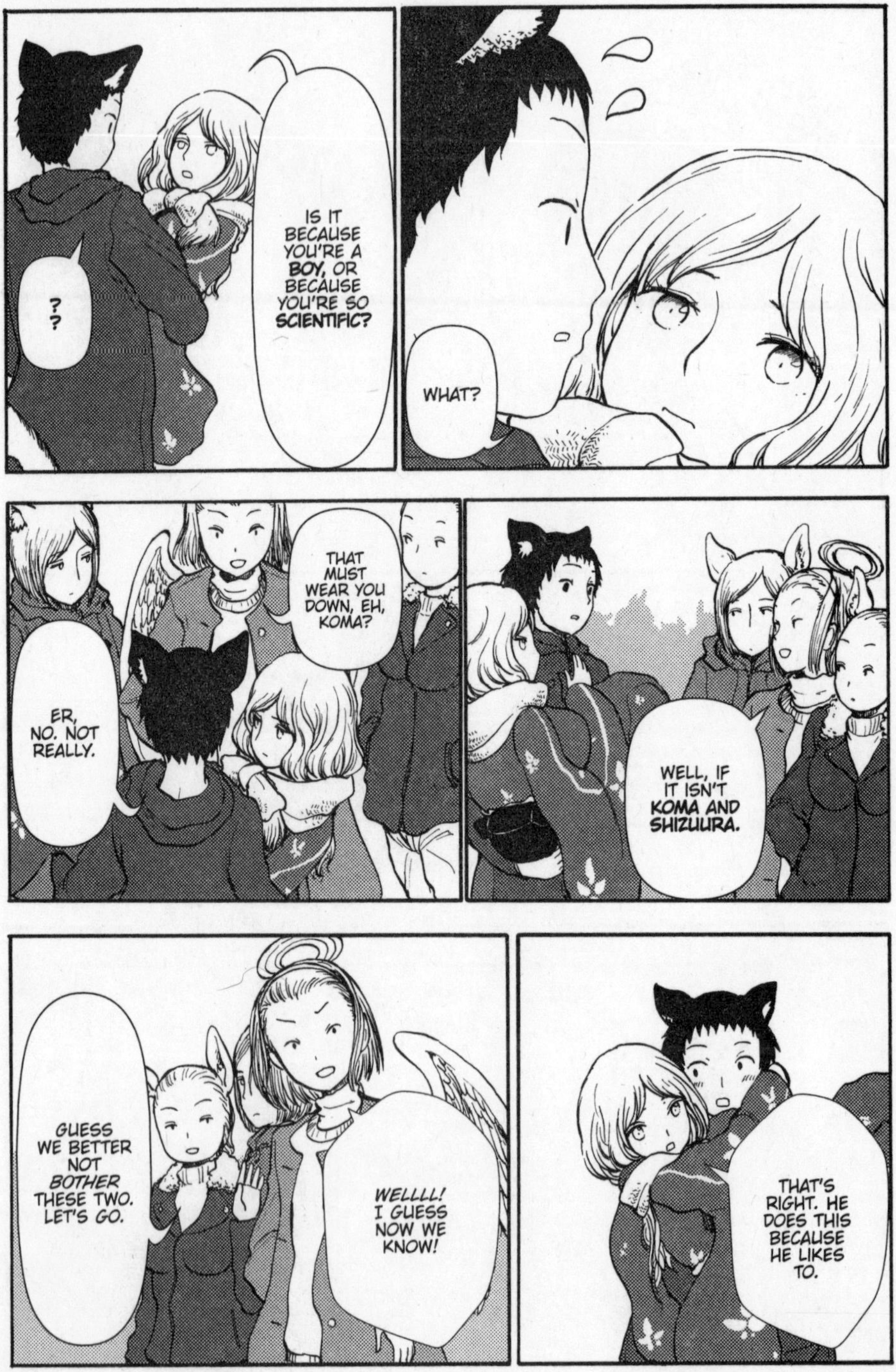
WHAT?
IS IT BECAUSE YOU'RE A BOY, OR BECAUSE YOU'RE SO SCIENTIFIC?
??
WELL, IF IT ISN'T KOMA AND SHIZUURA.
THAT MUST WEAR YOU DOWN, EH, KOMA?
ER, NO. NOT REALLY.
THAT'S RIGHT. HE DOES THIS BECAUSE HE LIKES TO.
WELLLL! I GUESS NOW WE KNOW!
GUESS WE BETTER NOT BOTHER THESE TWO. LET'S GO.

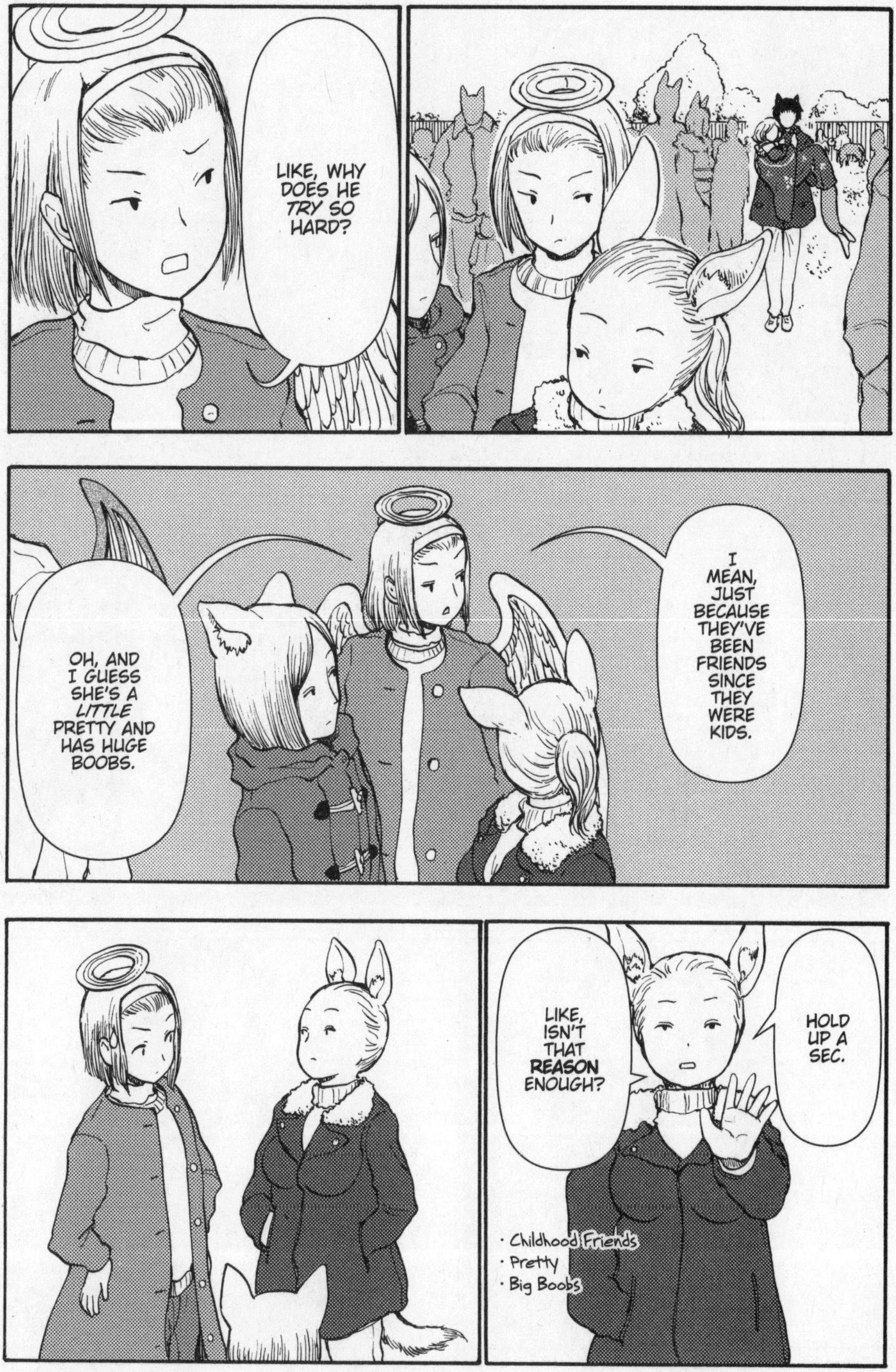
LIKE, WHY DOES HE *TRY* SO HARD?
I MEAN, JUST BECAUSE THEY'VE BEEN FRIENDS SINCE THEY WERE KIDS.
OH, AND I GUESS SHE'S A *LITTLE* PRETTY AND HAS HUGE BOOBS.
HOLD UP A SEC.
LIKE, ISN'T THAT **REASON** ENOUGH?
· Childhood Friends
· Pretty
· Big Boobs

CLONG
CLING
JINGLE
AKOYAKI
JUST ONE, THEN?
WELL, THAT'S ALL WE CAN HOLD.
HEH. I SUPPOSE SO. THAT'LL BE FIVE-HUN'RED YEN.
MUNCH

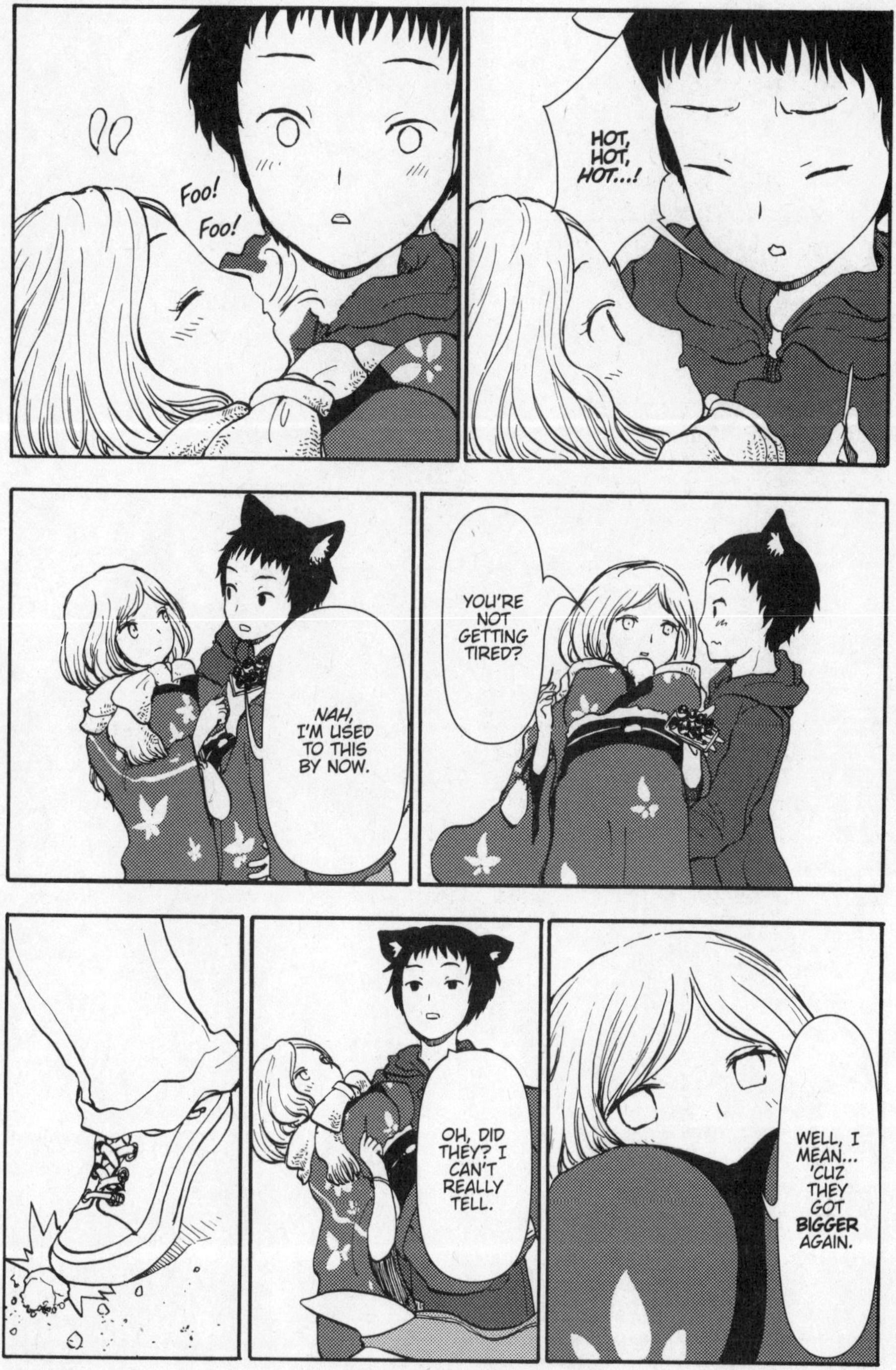
HOT, HOT, HOT...!
Foo! Foo!
YOU'RE NOT GETTING TIRED?
NAH, I'M USED TO THIS BY NOW.
WELL, I MEAN... 'CUZ THEY GOT BIGGER AGAIN.
OH, DID THEY? I CAN'T REALLY TELL.

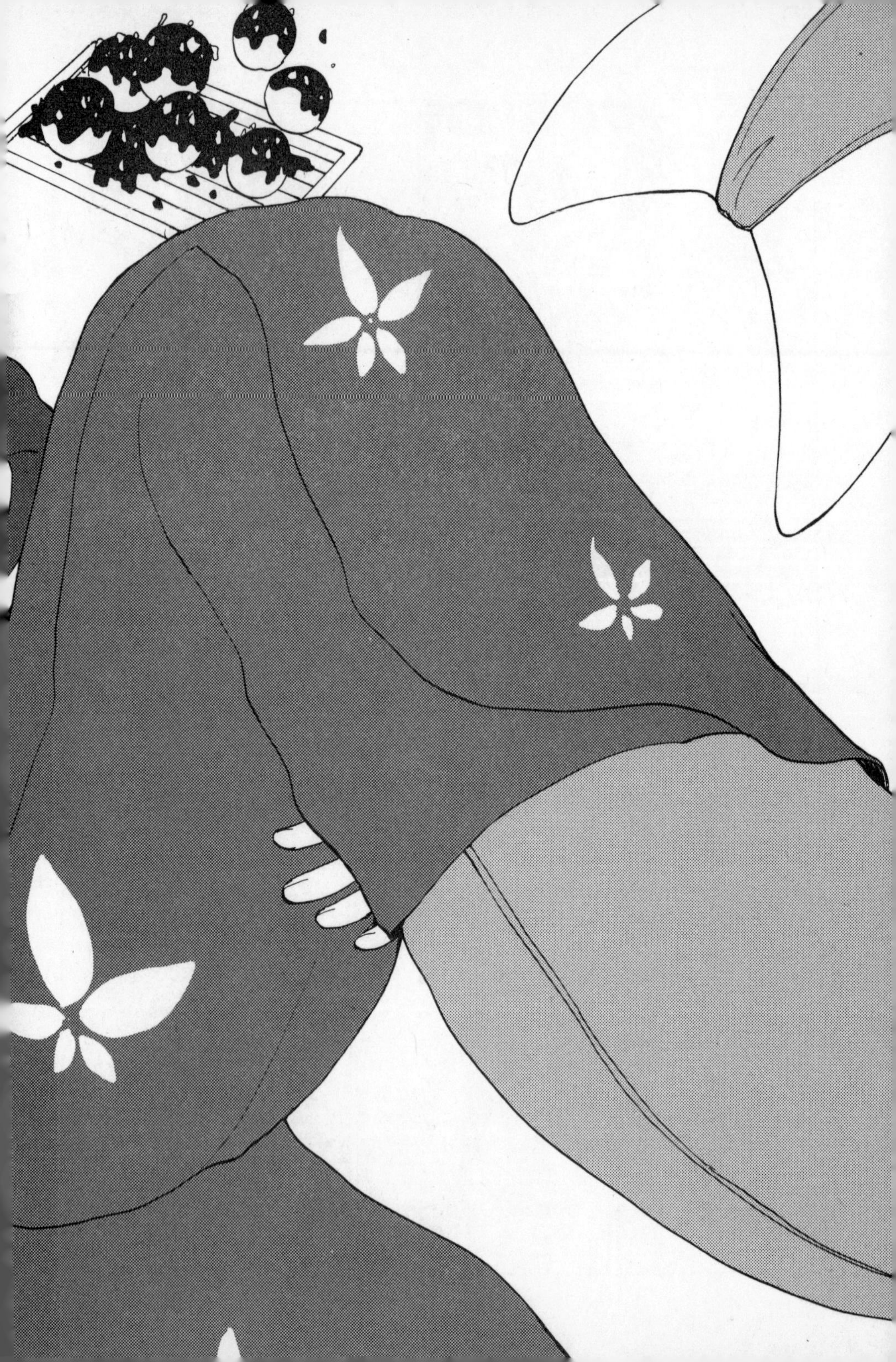

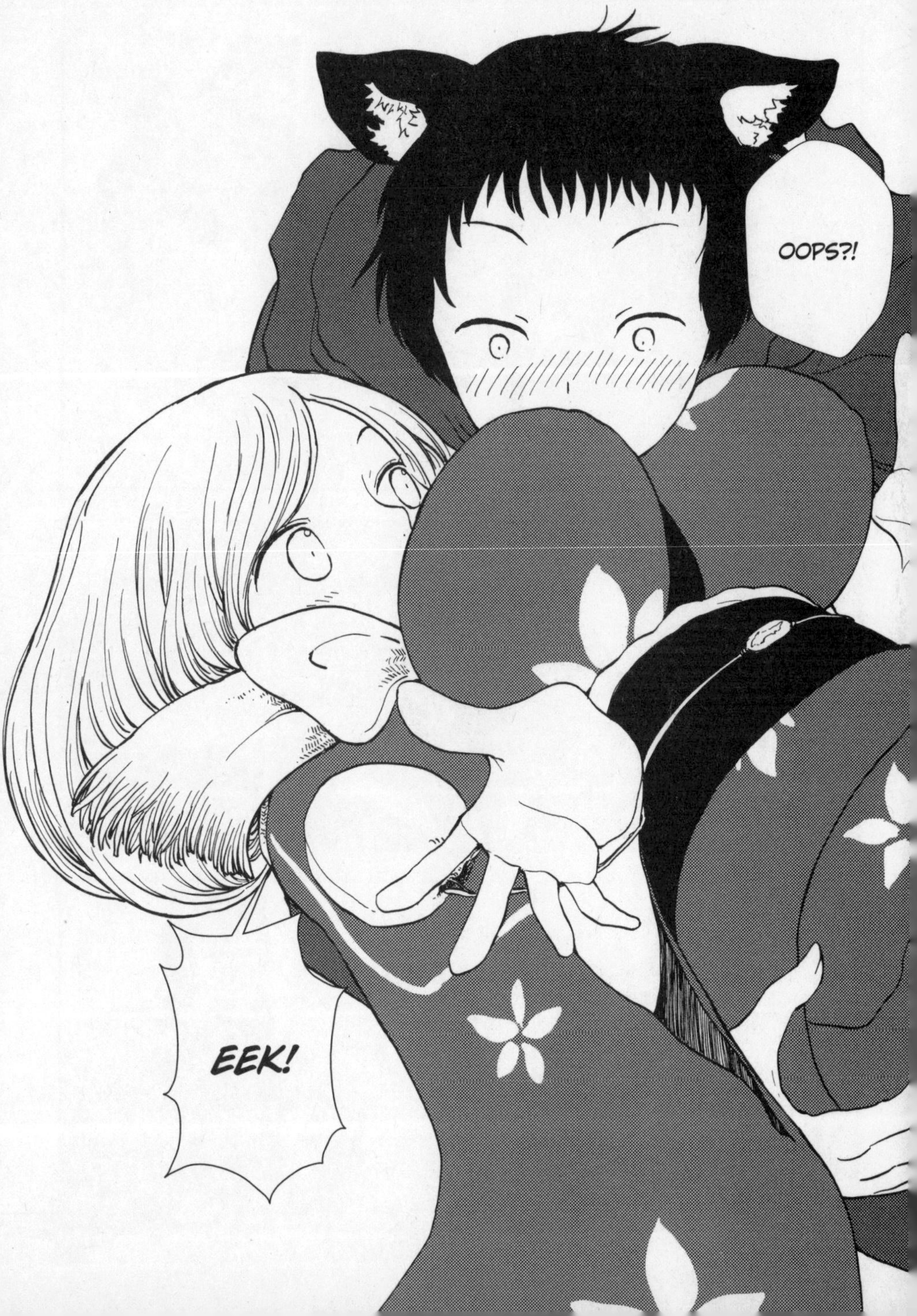
OOPS?!
EEK!

CATCH

YOU'RE
RIGHT,
THEY
DID GET
BIGGER.

WHOOp

WHOOp

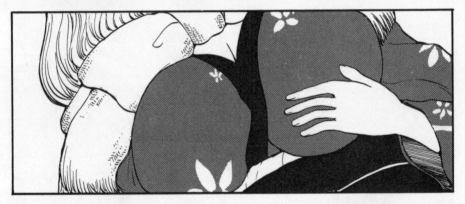

BUMP

IT'S
DANGEROUS
NOT TO
LOOK
WHERE
YOU'RE
GOING.

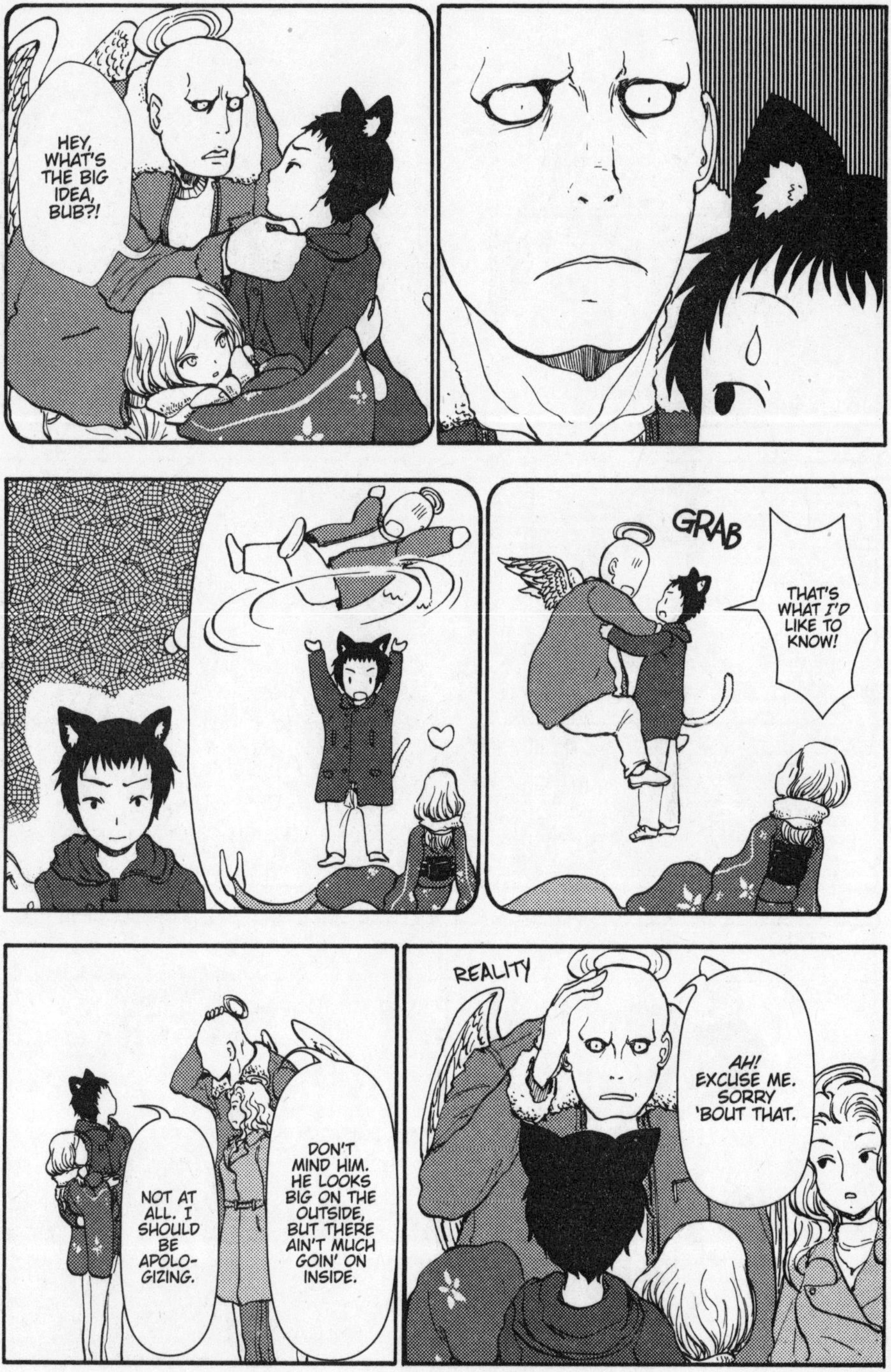
HEY, WHAT'S THE BIG IDEA, BUB?!
GRAB
THAT'S WHAT I'D LIKE TO KNOW!
REALITY
AH! EXCUSE ME. SORRY 'BOUT THAT.
DON'T MIND HIM. HE LOOKS BIG ON THE OUTSIDE, BUT THERE AIN'T MUCH GOIN' ON INSIDE.
NOT AT ALL. I SHOULD BE APOLO-GIZING.

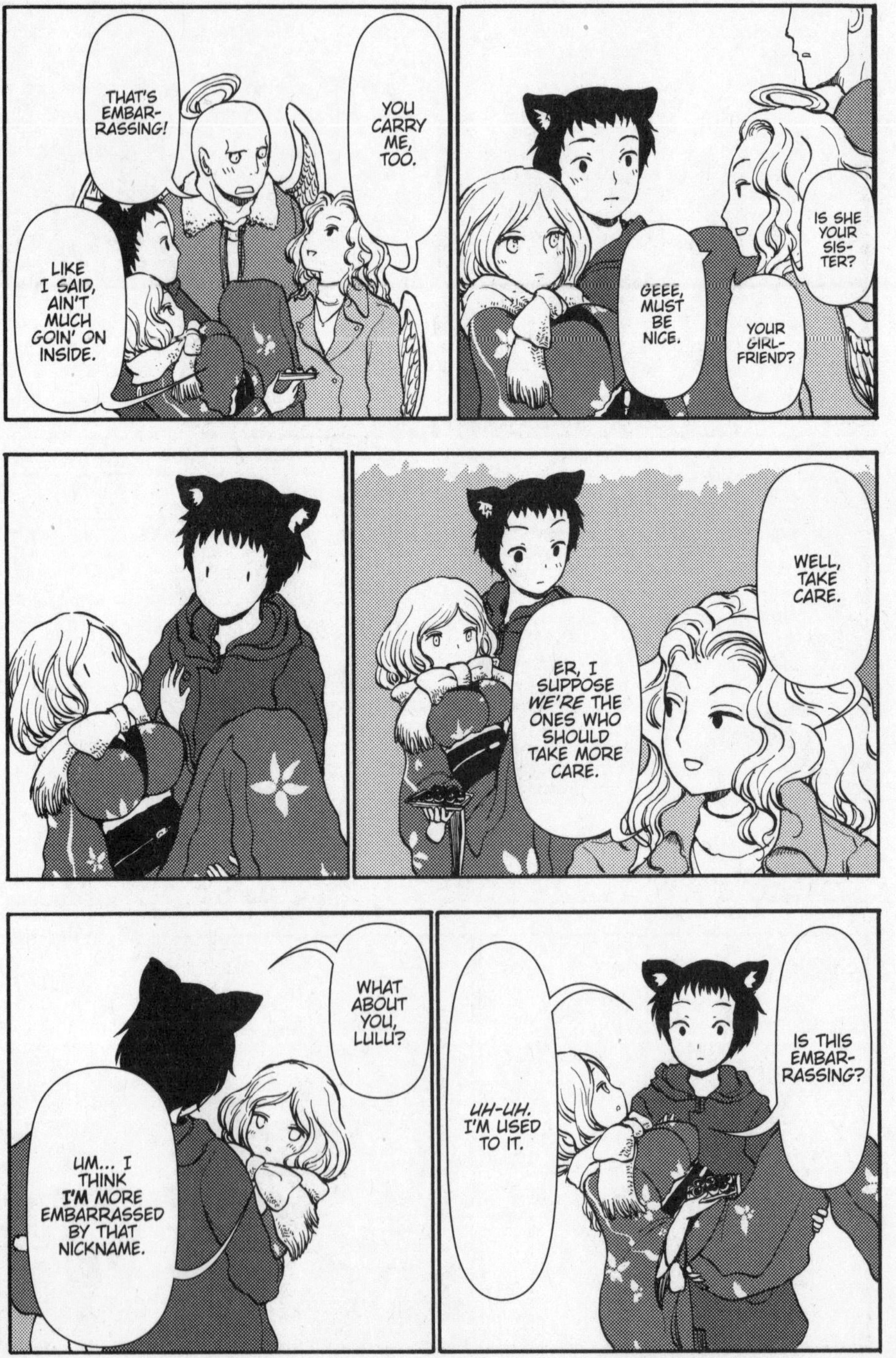
IS SHE YOUR SISTER?
YOUR GIRLFRIEND?
GEEE, MUST BE NICE.
YOU CARRY ME, TOO.
THAT'S EMBARRASSING!
LIKE I SAID, AIN'T MUCH GOIN' ON INSIDE.
WELL, TAKE CARE.
ER, I SUPPOSE *WE'RE* THE ONES WHO SHOULD TAKE MORE CARE.
IS THIS EMBARRASSING?
UH-UH. I'M USED TO IT.
WHAT ABOUT YOU, LULU?
UM... I THINK **I'M** MORE EMBARRASSED BY THAT NICKNAME.

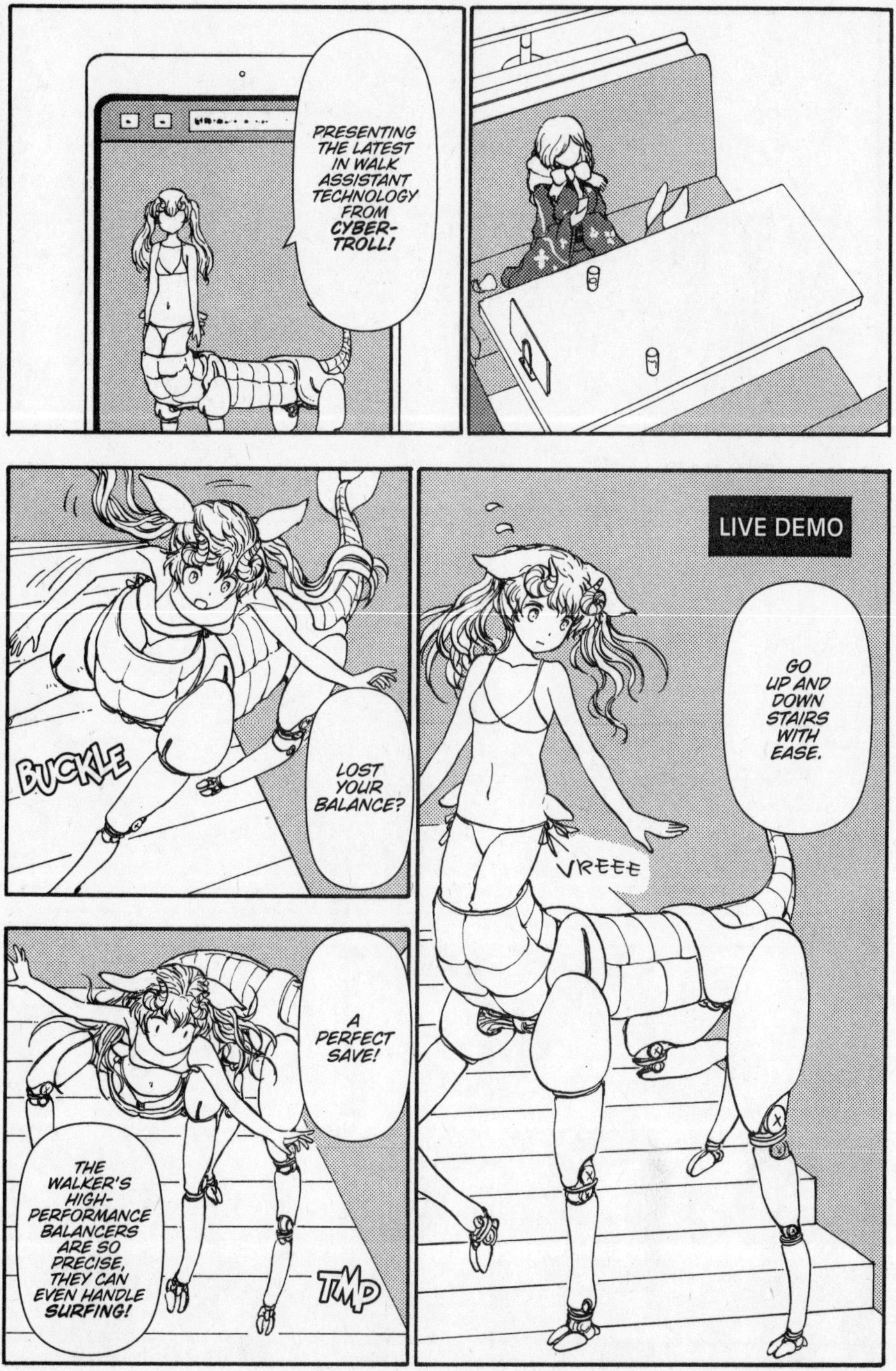
PRESENTING THE LATEST IN WALK ASSISTANT TECHNOLOGY FROM CYBER-TROLL!
LIVE DEMO
GO UP AND DOWN STAIRS WITH EASE.
VREEE
BUCKLE
LOST YOUR BALANCE?
A PERFECT SAVE!
THE WALKER'S HIGH-PERFORMANCE BALANCERS ARE SO PRECISE, THEY CAN EVEN HANDLE SURFING!
TMP

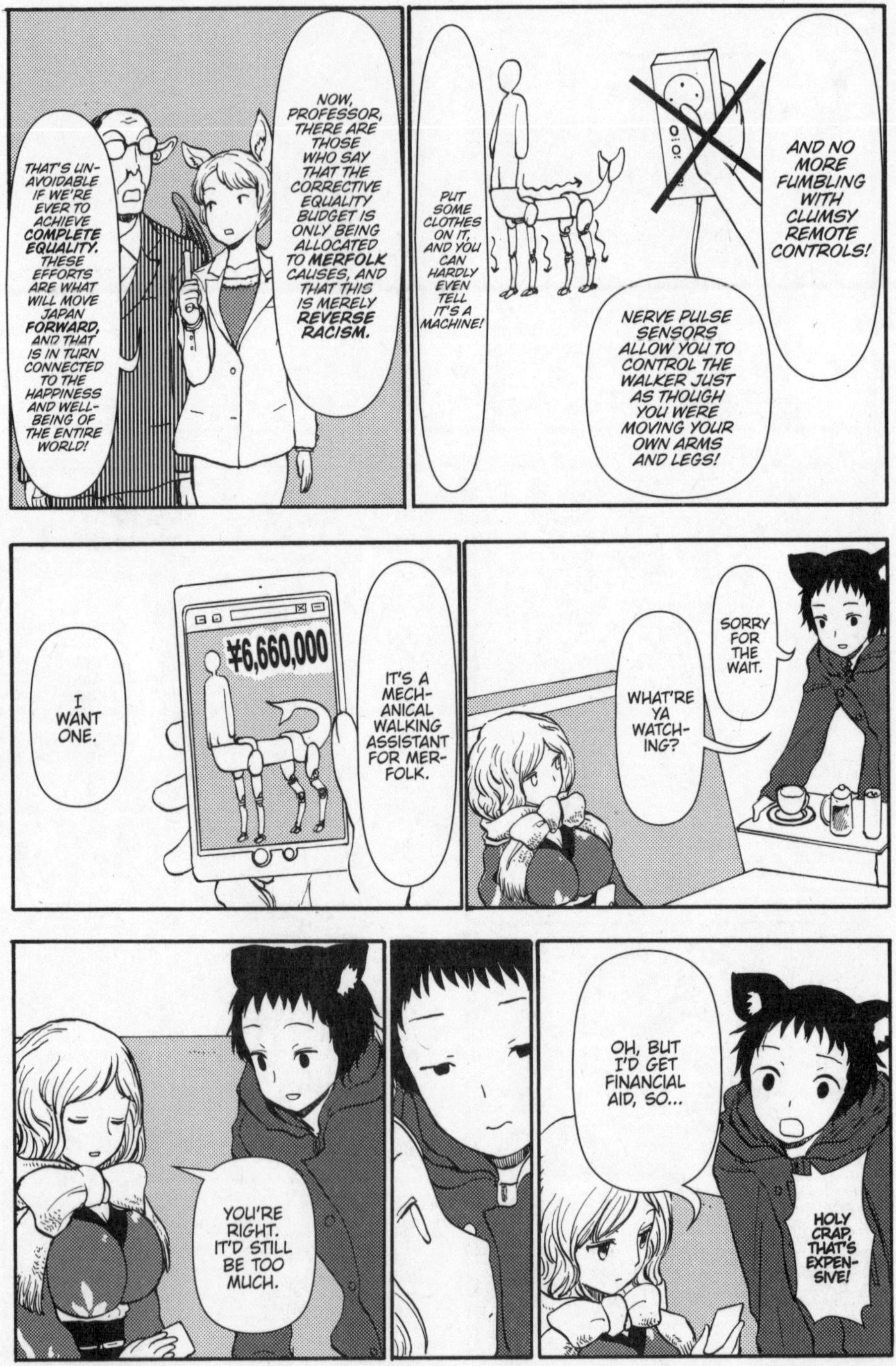
AND NO MORE FUMBLING WITH CLUMSY REMOTE CONTROLS!
NERVE PULSE SENSORS ALLOW YOU TO CONTROL THE WALKER JUST AS THOUGH YOU WERE MOVING YOUR OWN ARMS AND LEGS!
PUT SOME CLOTHES ON IT, AND YOU CAN HARDLY EVEN TELL IT'S A MACHINE!
NOW, PROFESSOR, THERE ARE THOSE WHO SAY THAT THE CORRECTIVE EQUALITY BUDGET IS ONLY BEING ALLOCATED TO **MERFOLK** CAUSES, AND THAT THIS IS MERELY **REVERSE RACISM.**
THAT'S UN-AVOIDABLE IF WE'RE EVER TO ACHIEVE **COMPLETE EQUALITY.** THESE EFFORTS ARE WHAT WILL MOVE JAPAN **FORWARD,** AND THAT IS IN TURN CONNECTED TO THE HAPPINESS AND WELL-BEING OF THE ENTIRE WORLD!
SORRY FOR THE WAIT.
WHAT'RE YA WATCHING?
IT'S A MECH-ANICAL WALKING ASSISTANT FOR MER-FOLK.
¥6,660,000
I WANT ONE.
HOLY CRAP, THAT'S EXPEN-SIVE!
OH, BUT I'D GET FINANCIAL AID, SO...
YOU'RE RIGHT. IT'D STILL BE TOO MUCH.

A Centaur's Life

TRADITIONAL DRESS FROM AROUND THE WORLD (ERITREA)

THE RASHAIDA TRIBE, WHICH ACCOUNTS FOR TWO PERCENT OF THE ERITREAN POPULATION, ORIGINALLY MADE THEIR HOME IN THE ARABIAN PENINSULA, BUT WERE DRIVEN BY WAR ACROSS THE RED SEA AND INTO AFRICA. CENTERED ON THE NUBIAN DESERT, THEY CAME TO LIVE NOMADICALLY, AND EVEN NOW SOME MEMBERS OF THE TRIBE MAKE THEIR HOME IN THE MIDDLE EAST, CARRYING OUT TRADE WITH ERITREA AND THE NEIGHBORING SUDAN, AS WELL AS THE ARABIAN PENINSULA. BECAUSE OF THIS BACKGROUND, MANY ARABIC CUSTOMS HAVE TAKEN DEEP ROOT WITHIN THE RASHAIDA CULTURE, SUCH AS THE DONNING OF FACE-CONCEALING BURQAS BY FEMALE MEMBERS. THESE, HOWEVER, ARE NOT THE PLAIN, SOLID BLACK BURQAS TYPICALLY PICTURED BY OUTSIDERS, BUT ARE IN FACT ADORNED "SO HEAVILY AS TO IMPEDE MOBILITY" IN BEAUTIFUL DECORATIONS PRIMARILY MADE OF SILVER.

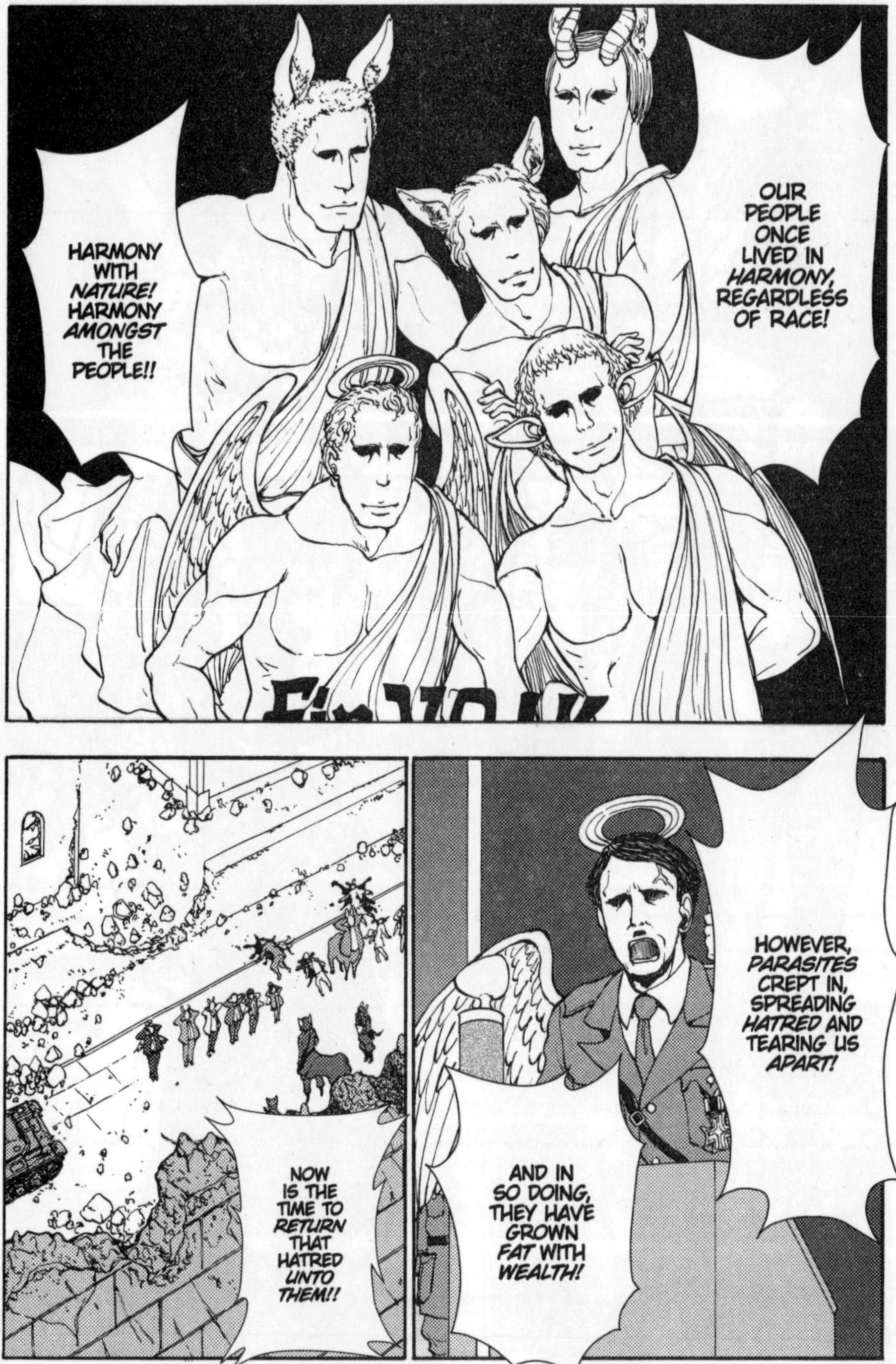
OUR PEOPLE ONCE LIVED IN *HARMONY*, REGARDLESS OF RACE!
HARMONY WITH *NATURE!* HARMONY *AMONGST* THE PEOPLE!!
HOWEVER, *PARASITES* CREPT IN, SPREADING *HATRED* AND TEARING US *APART!*
AND IN SO DOING, THEY HAVE GROWN *FAT* WITH *WEALTH!*
NOW IS THE TIME TO *RETURN* THAT HATRED *UNTO THEM!!*

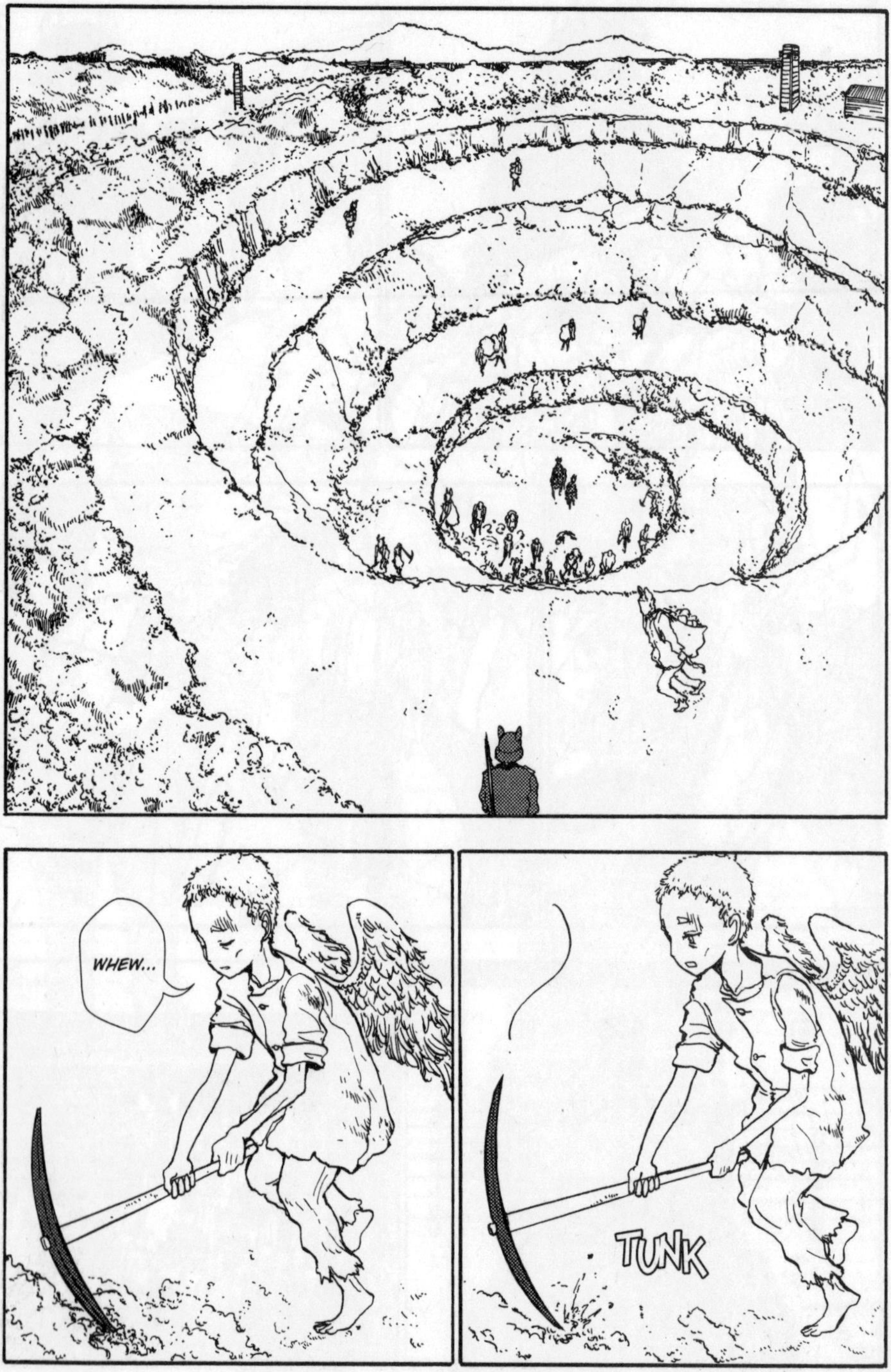
TUNK
WHEW...

WHUMP
DO NOT REST!
HEY! YOU THINK YOU GET TO LAZE AROUND WHILE THE REST OF US WORK?!
WHUD
WHUD
STAND.
WORK!
WHUMP
THAT'S RIGHT. IT IS LABOR THAT WILL SET YOU FREE.

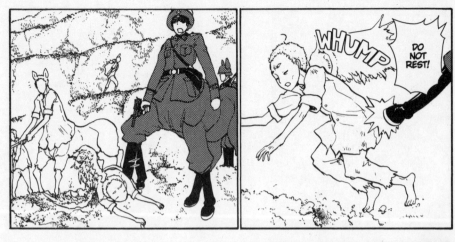

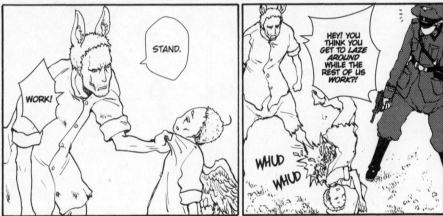

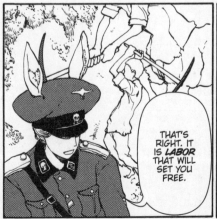

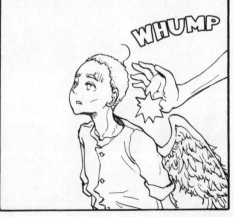

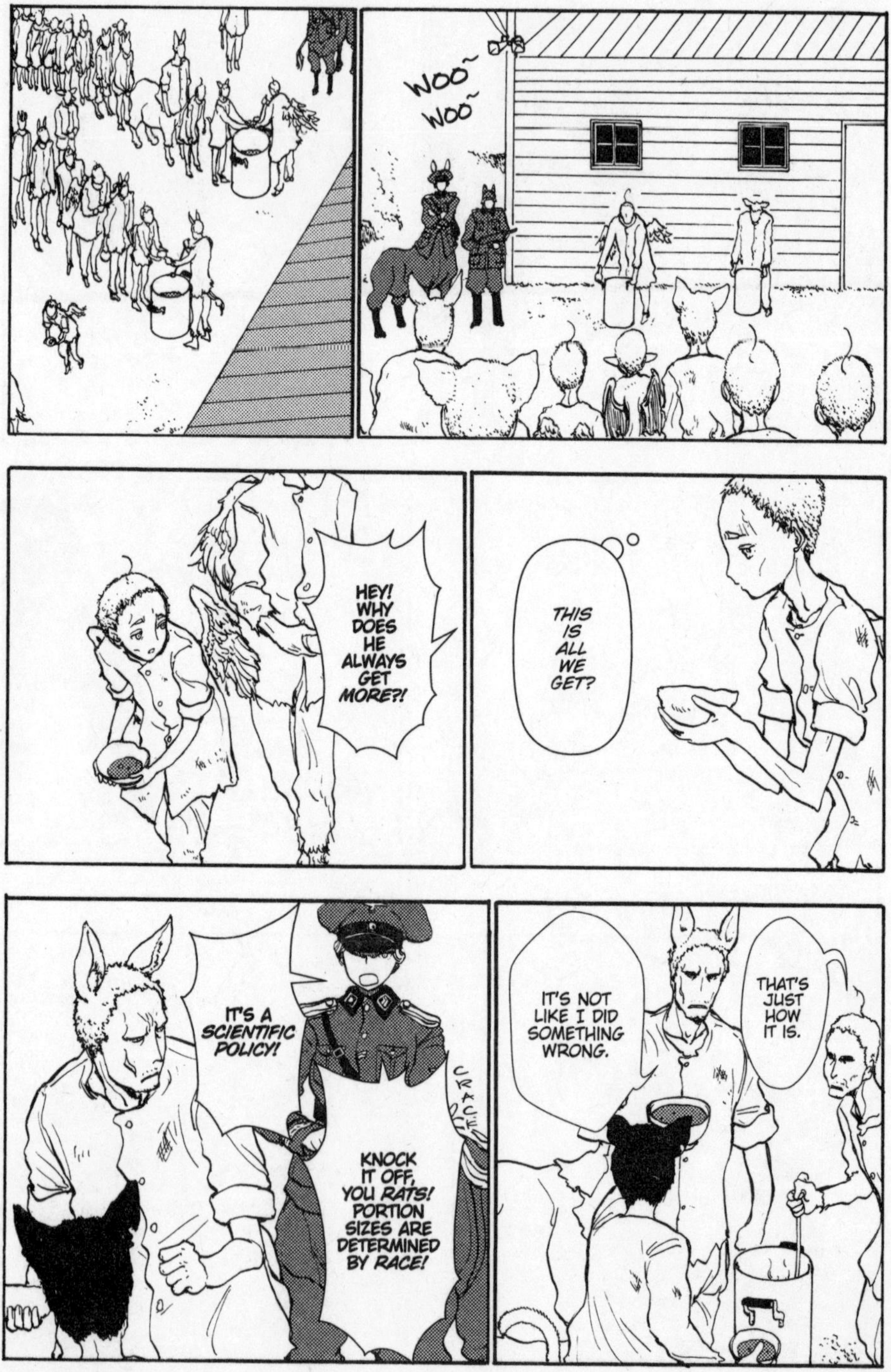
WOO~
WOO~
THIS IS ALL WE GET?
HEY! WHY DOES HE ALWAYS GET MORE?!
THAT'S JUST HOW IT IS.
IT'S NOT LIKE I DID SOMETHING WRONG.
IT'S A SCIENTIFIC POLICY!
CRACK
KNOCK IT OFF, YOU RATS! PORTION SIZES ARE DETERMINED BY RACE!

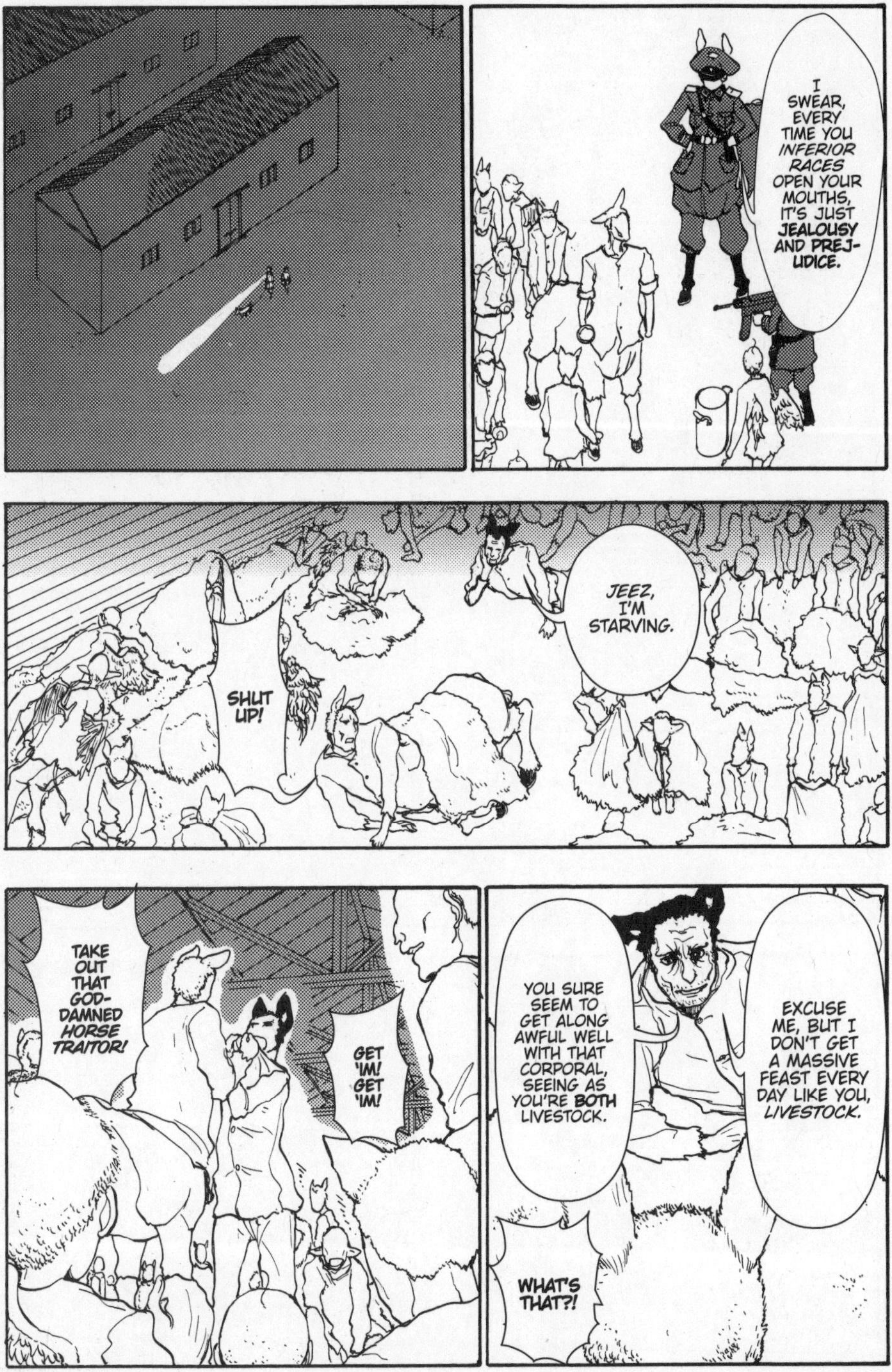
I SWEAR, EVERY TIME YOU *INFERIOR RACES* OPEN YOUR MOUTHS, IT'S JUST **JEALOUSY AND PREJUDICE.**
JEEZ, I'M STARVING.
SHUT UP!
EXCUSE ME, BUT I DON'T GET A MASSIVE FEAST EVERY DAY LIKE YOU, *LIVESTOCK.*
YOU SURE SEEM TO GET ALONG AWFUL WELL WITH THAT CORPORAL, SEEING AS YOU'RE **BOTH** LIVESTOCK.
WHAT'S THAT?!
TAKE OUT THAT GOD-DAMNED *HORSE TRAITOR!*
GET 'IM! GET 'IM!

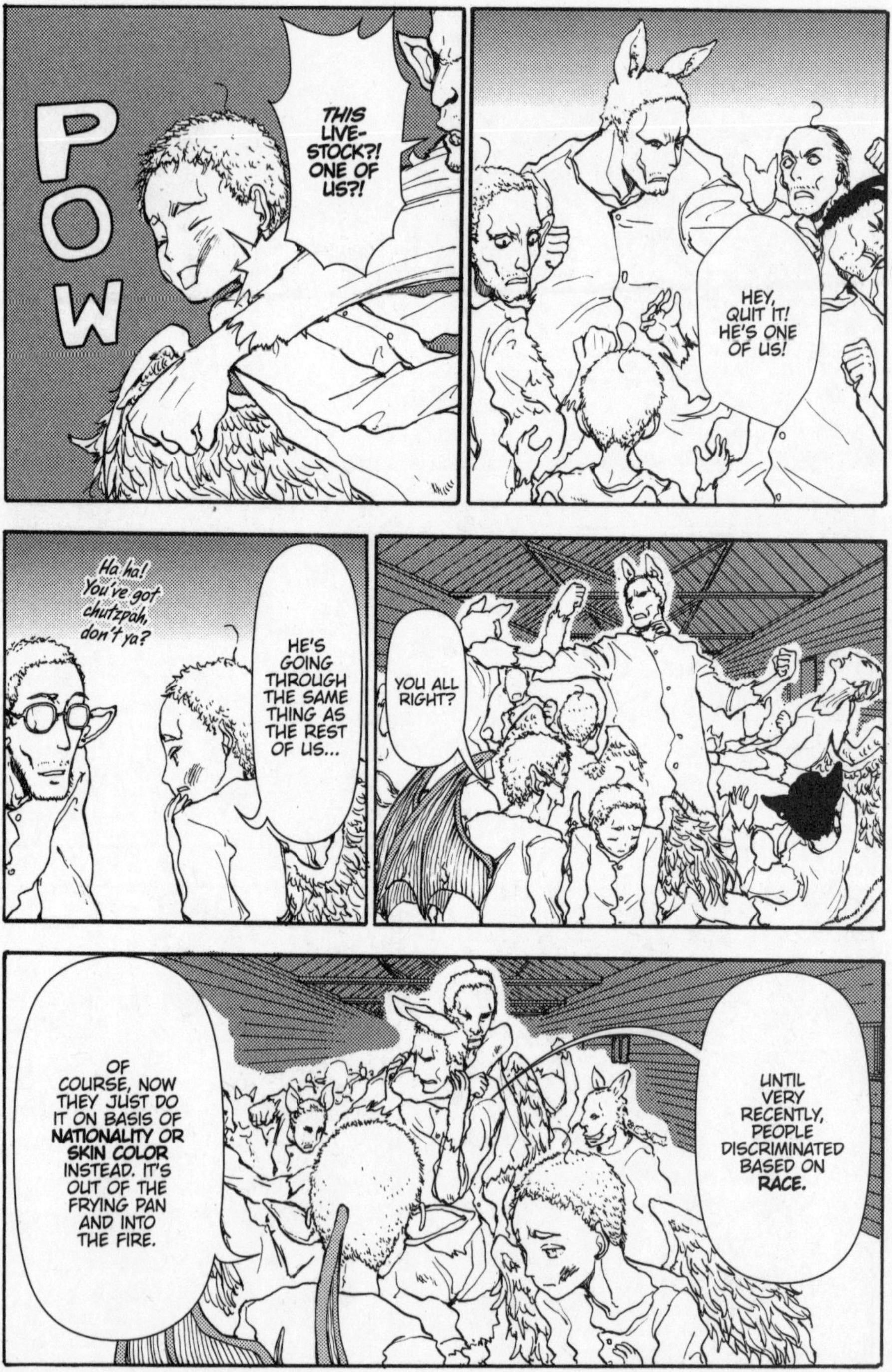
HEY, QUIT IT! HE'S ONE OF US!
THIS LIVE-STOCK?! ONE OF US?!
POW
YOU ALL RIGHT?
HE'S GOING THROUGH THE SAME THING AS THE REST OF US...
Ha ha! You've got chutzpah, don't ya?
UNTIL VERY RECENTLY, PEOPLE DISCRIMINATED BASED ON RACE.
OF COURSE, NOW THEY JUST DO IT ON BASIS OF NATIONALITY OR SKIN COLOR INSTEAD. IT'S OUT OF THE FRYING PAN AND INTO THE FIRE.

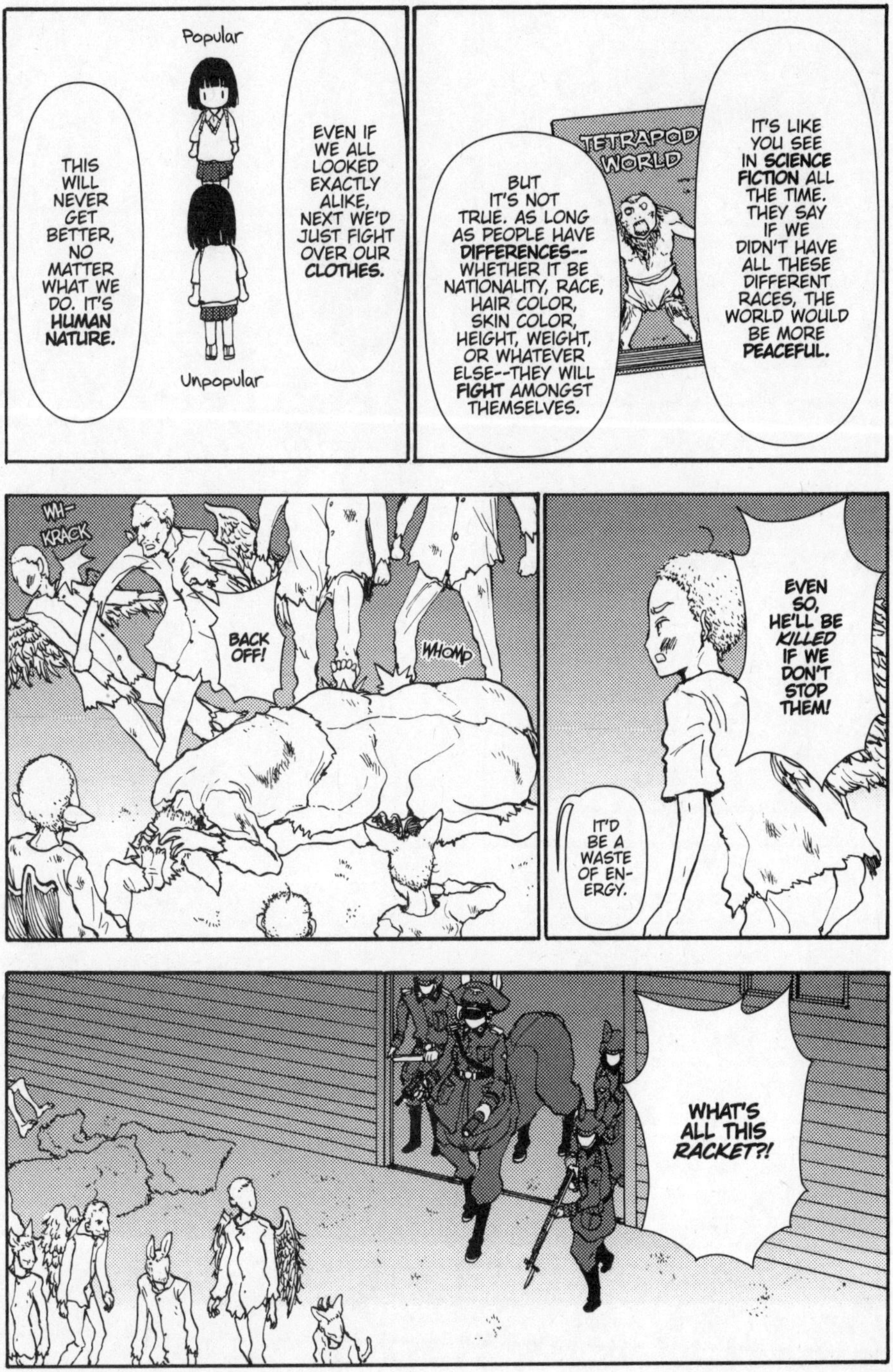

IT'S LIKE YOU SEE IN SCIENCE FICTION ALL THE TIME. THEY SAY IF WE DIDN'T HAVE ALL THESE DIFFERENT RACES, THE WORLD WOULD BE MORE PEACEFUL.
TETRAPOD WORLD
BUT IT'S NOT TRUE. AS LONG AS PEOPLE HAVE DIFFERENCES--WHETHER IT BE NATIONALITY, RACE, HAIR COLOR, SKIN COLOR, HEIGHT, WEIGHT, OR WHATEVER ELSE--THEY WILL FIGHT AMONGST THEMSELVES.
EVEN IF WE ALL LOOKED EXACTLY ALIKE, NEXT WE'D JUST FIGHT OVER OUR CLOTHES.
Popular
Unpopular
THIS WILL NEVER GET BETTER, NO MATTER WHAT WE DO. IT'S HUMAN NATURE.
EVEN SO, HE'LL BE KILLED IF WE DON'T STOP THEM!
IT'D BE A WASTE OF EN-ERGY.
WH-KRACK
BACK OFF!
WHOMP
WHAT'S ALL THIS RACKET?!

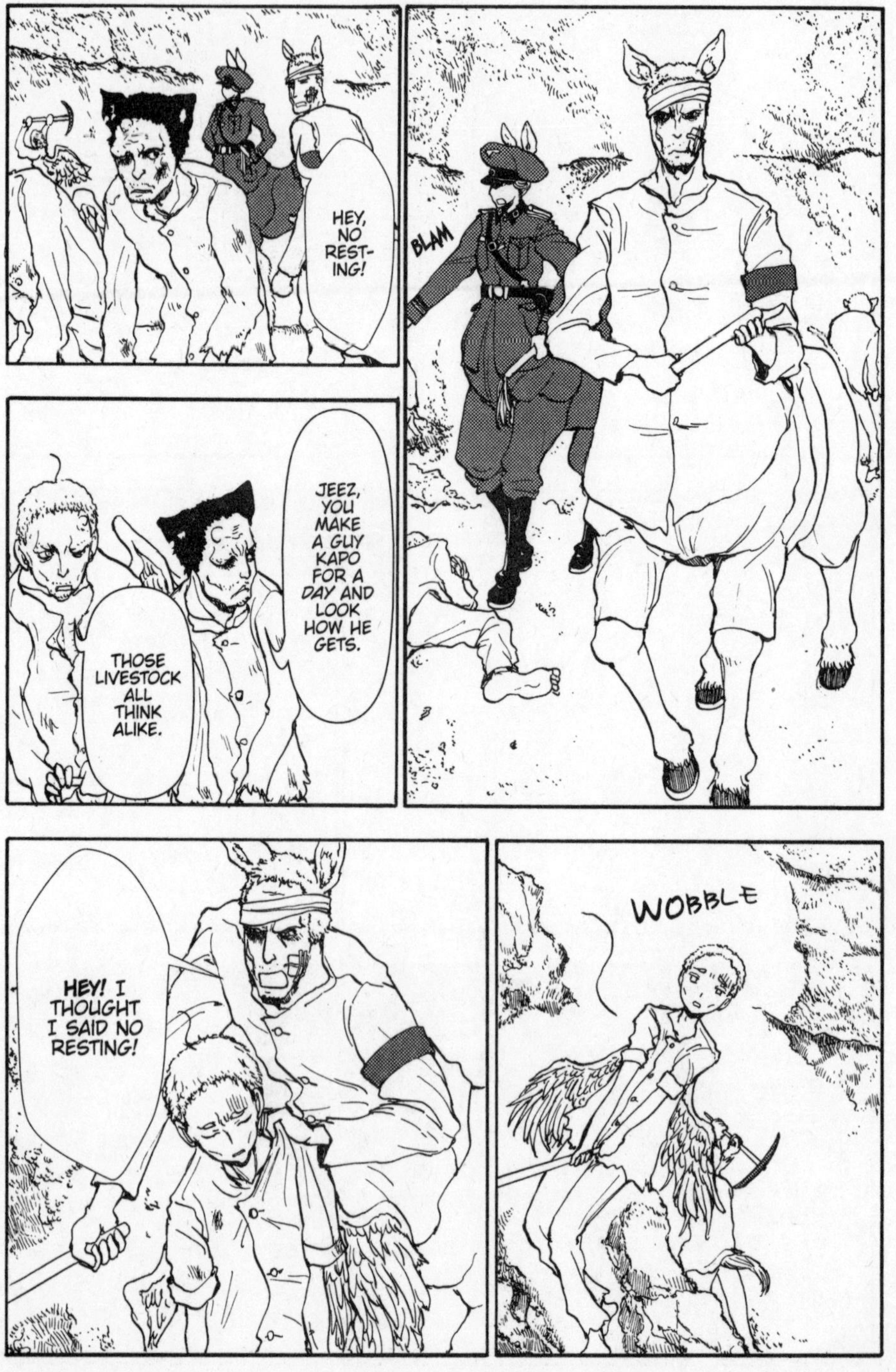
BLAM
HEY, NO RESTING!
JEEZ, YOU MAKE A GUY KAPO FOR A *DAY* AND LOOK HOW HE GETS.
THOSE LIVESTOCK ALL THINK ALIKE.
WOBBLE
HEY! I THOUGHT I SAID NO RESTING!

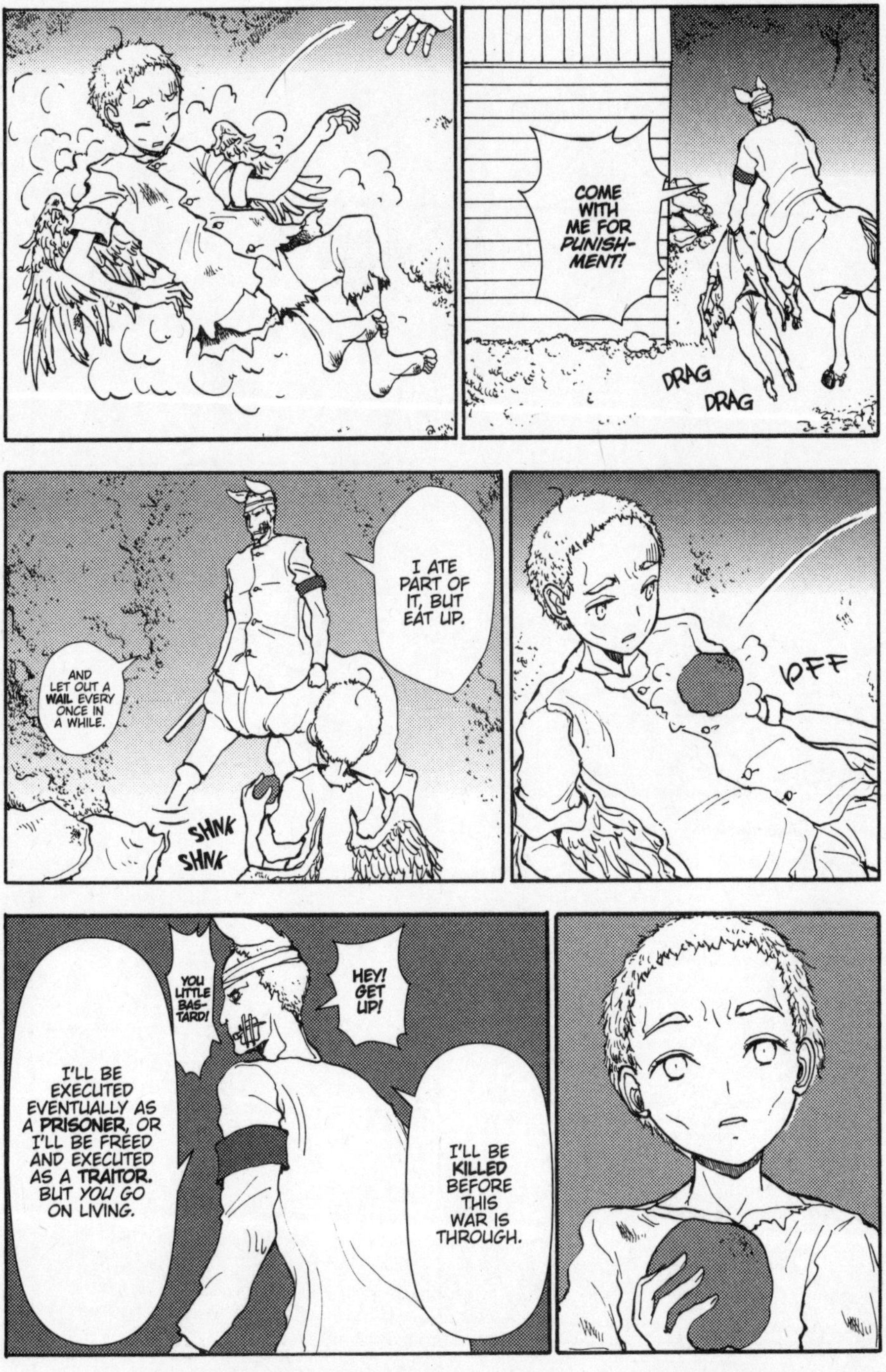
COME WITH ME FOR PUNISH-MENT!
DRAG
DRAG
PFF
I ATE PART OF IT, BUT EAT UP.
AND LET OUT A WAIL EVERY ONCE IN A WHILE.
SHNK
SHNK
HEY! GET UP!
YOU LITTLE BAS-TARD!
I'LL BE KILLED BEFORE THIS WAR IS THROUGH.
I'LL BE EXECUTED EVENTUALLY AS A PRISONER, OR I'LL BE FREED AND EXECUTED AS A TRAITOR. BUT YOU GO ON LIVING.

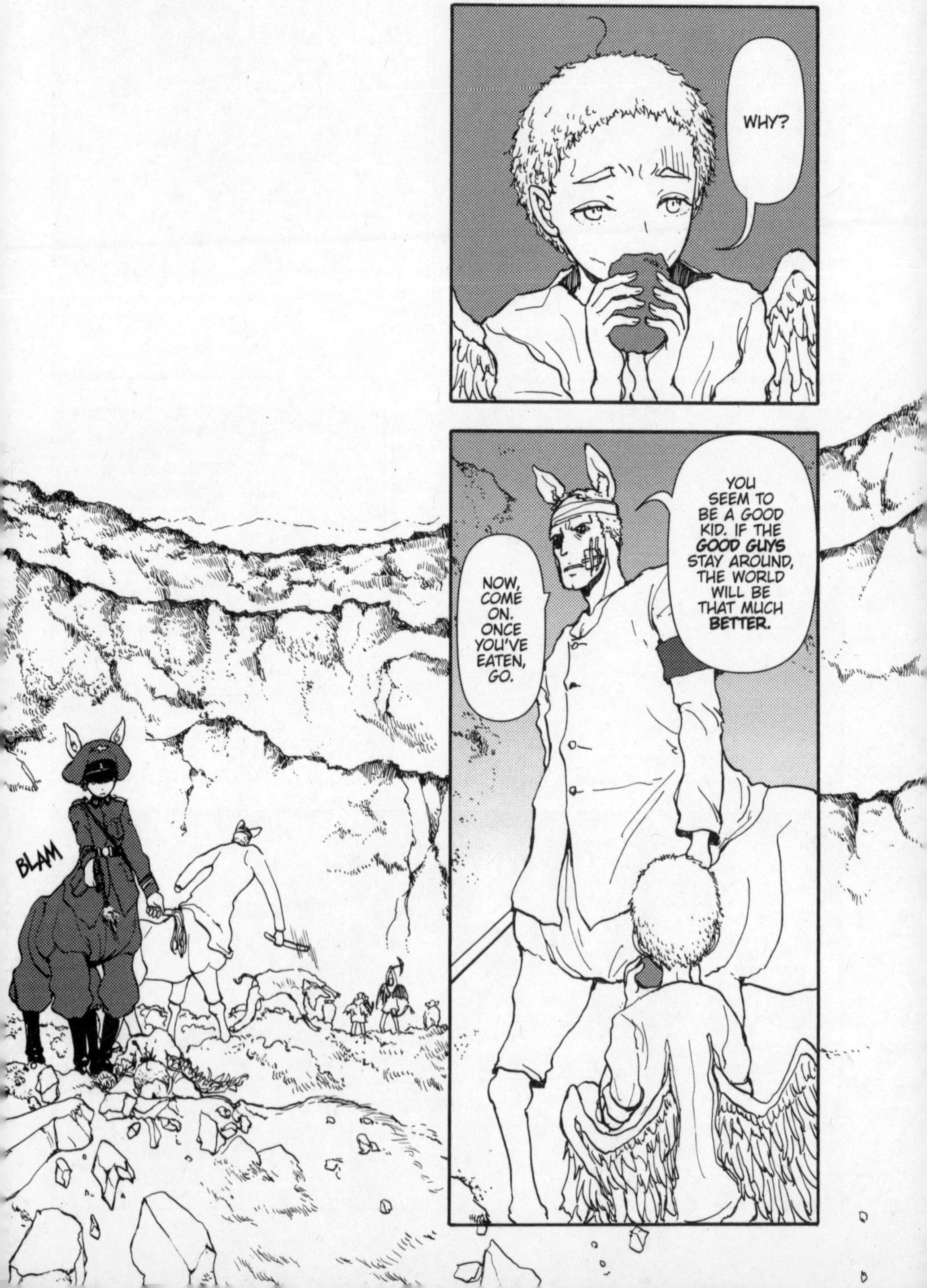
WHY?
YOU SEEM TO BE A GOOD KID. IF THE **GOOD GUYS** STAY AROUND, THE WORLD WILL BE THAT MUCH **BETTER.**
NOW, COME ON. ONCE YOU'VE EATEN, GO.
BLAM

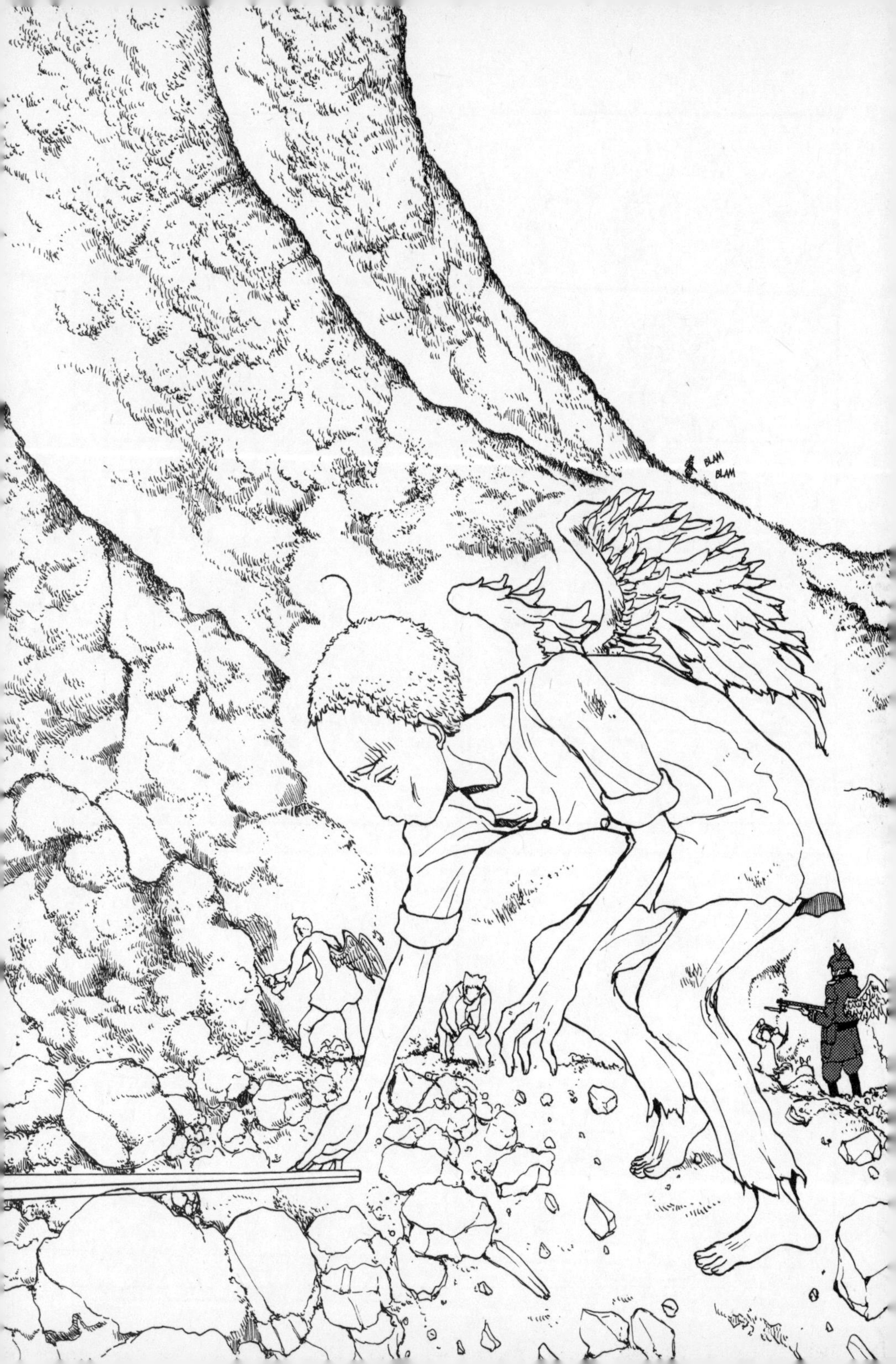
BLAM
BLAM

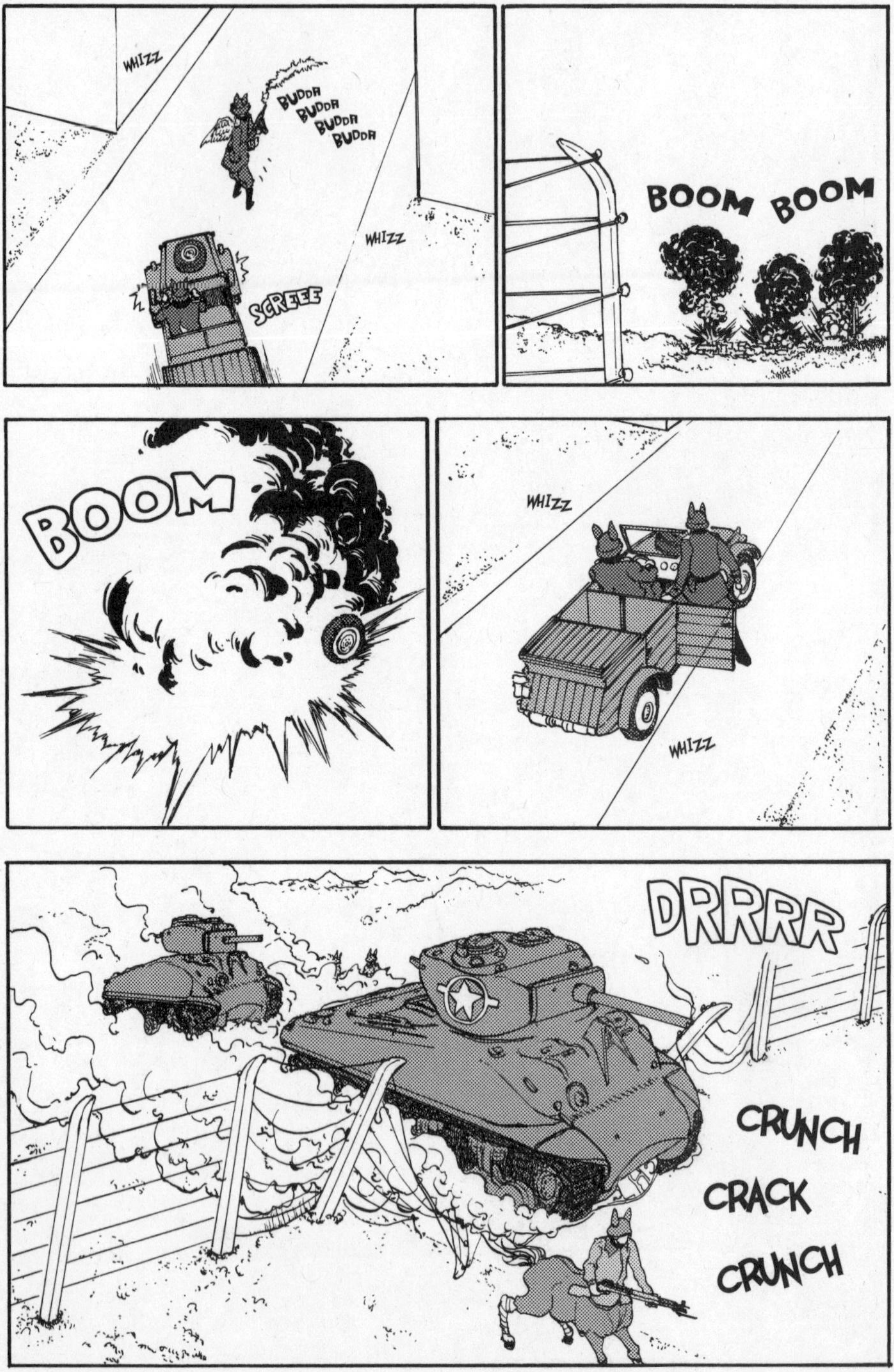
BOOM BOOM
WHIZZ
BUDDA
BUDDA
BUDDA
BUDDA
WHIZZ
SCREEE
WHIZZ
WHIZZ
BOOM
DRRRR
CRUNCH
CRACK
CRUNCH

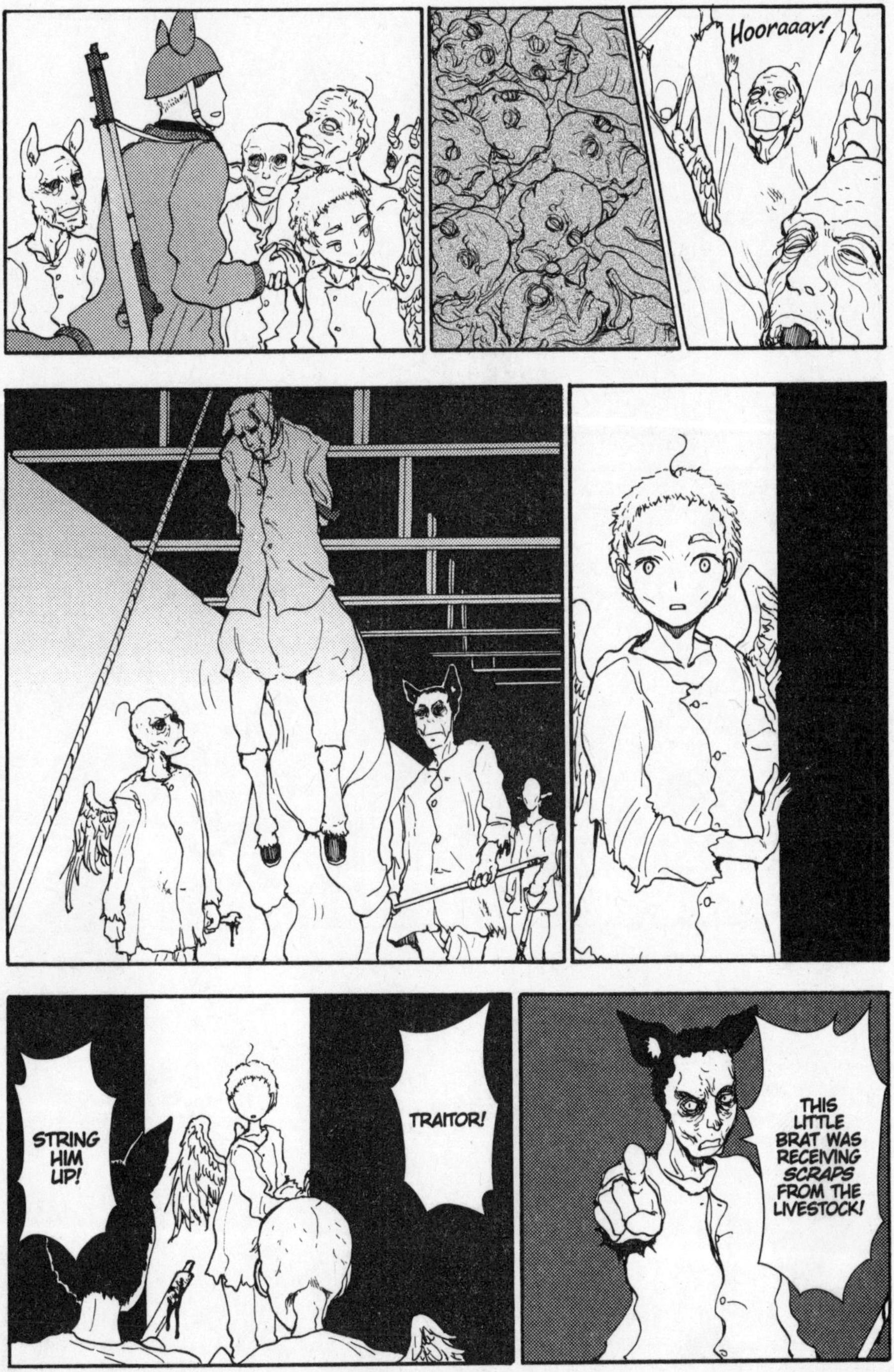
Hooraaay!
THIS LITTLE BRAT WAS RECEIVING SCRAPS FROM THE LIVESTOCK!
TRAITOR!
STRING HIM UP!

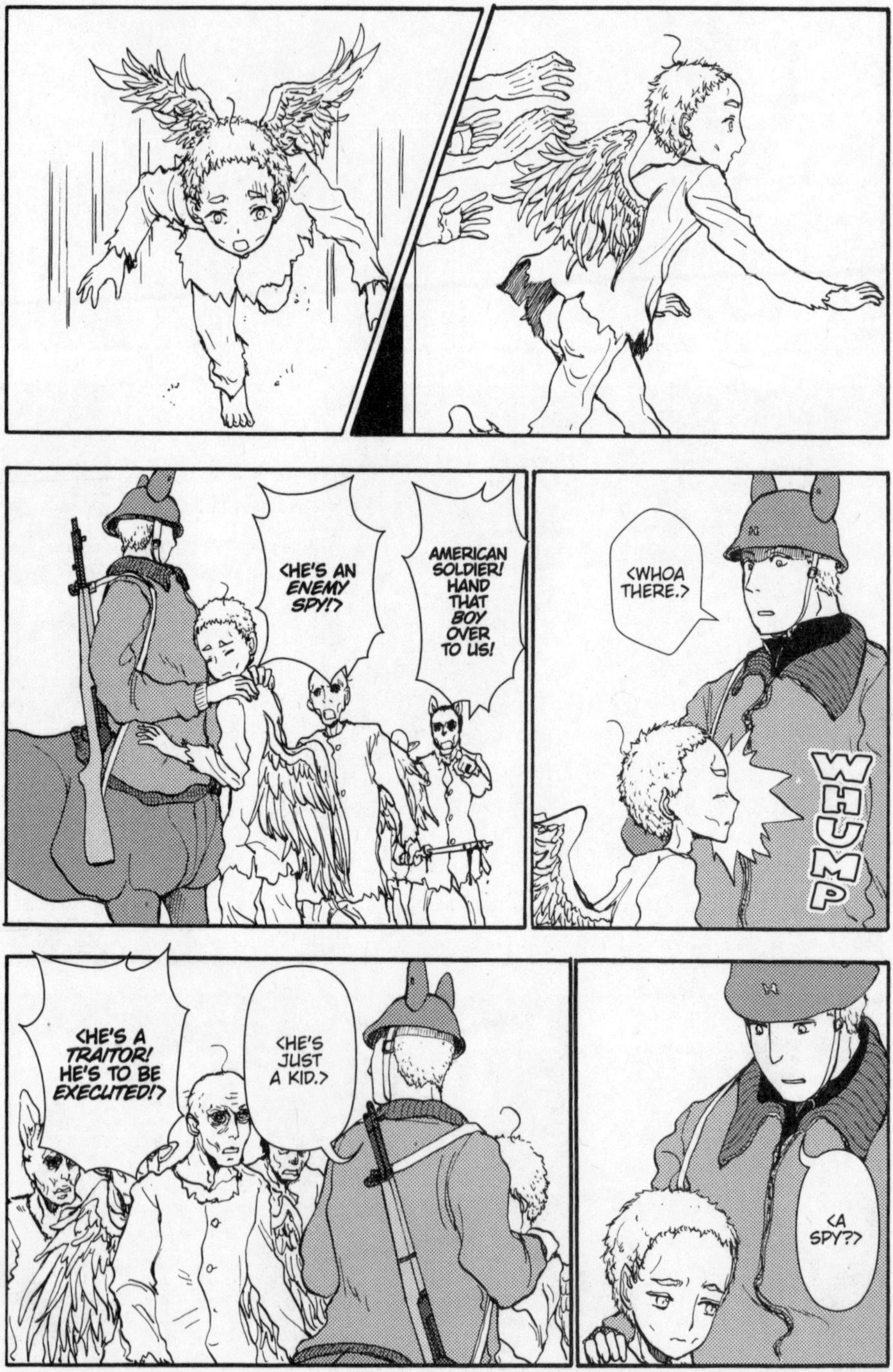
<WHOA THERE.>
WHUMP
AMERICAN SOLDIER! HAND THAT BOY OVER TO US!
<HE'S AN ENEMY SPY!?>
<A SPY??>
<HE'S JUST A KID.>
<HE'S A TRAITOR! HE'S TO BE EXECUTED!?>

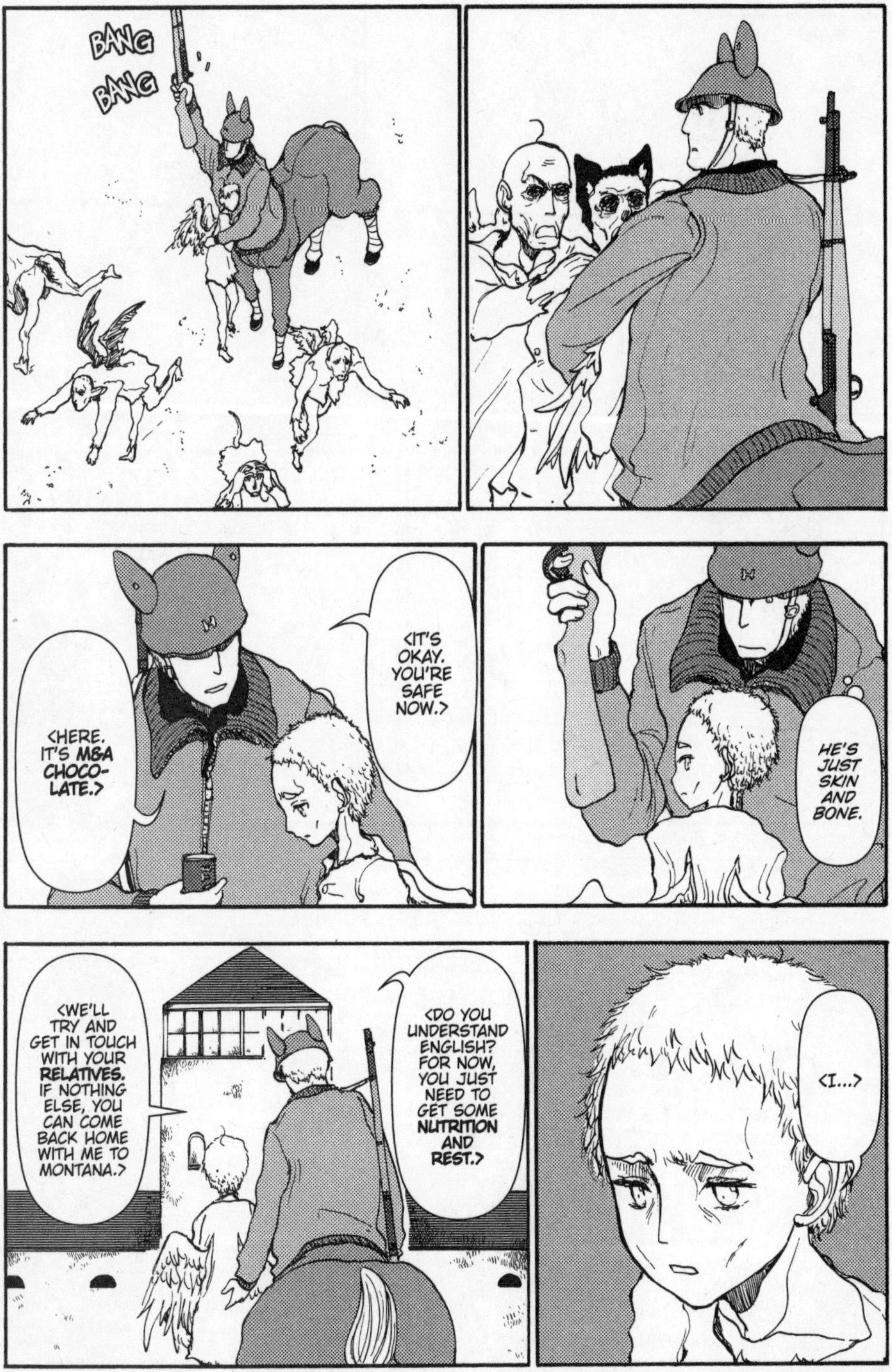
BANG
BANG
HE'S JUST SKIN AND BONE.
<IT'S OKAY. YOU'RE SAFE NOW.>
<HERE. IT'S M&A CHOCOLATE.>
<I...>
<DO YOU UNDERSTAND ENGLISH? FOR NOW, YOU JUST NEED TO GET SOME NUTRITION AND REST.>
<WE'LL TRY AND GET IN TOUCH WITH YOUR RELATIVES. IF NOTHING ELSE, YOU CAN COME BACK HOME WITH ME TO MONTANA.>

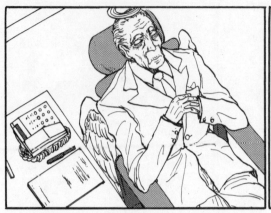

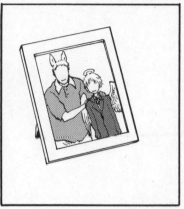

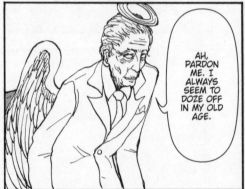

SIR, MR. ROUSSEAU IS HERE.
AH, PARDON ME. I ALWAYS SEEM TO DOZE OFF IN MY OLD AGE.

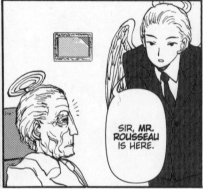

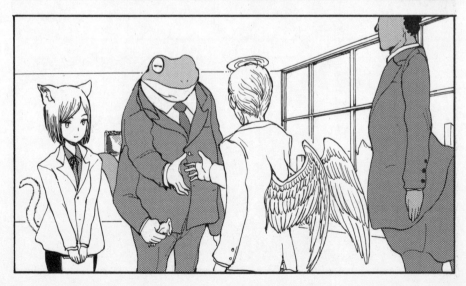

A Centaur's Life

TRADITIONAL DRESS FROM AROUND THE WORLD (THE AZTECS)

IN THE FIFTEENTH CENTURY, THE MOST MENACING THING BROUGHT INTO THIS CENTRAL AMERICAN EMPIRE BY EUROPEAN CONQUERORS (CONQUISTADORS) WAS NEITHER METAL WEAPONS NOR FIREARMS, NOR HORSES, NOR CENTAUR SLAVES. IT WAS DISEASE. THE NATIVES, WHOSE BODIES HAD NO RESISTANCE TO THE FOREIGN PATHOGENS BROUGHT IN, WERE KILLED IN DROVES. IF THE ANTARCTICANS HAD NOT COME TO THEIR AID, THE *MEXIHCAH* PEOPLE AND THEIR EMPIRE WOULD HAVE VANISHED COMPLETELY, LEAVING ONLY DEAD CITIES AND TEMPLES IN THEIR WAKE. NEVERTHELESS, THE EMPIRE DID ULTIMATELY COLLAPSE, AND THE FRAMEWORK OF THE AZTEC CIVILIZATION WAS USED TO FORM A UNION OF MULTIPLE TRIBES WHICH CLAIMED THE ALL BUT OBSOLETE EMPEROR AS ITS SYMBOLIC FIGUREHEAD. THE EMPEROR'S CLOTHING IS CHARACTERIZED BY THE LAVISH ADORNMENT OF GOLDEN DECORATIONS, AS WELL AS A CLOAK DECORATED WITH DESIGNS SOME THEORIZE ARE REFERENCES TO SECRET ANTARCTICAN KNOWLEDGE OTHERWISE UNKNOWN TO MAMMALIAN MANKIND. THESE ARTICLES, LIKE THE MANY MYSTERY-LADEN RITUALS OF THIS CIVILIZATION, ARE RARELY VIEWED BY THE EYES OF OUTSIDERS.

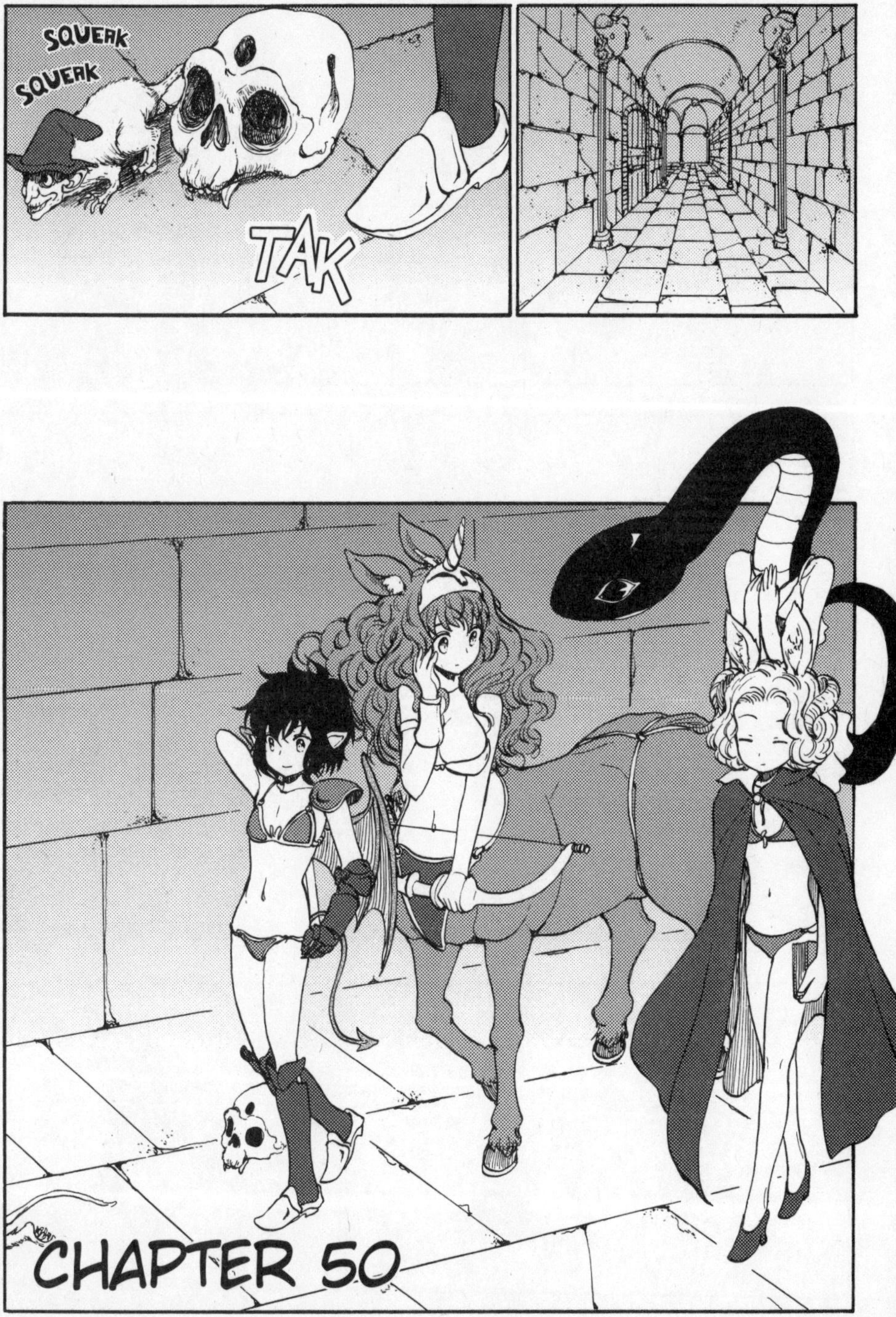
SQUEAK
SQUEAK
TAK
CHAPTER 50

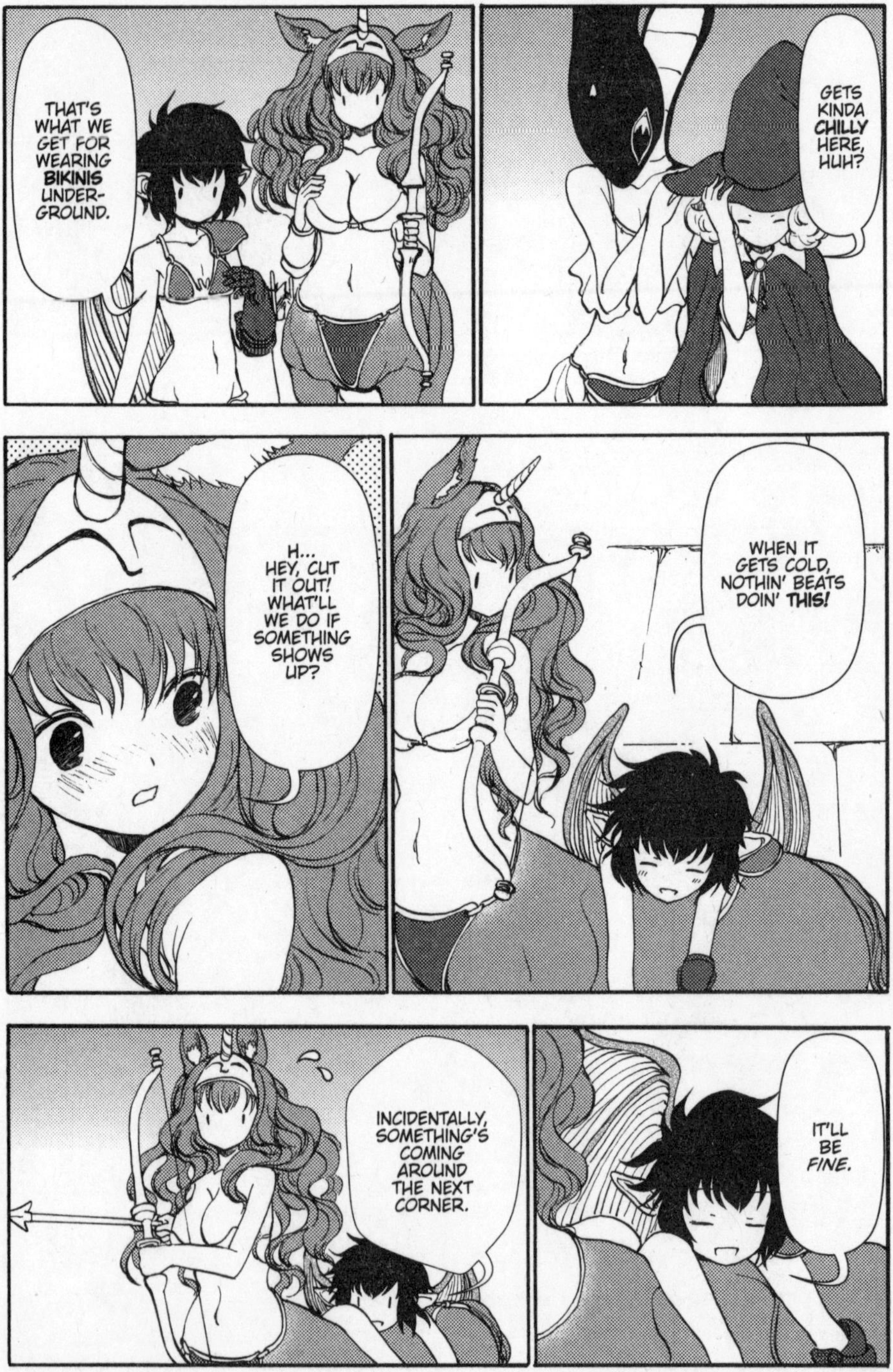
GETS KINDA CHILLY HERE, HUH?
THAT'S WHAT WE GET FOR WEARING BIKINIS UNDERGROUND.
WHEN IT GETS COLD, NOTHIN' BEATS DOIN' THIS!
H... HEY, CUT IT OUT! WHAT'LL WE DO IF SOMETHING SHOWS UP?
IT'LL BE FINE.
INCIDENTALLY, SOMETHING'S COMING AROUND THE NEXT CORNER.

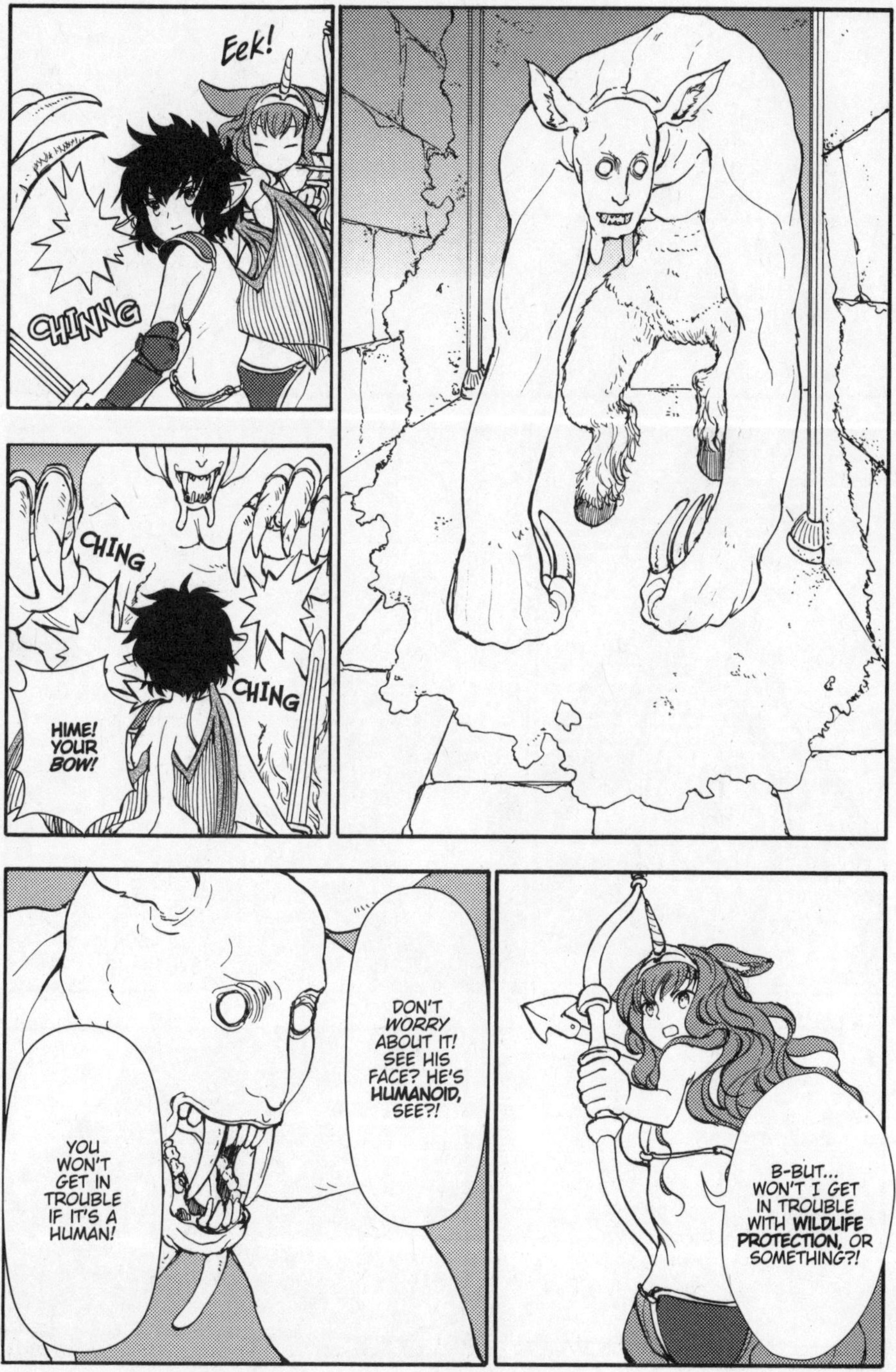
Eek!
CHINNG
CHING
CHING
HIME! YOUR BOW!
B-BUT... WON'T I GET IN TROUBLE WITH WILDLIFE PROTECTION, OR SOMETHING?!
DON'T WORRY ABOUT IT! SEE HIS FACE? HE'S HUMANOID, SEE?!
YOU WON'T GET IN TROUBLE IF IT'S A HUMAN!

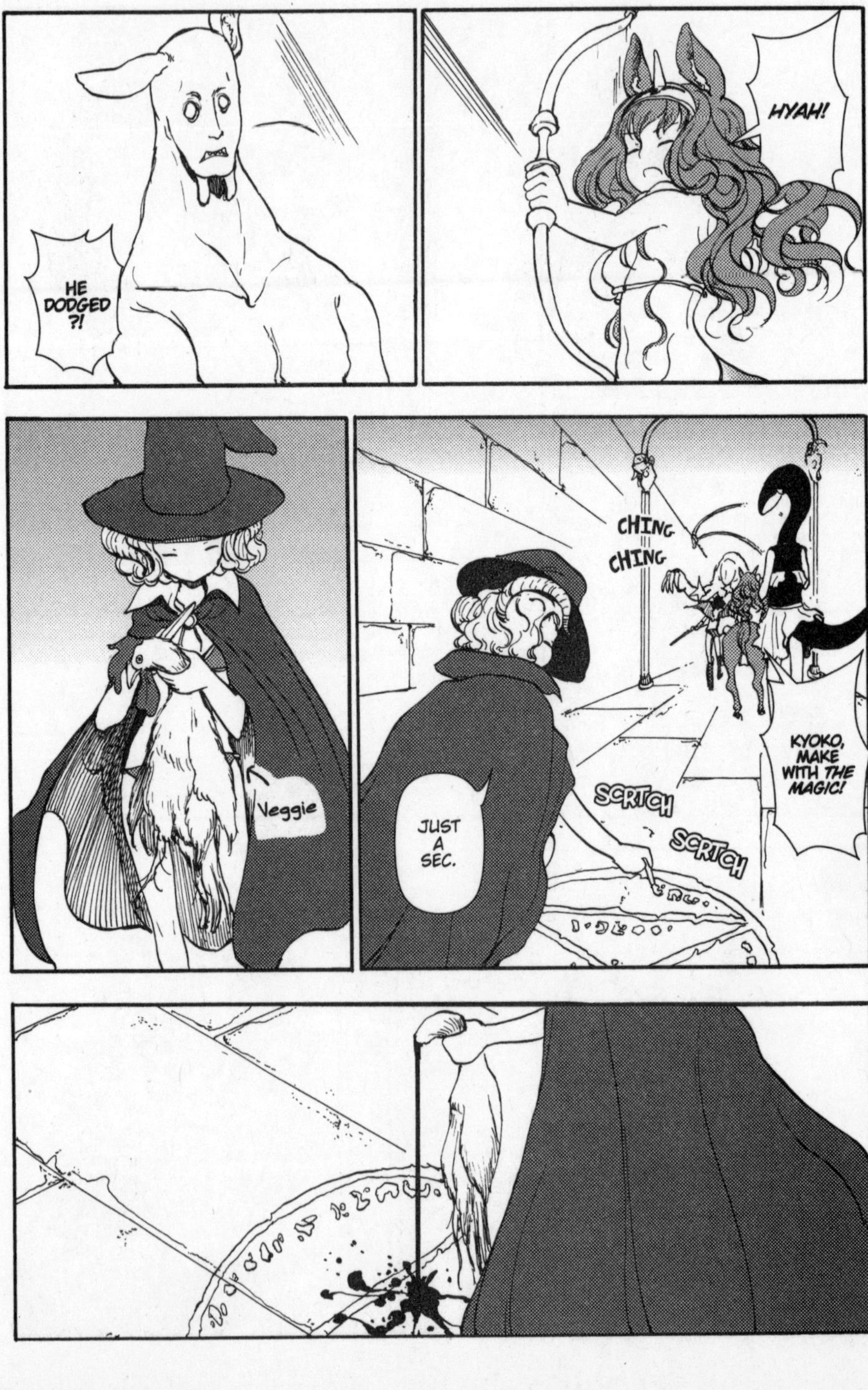
HYAH!
HE DODGED ?!
CHING CHING
KYOKO, MAKE WITH *THE MAGIC!*
SCRTCH SCRTCH
JUST A SEC.
Veggie

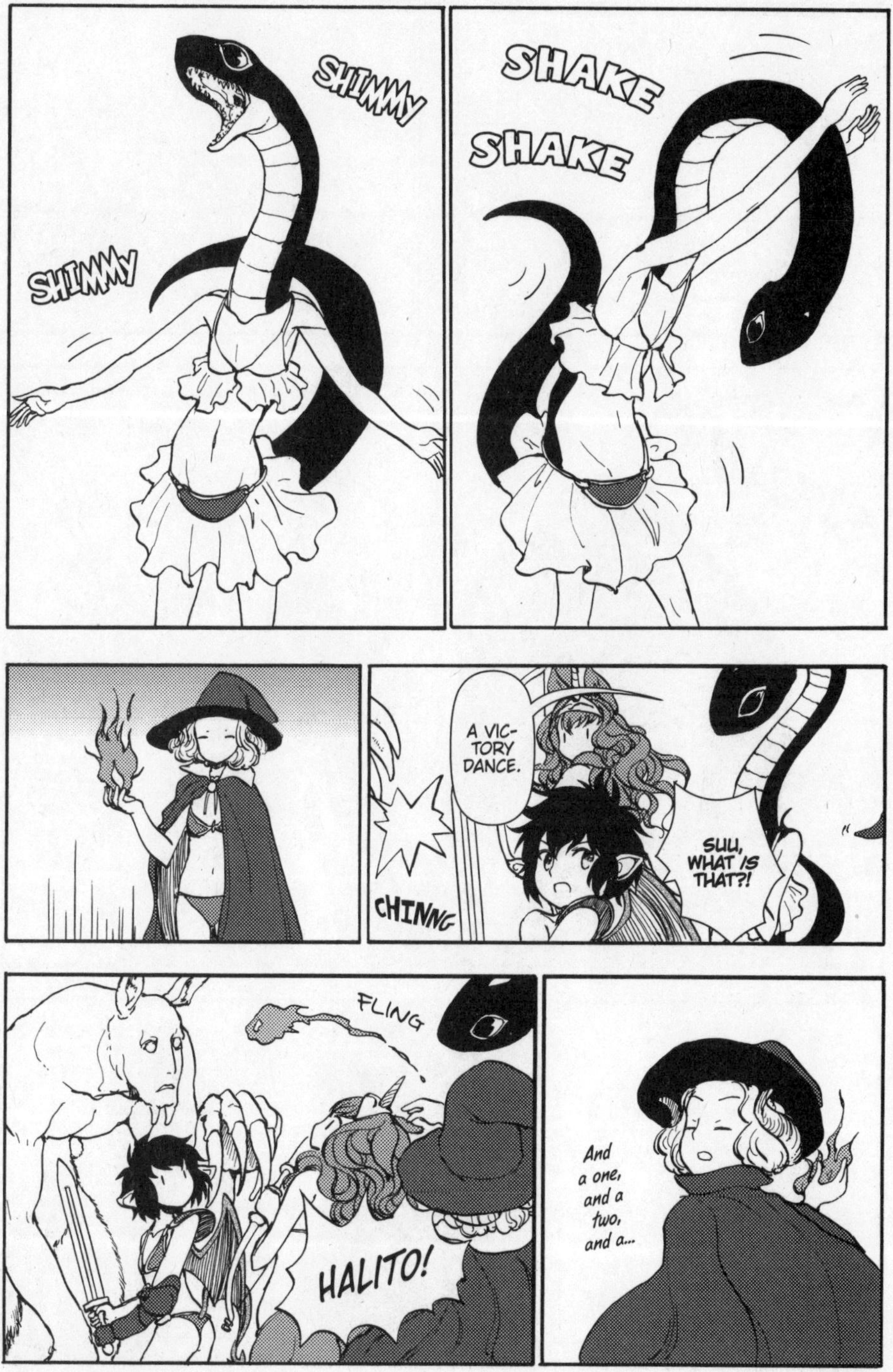
SHAKE
SHAKE
SHIMMY
SHIMMY
SUU, WHAT IS THAT?!
A VIC-TORY DANCE.
CHINNG
And a one, and a two, and a...
FLING
HALITO!

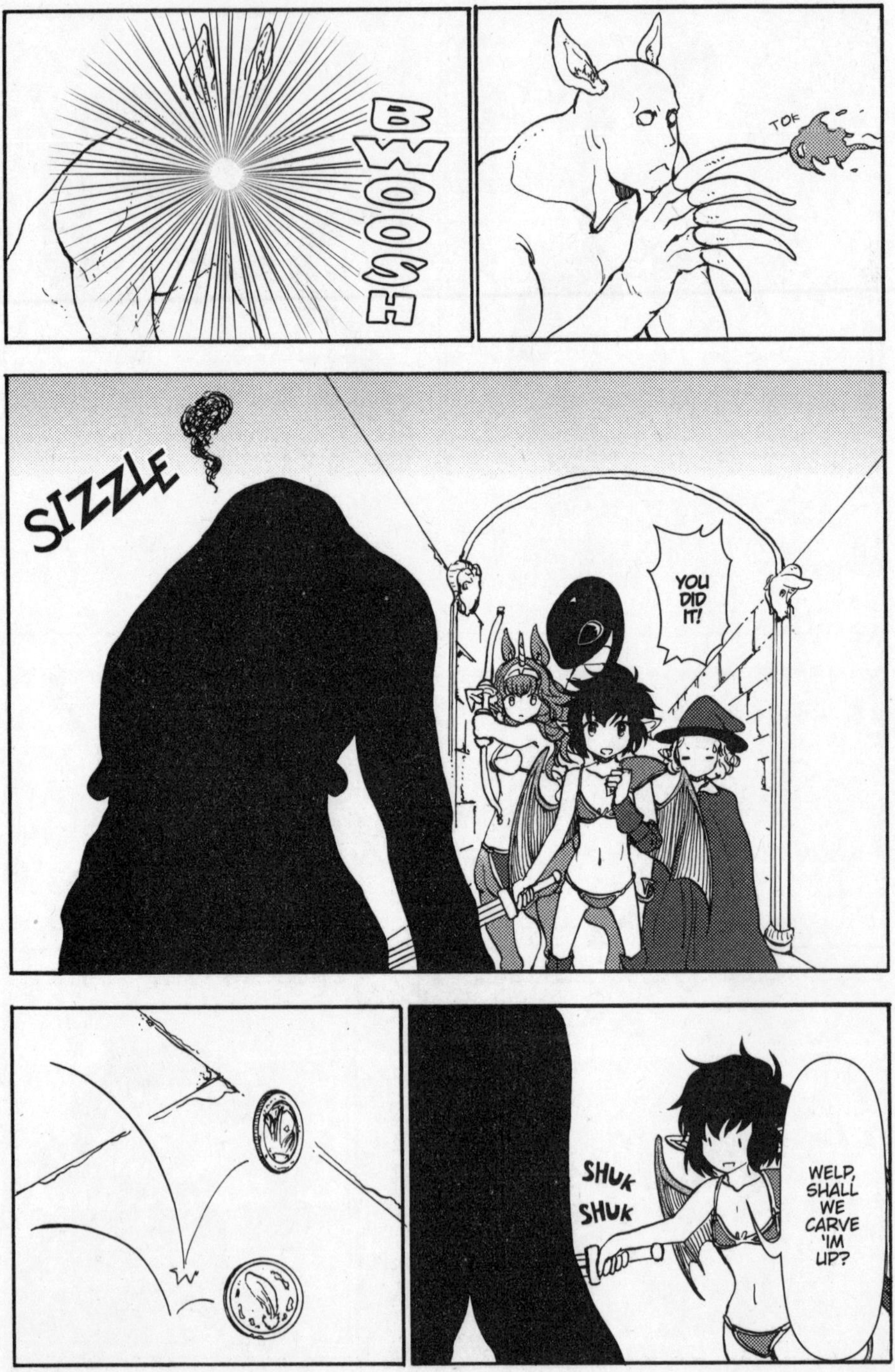
TOK
BWOOSH
SIZZLE
YOU DID IT!
WELP, SHALL WE CARVE 'IM UP?
SHUK SHUK

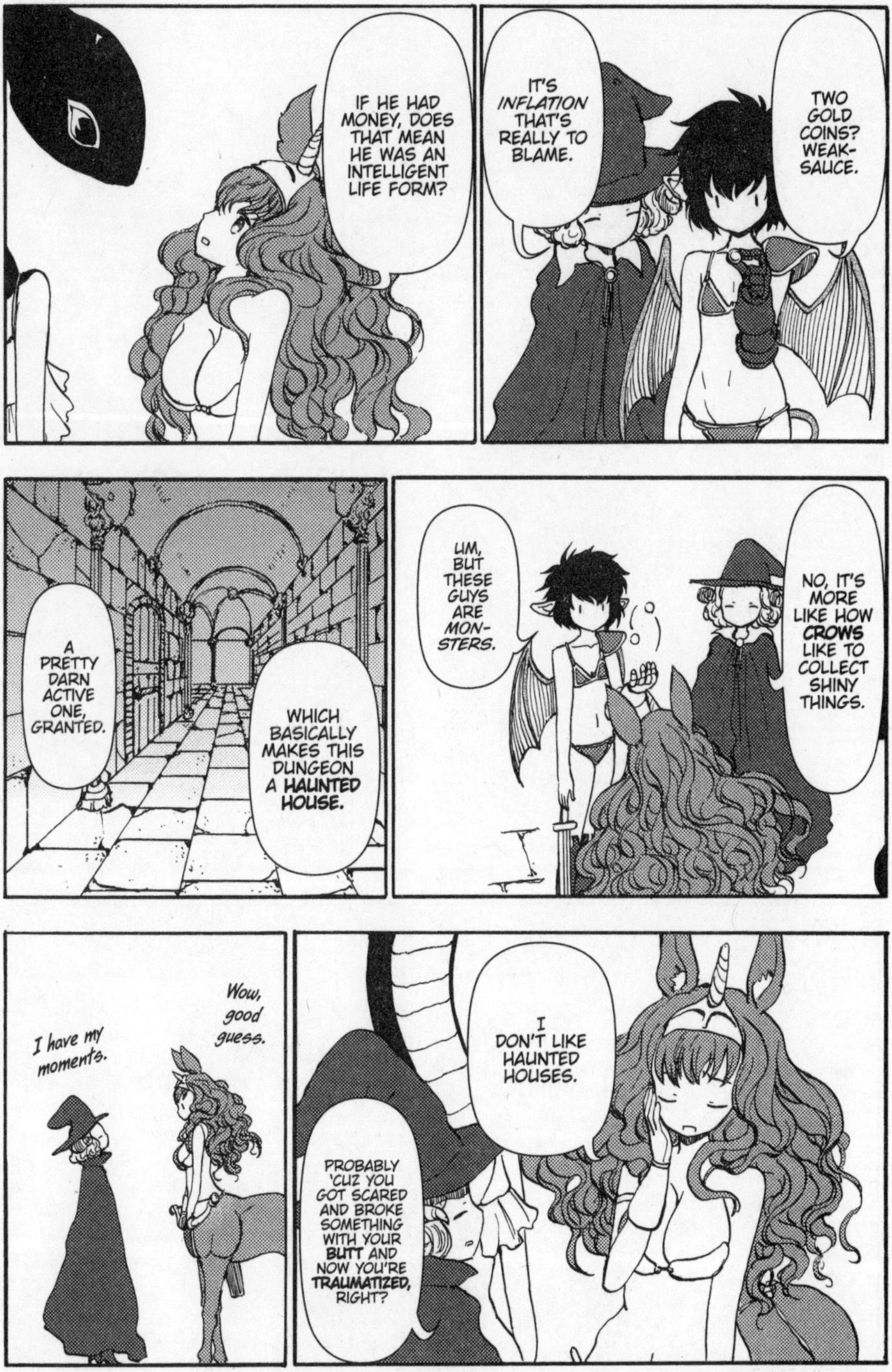
TWO GOLD COINS? WEAK-SAUCE.
IT'S *INFLATION* THAT'S REALLY TO BLAME.
IF HE HAD MONEY, DOES THAT MEAN HE WAS AN INTELLIGENT LIFE FORM?
NO, IT'S MORE LIKE HOW **CROWS** LIKE TO COLLECT SHINY THINGS.
UM, BUT THESE GUYS ARE *MON-STERS.*
WHICH BASICALLY MAKES THIS DUNGEON A **HAUNTED HOUSE.**
A PRETTY DARN ACTIVE ONE, GRANTED.
I DON'T LIKE HAUNTED HOUSES.
PROBABLY 'CUZ YOU GOT SCARED AND BROKE SOMETHING WITH YOUR **BUTT** AND NOW YOU'RE **TRAUMATIZED,** RIGHT?
Wow, good guess.
I have my moments.

HERE COME MORE OF 'EM!

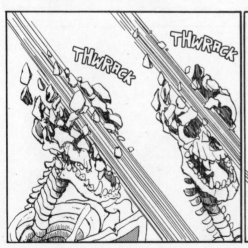

THWRACK

THWRACK

MM!

YOU CAN **SHOOT** THESE GUYS, RIGHT?

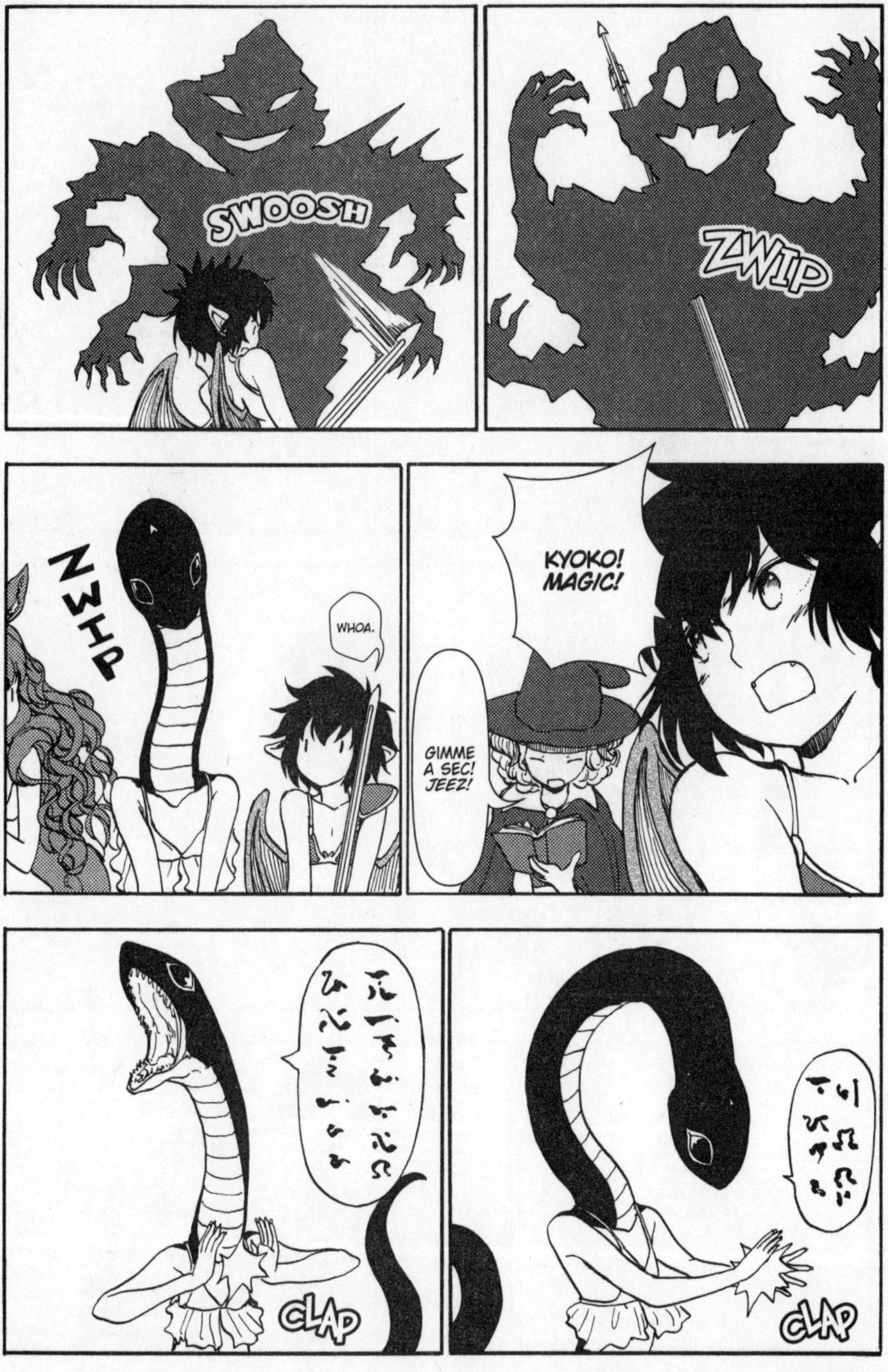
ZWIP
SWOOSH
KYOKO! MAGIC!
GIMME A SEC! JEEZ!
WHOA.
ZWIP
CLAP
CLAP

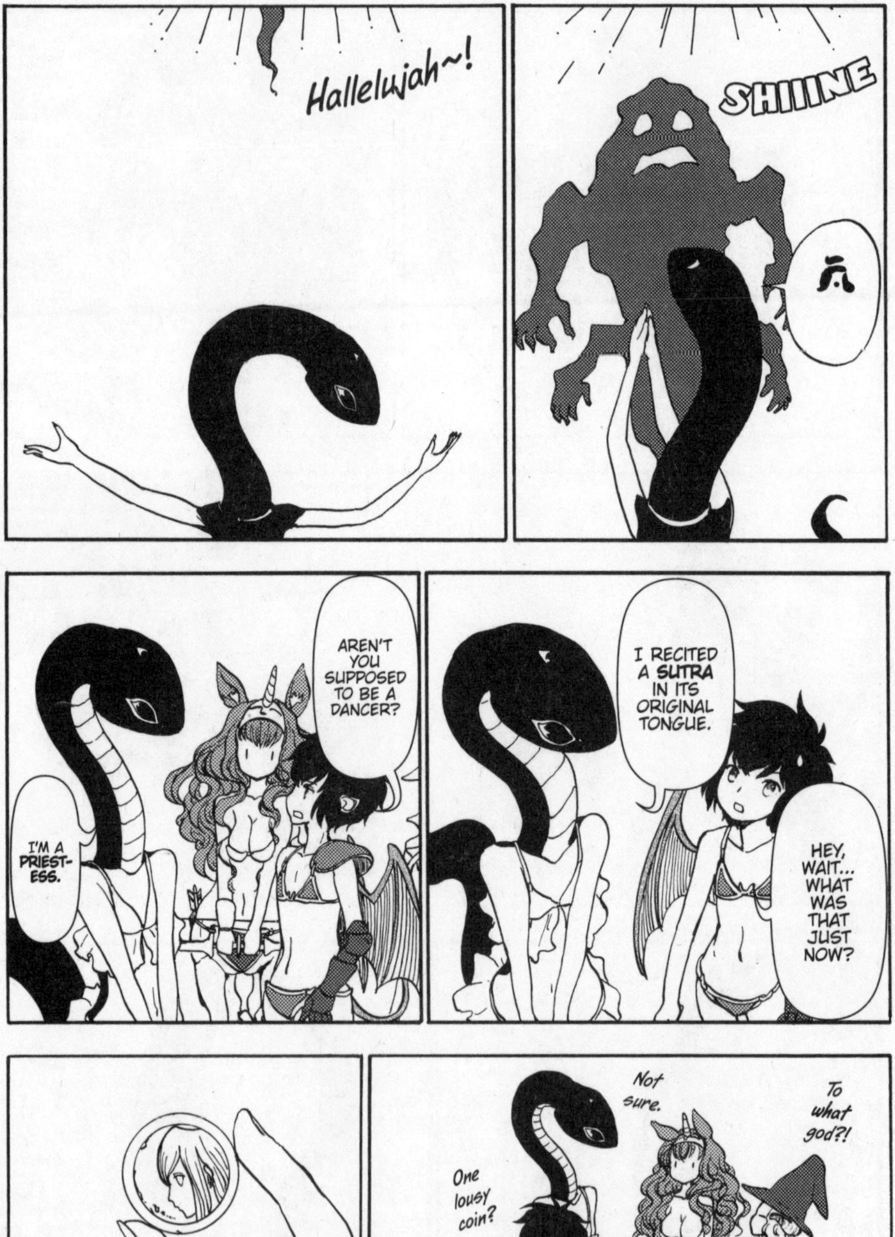
SHIIINE
Hallelujah~!
HEY, WAIT... WHAT WAS THAT JUST NOW?
I RECITED A SUTRA IN ITS ORIGINAL TONGUE.
AREN'T YOU SUPPOSED TO BE A DANCER?
I'M A PRIEST-ESS.
To what god?!
Not sure.
One lousy coin?

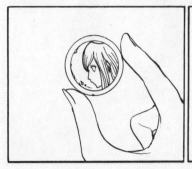

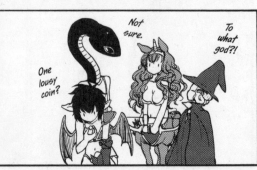

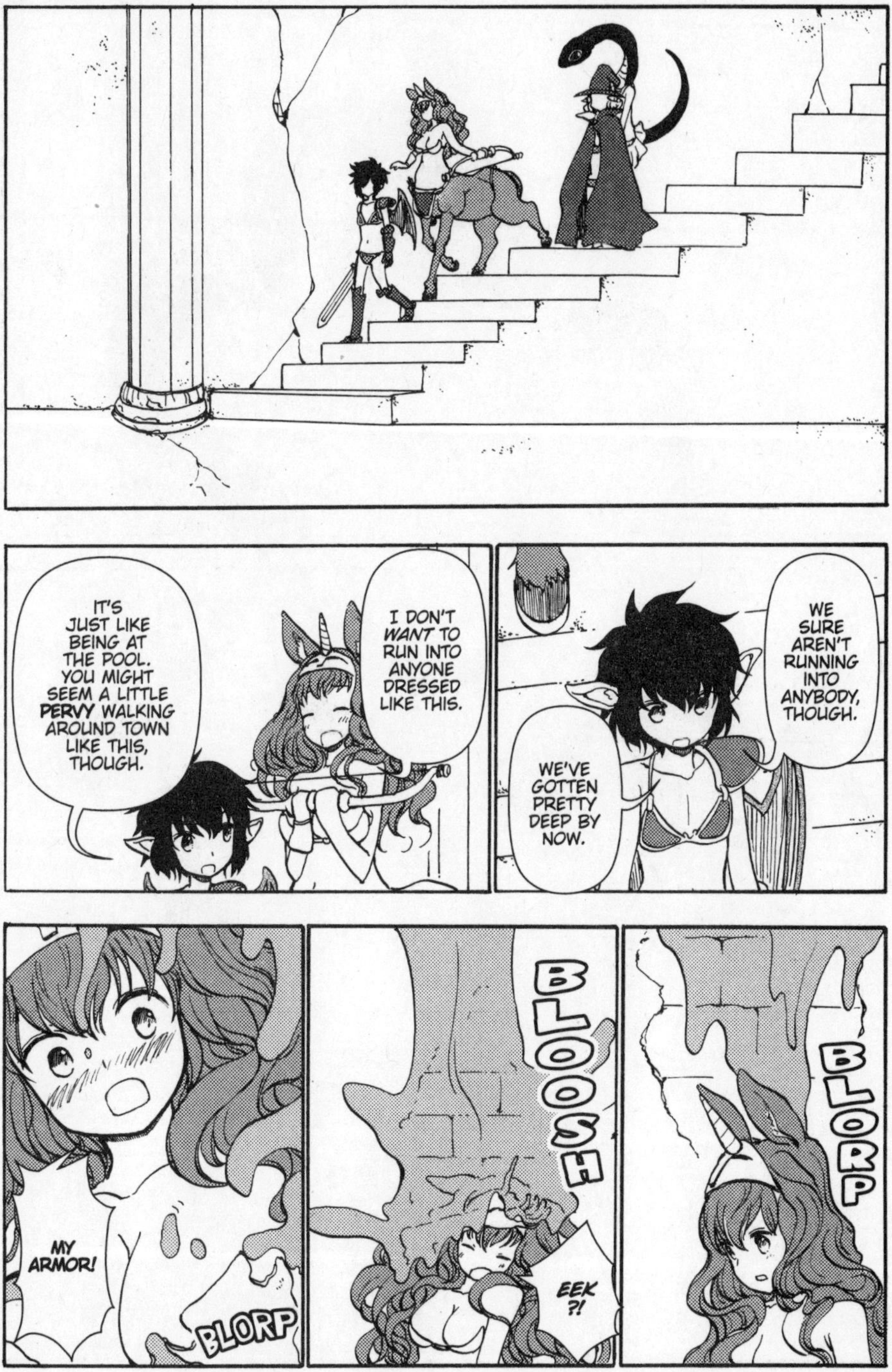
WE SURE AREN'T RUNNING INTO ANYBODY, THOUGH.
WE'VE GOTTEN PRETTY DEEP BY NOW.
I DON'T *WANT* TO RUN INTO ANYONE DRESSED LIKE THIS.
IT'S JUST LIKE BEING AT THE POOL. YOU MIGHT SEEM A LITTLE **PERVY** WALKING AROUND TOWN LIKE THIS, THOUGH.
BLORP
BLOOSH
EEK ?!
MY ARMOR!
BLORP

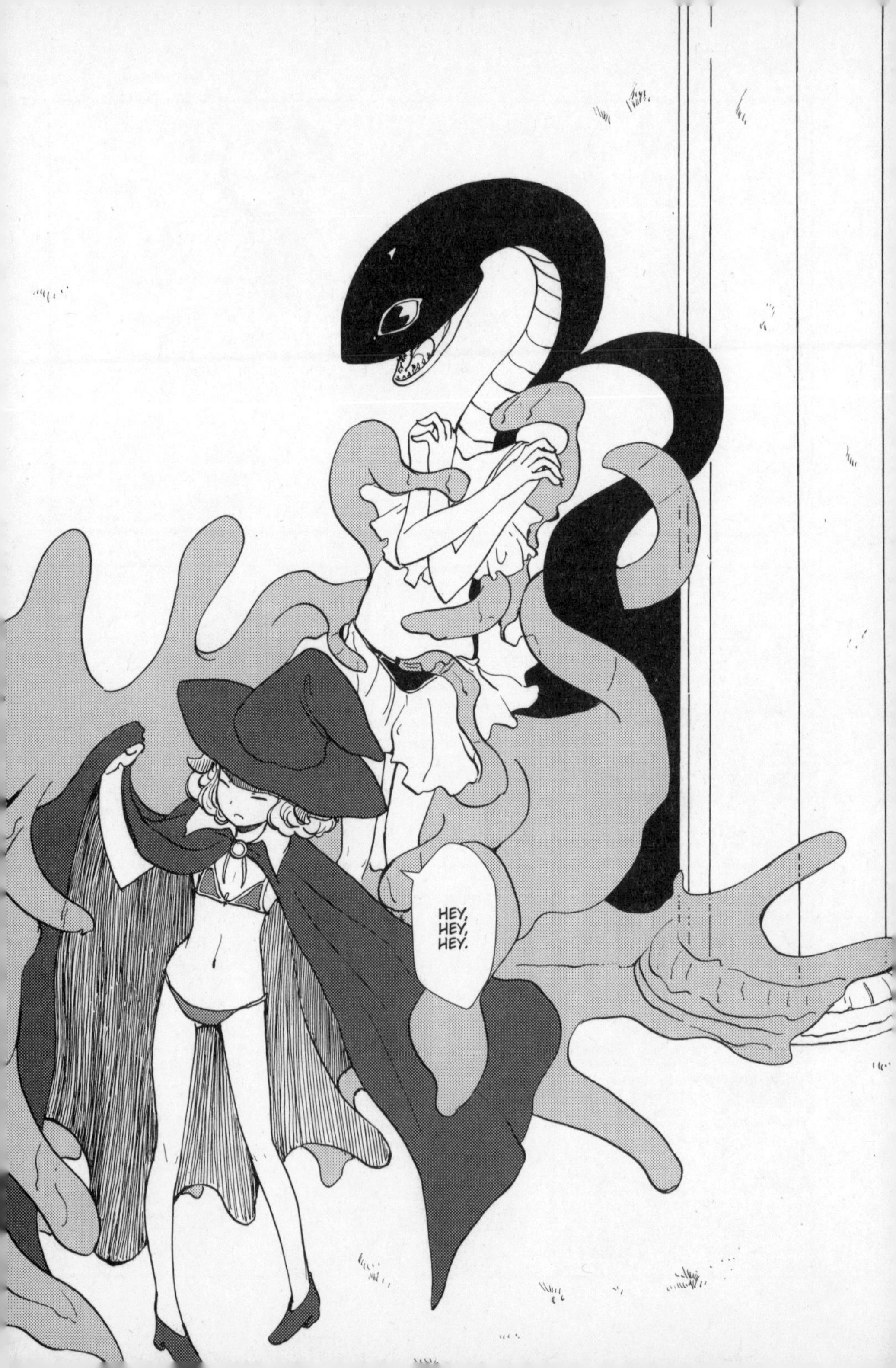
HEY, HEY, HEY.

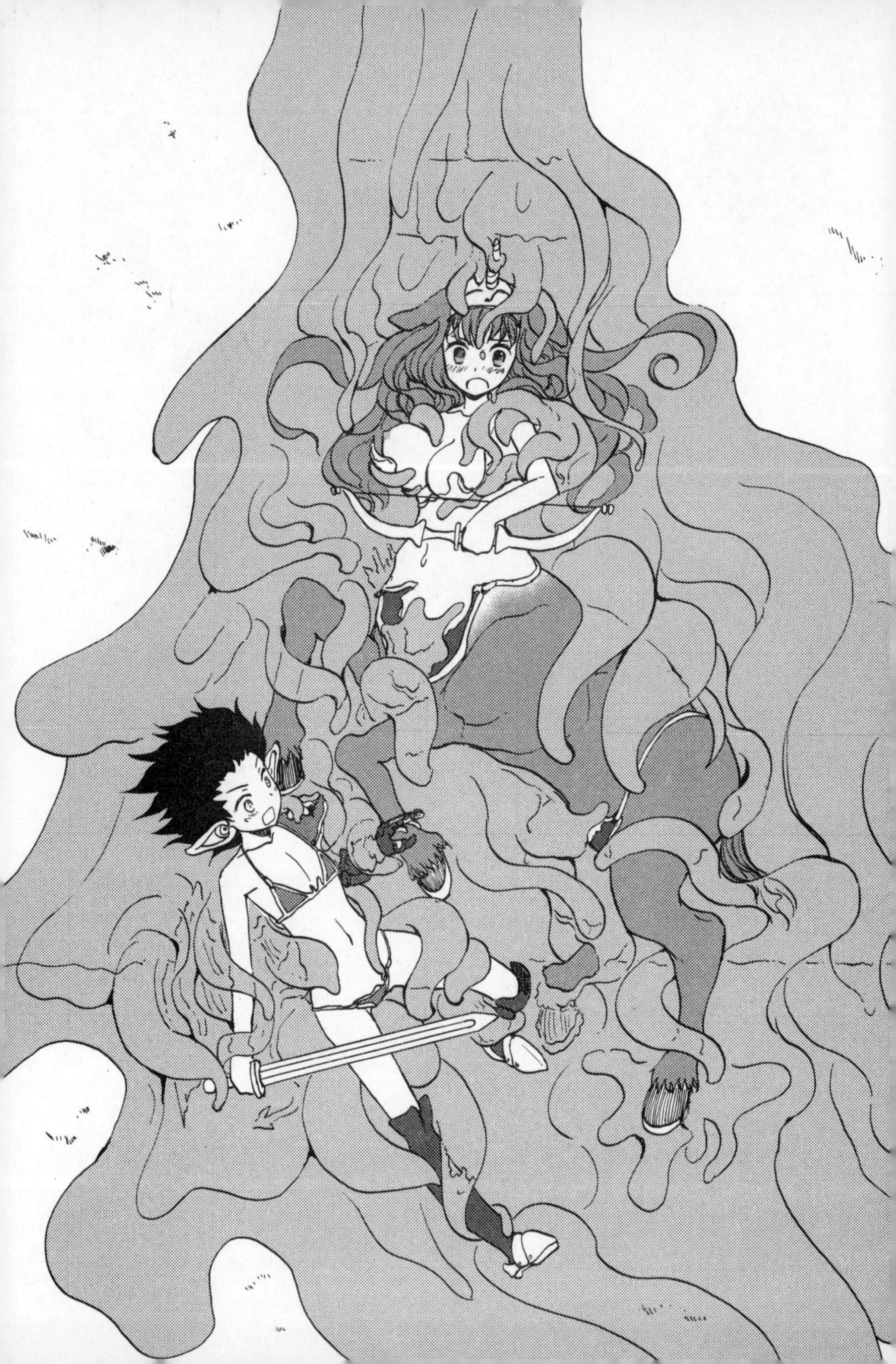

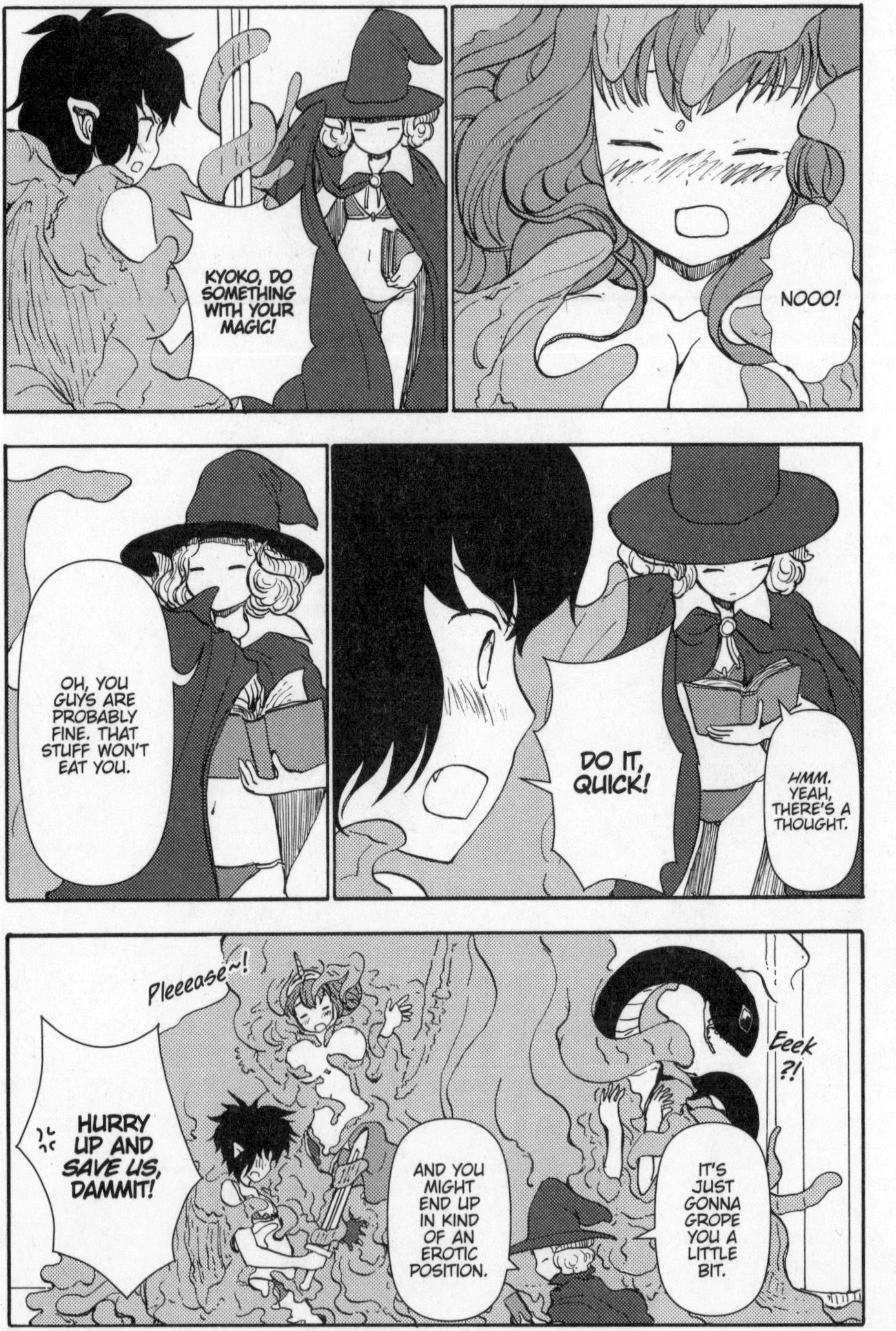
NOOO!
KYOKO, DO SOMETHING WITH YOUR MAGIC!
DO IT, QUICK!
HMM. YEAH, THERE'S A THOUGHT.
OH, YOU GUYS ARE PROBABLY FINE. THAT STUFF WON'T EAT YOU.
Eeek ?!
IT'S JUST GONNA GROPE YOU A LITTLE BIT.
AND YOU MIGHT END UP IN KIND OF AN EROTIC POSITION.
Pleeease~!
HURRY UP AND SAVE US, DAMMIT!

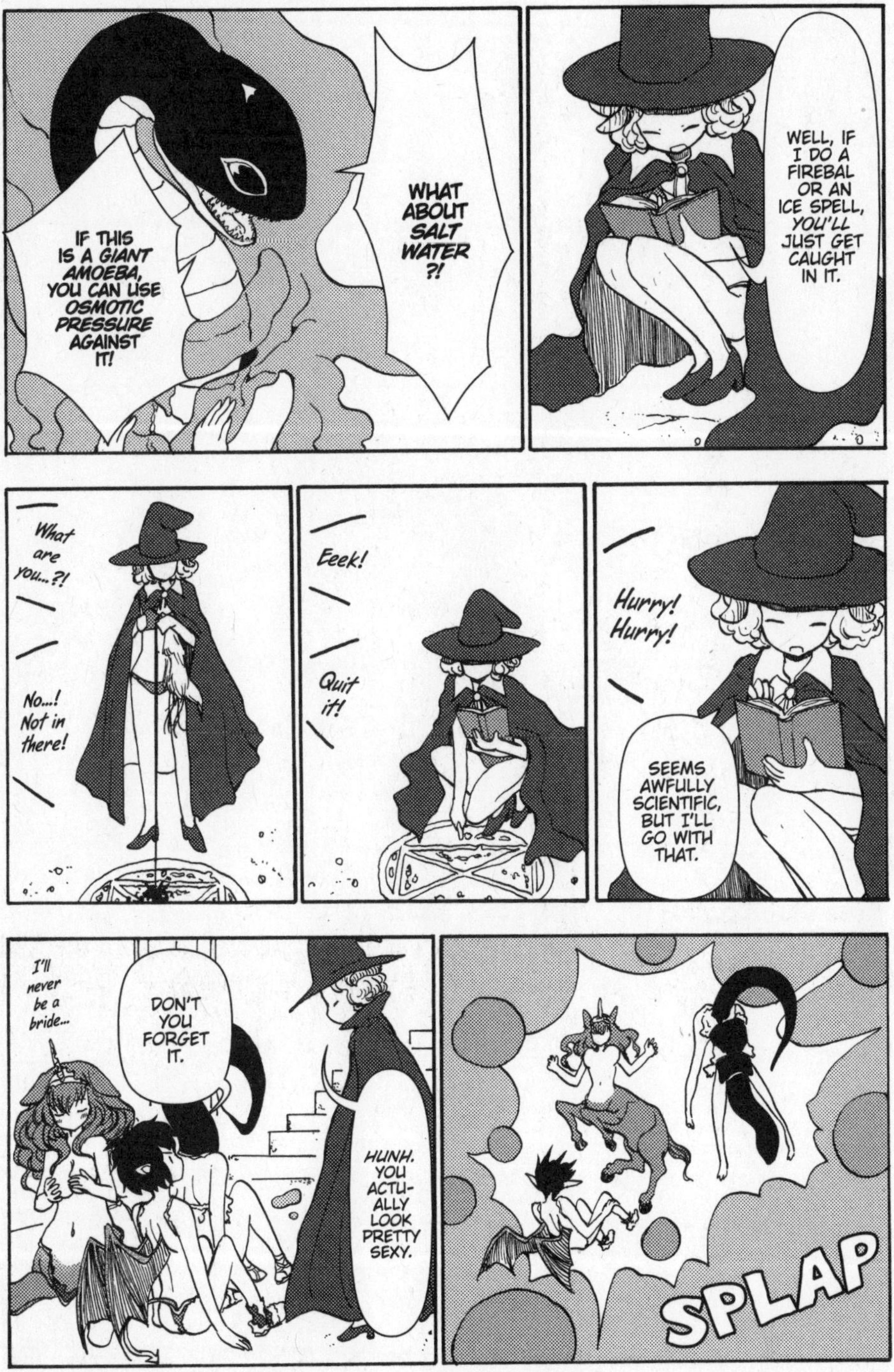
WELL, IF I DO A FIREBAL OR AN ICE SPELL, YOU'LL JUST GET CAUGHT IN IT.
WHAT ABOUT SALT WATER?!
IF THIS IS A GIANT AMOEBA, YOU CAN USE OSMOTIC PRESSURE AGAINST IT!
Hurry! Hurry!
SEEMS AWFULLY SCIENTIFIC, BUT I'LL GO WITH THAT.
Eeek!
Quit it!
What are you...?!
No...! Not in there!
SPLAP
HUNH. YOU ACTU-ALLY LOOK PRETTY SEXY.
I'll never be a bride...
DON'T YOU FORGET IT.

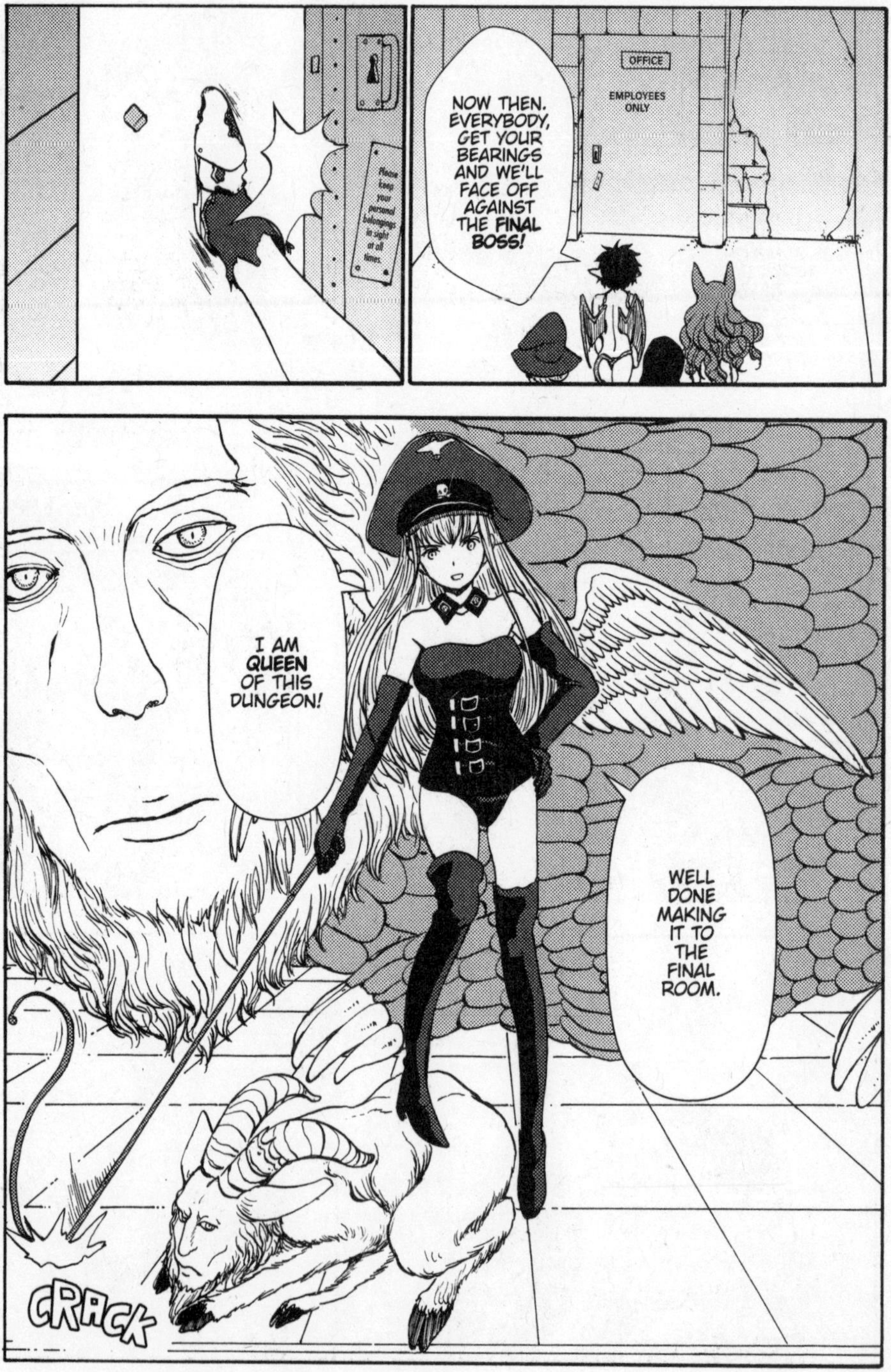
OFFICE
EMPLOYEES ONLY
NOW THEN. EVERYBODY, GET YOUR BEARINGS AND WE'LL FACE OFF AGAINST THE **FINAL BOSS!**
Please keep your personal belongings in sight at all times.
WELL DONE MAKING IT TO THE FINAL ROOM.
I AM **QUEEN** OF THIS DUNGEON!
CRACK

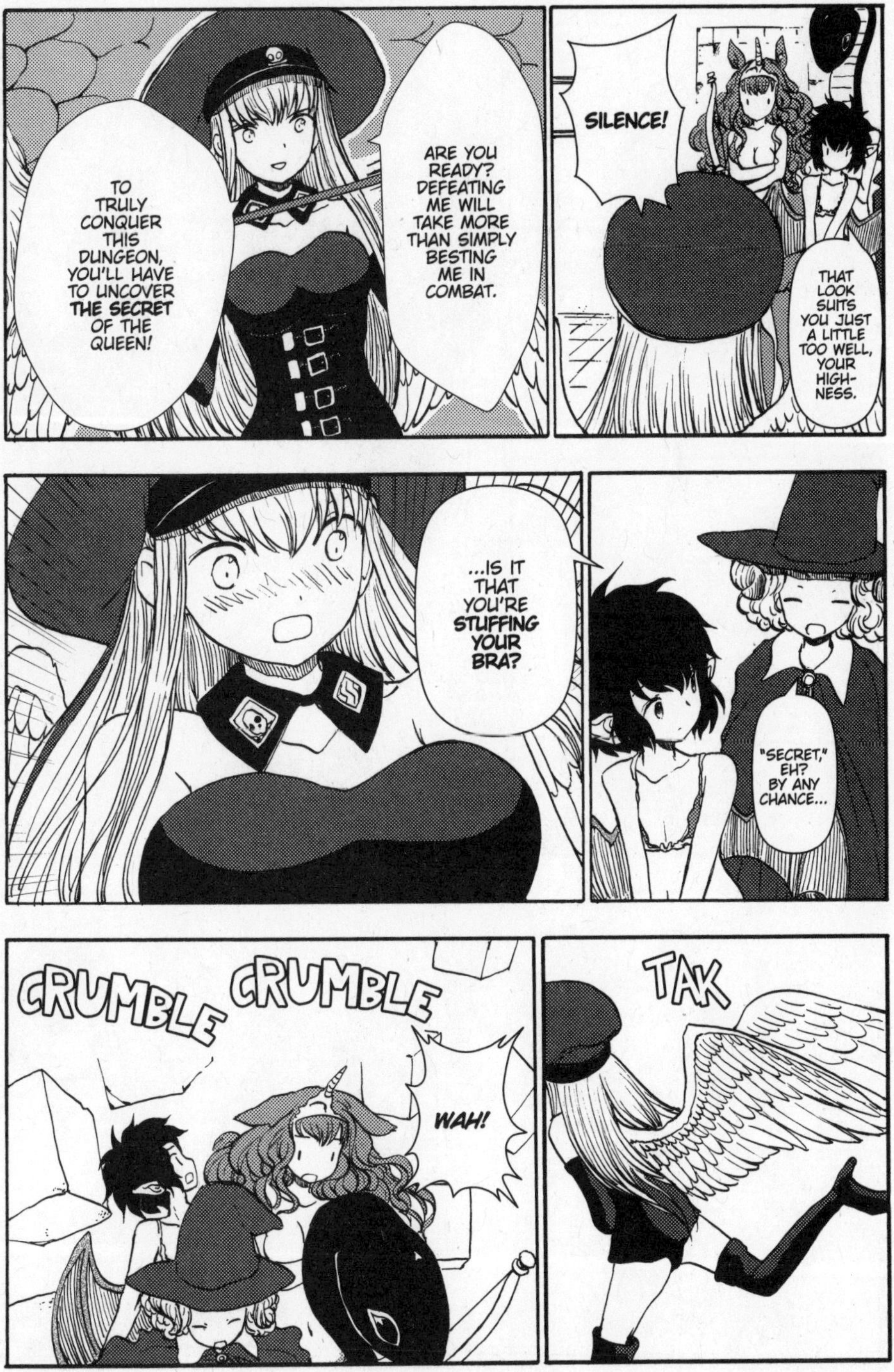
THAT LOOK SUITS YOU JUST A LITTLE TOO WELL, YOUR HIGHNESS.
SILENCE!
ARE YOU READY? DEFEATING ME WILL TAKE MORE THAN SIMPLY BESTING ME IN COMBAT.
TO TRULY CONQUER THIS DUNGEON, YOU'LL HAVE TO UNCOVER **THE SECRET** OF THE QUEEN!
"SECRET," EH? BY ANY CHANCE...
...IS IT THAT YOU'RE **STUFFING YOUR BRA?**
TAK
CRUMBLE
CRUMBLE
WAH!

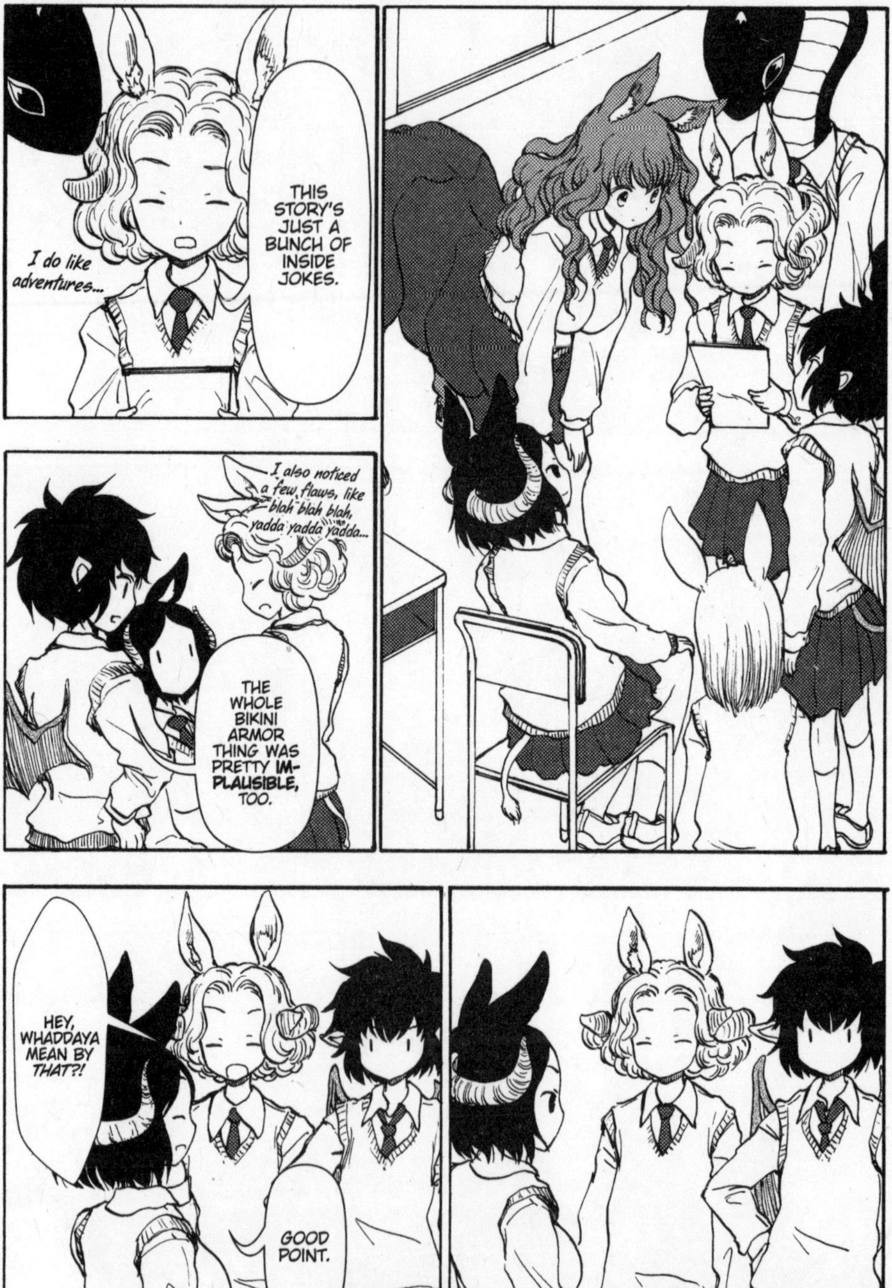
THIS STORY'S JUST A BUNCH OF INSIDE JOKES.
I do like adventures...
I also noticed a few flaws, like blah blah blah, yadda yadda yadda...
THE WHOLE BIKINI ARMOR THING WAS PRETTY **IM-PLAUSIBLE,** TOO.
HEY, WHADDAYA MEAN BY *THAT?!*
GOOD POINT.

A CentaUr's Life

TRADITIONAL DRESS FROM AROUND THE WORLD (JAPAN)

GARMENTS SUCH AS THE *ETCHU FUNDOSHI* AND *ROKUSHAKU FUNDOSHI* (DIFFERENT STYLES OF LOINCLOTH) ARE THOUGHT TO BE AGE-OLD, AND INDEED THERE WERE SUCH GARMENTS IN ANCIENT TIMES. HOWEVER, IT WAS NOT UNTIL RELATIVELY RECENTLY THAT THEY BECAME WIDESPREAD AMONGST THE COMMON MAN. CLOTH WAS ONCE AN EXTRAVAGANT ITEM-- SO MUCH SO THAT TO WEAR IT SOMEWHERE UNSEEN TO PROTECT ONLY ONE SPECIFIC PART OF THE BODY WAS A PRACTICE RESERVED FOR THE WELL-TO-DO.

ANOTHER KNOWN FALLACY IS THAT MERFOLK OFTEN WORE *FUNDOSHI*. IN FACT, IT IS LIKELY THAT THE PRACTICE OF WEARING CLOTHES WAS NOT COMMON AMONGST MERFOLK UNTIL THE ADVENT OF BATHING SUITS MADE WITH SYNTHETIC FIBERS. WHEN INTERACTING WITH OTHER, LAND-BASED RACES, MERFOLK DO MAKE AN EFFORT TO WEAR APPROPRIATE CLOTHING, AND LAND-BASED MERFOLK WHO LIVE AMONGST OTHER RACES DAY-TO-DAY DO WEAR REGULAR CLOTHES AS A DAILY HABIT. IN EITHER CASE, FEMALE MERFOLK TYPICALLY DRESS APPROPRIATELY IN PUBLIC--IT'S UNLIKELY THAT ONE WOULD REVEAL HERSELF IN JUST HER UNDERWEAR. HENCE, ILLUSTRATIONS LIKE THE ONE BELOW ARE LIKELY JUST DESIGNED TO BE SUGGESTIVE.

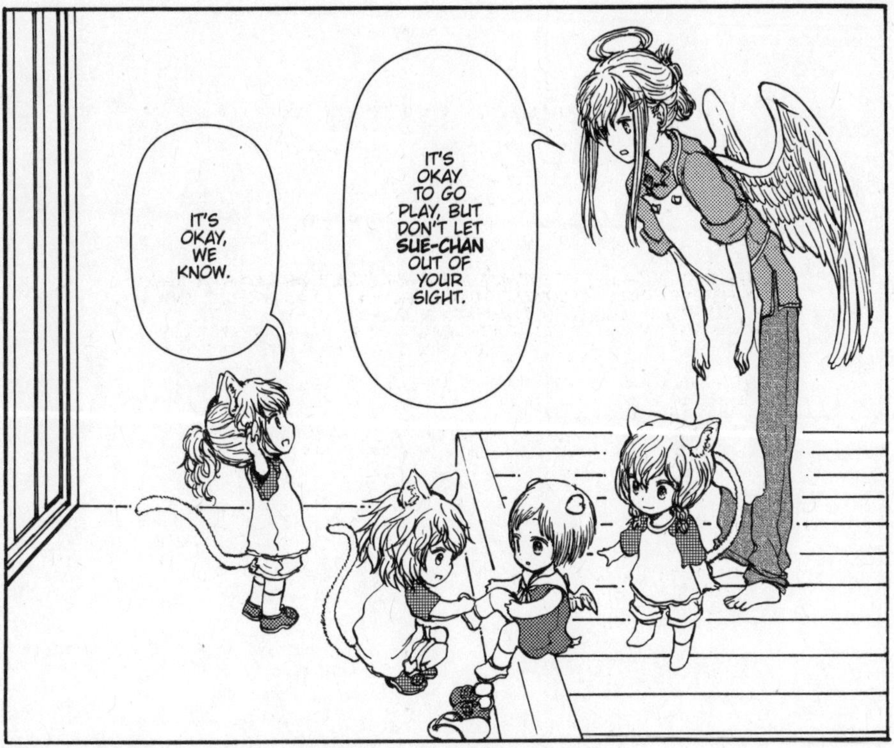
IT'S OKAY TO GO PLAY, BUT DON'T LET **SUE-CHAN** OUT OF YOUR SIGHT.
IT'S OKAY, WE KNOW.

CHAPTER 51

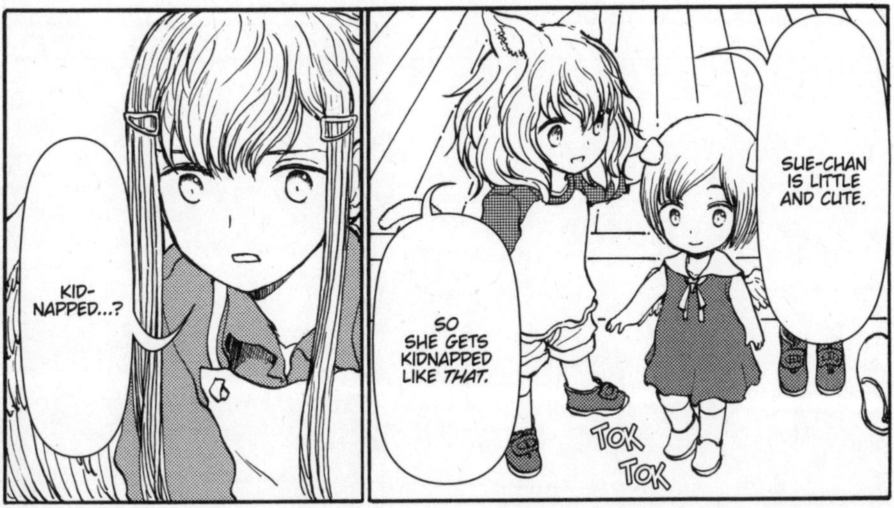
SUE-CHAN IS LITTLE AND CUTE.
SO SHE GETS KIDNAPPED LIKE *THAT.*
TOK TOK
KID-NAPPED...?

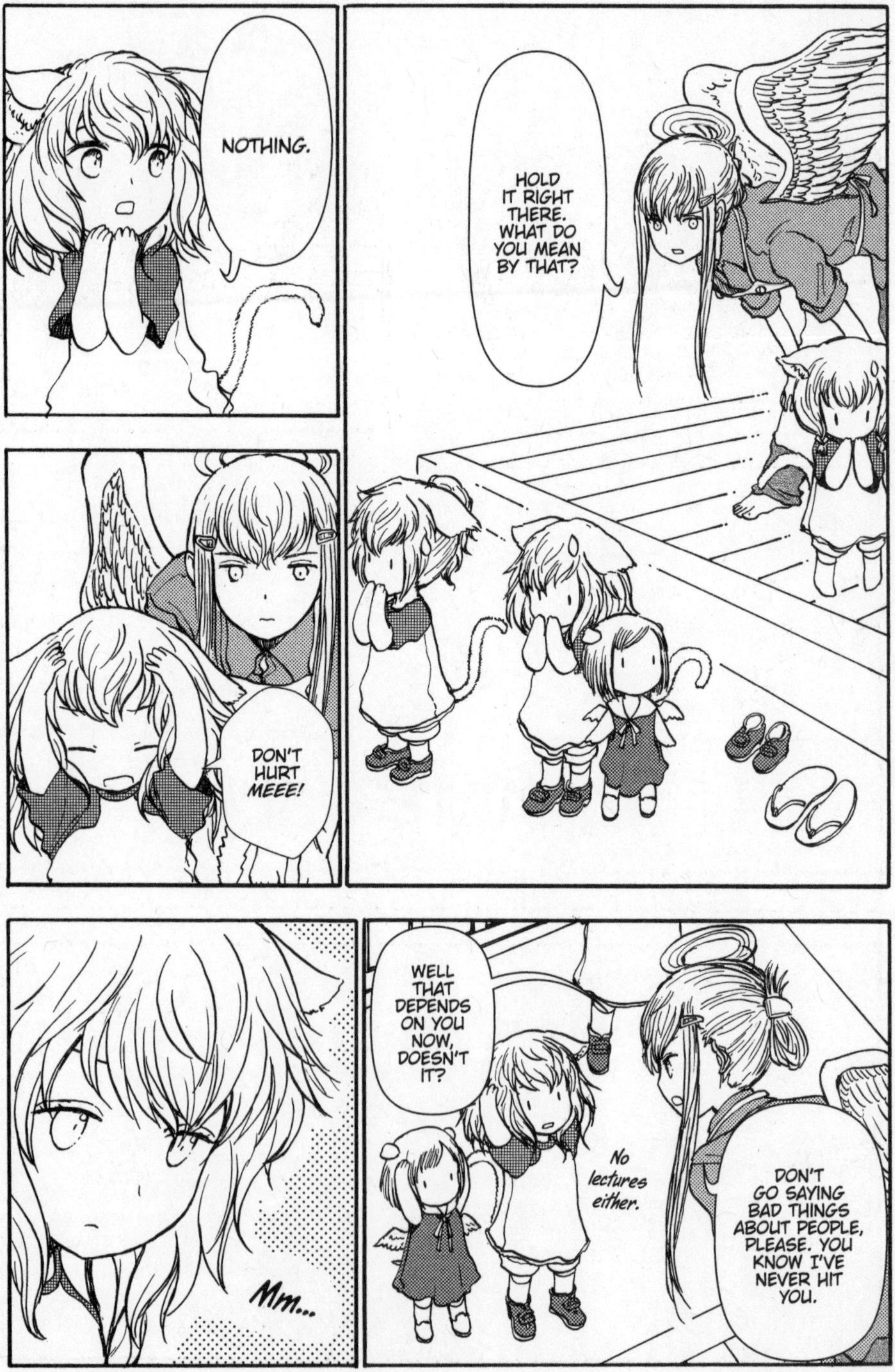
HOLD IT RIGHT THERE. WHAT DO YOU MEAN BY THAT?
NOTHING.
DON'T HURT MEEE!
DON'T GO SAYING BAD THINGS ABOUT PEOPLE, PLEASE. YOU KNOW I'VE NEVER HIT YOU.
WELL THAT DEPENDS ON YOU NOW, DOESN'T IT?
No lectures either.
Mm...

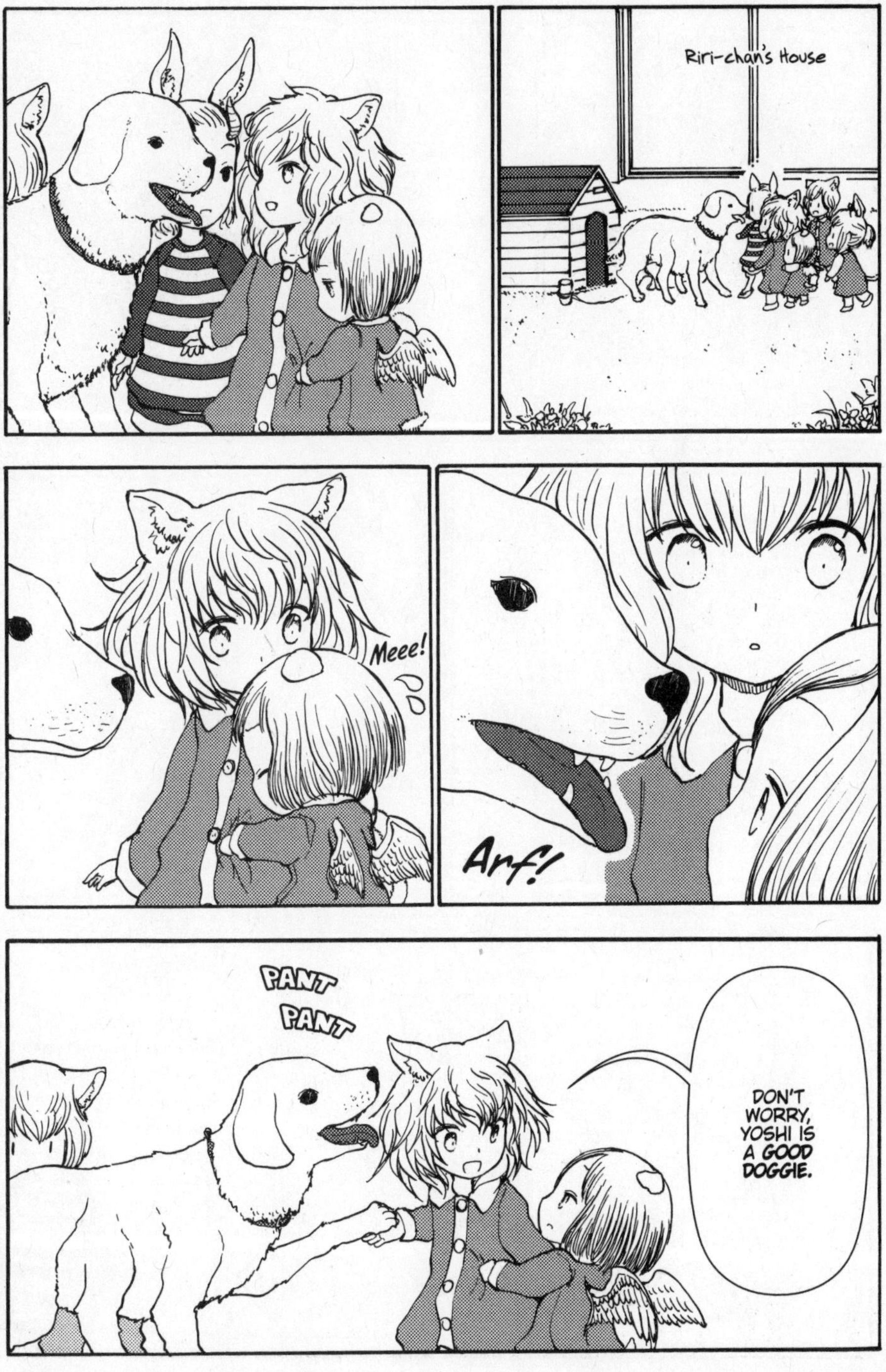
Riri-chan's House
Arf!
Meee!
PANT
PANT
DON'T WORRY, YOSHI IS A **GOOD DOGGIE.**

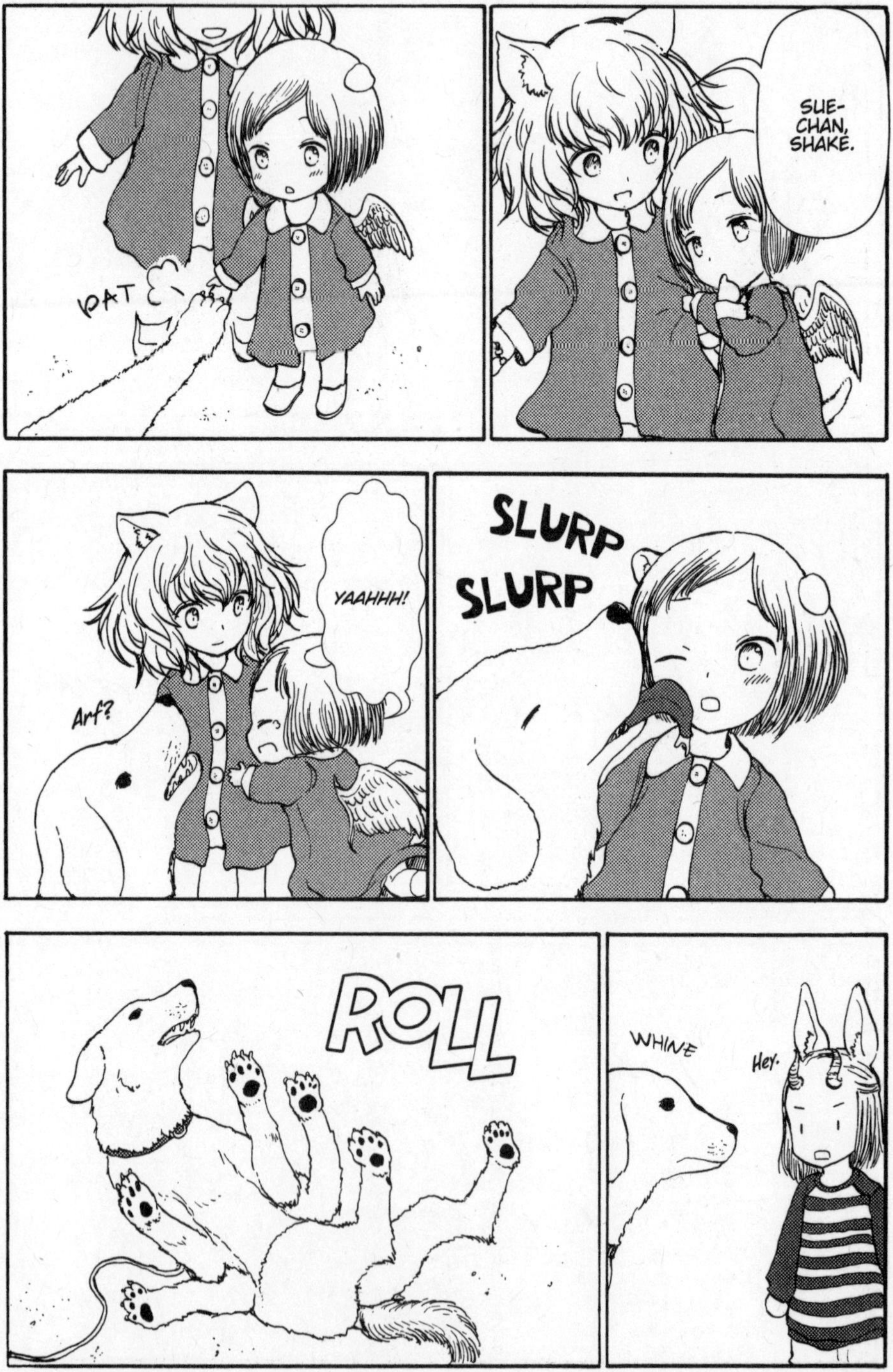
SUE-CHAN, SHAKE.
PAT
SLURP
SLURP
YAAHHH!
Arf?
WHINE
Hey.
ROLL

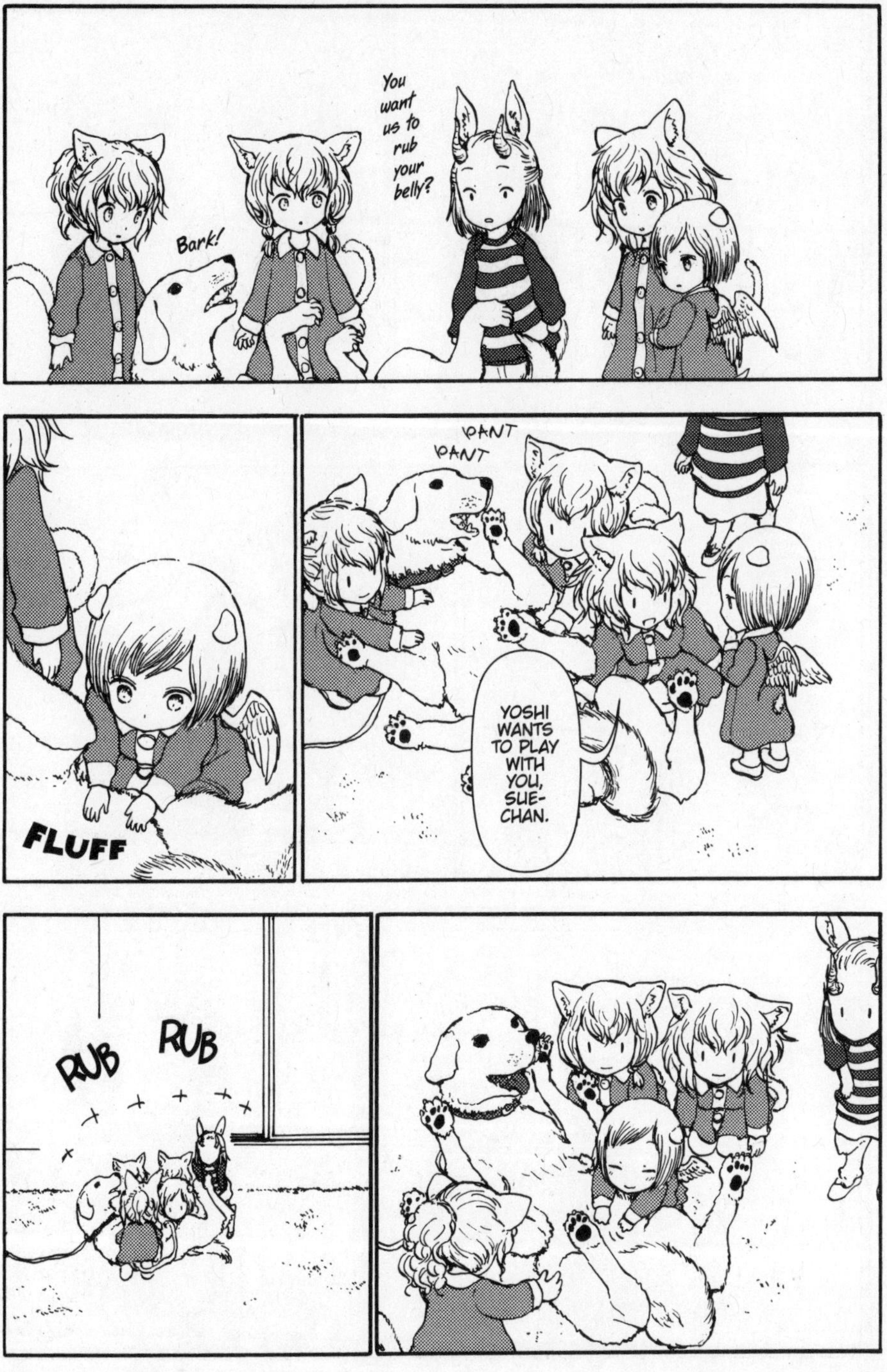
You want us to rub your belly?
Bark!
PANT PANT
YOSHI WANTS TO PLAY WITH YOU, SUE-CHAN.
FLUFF
RUB RUB

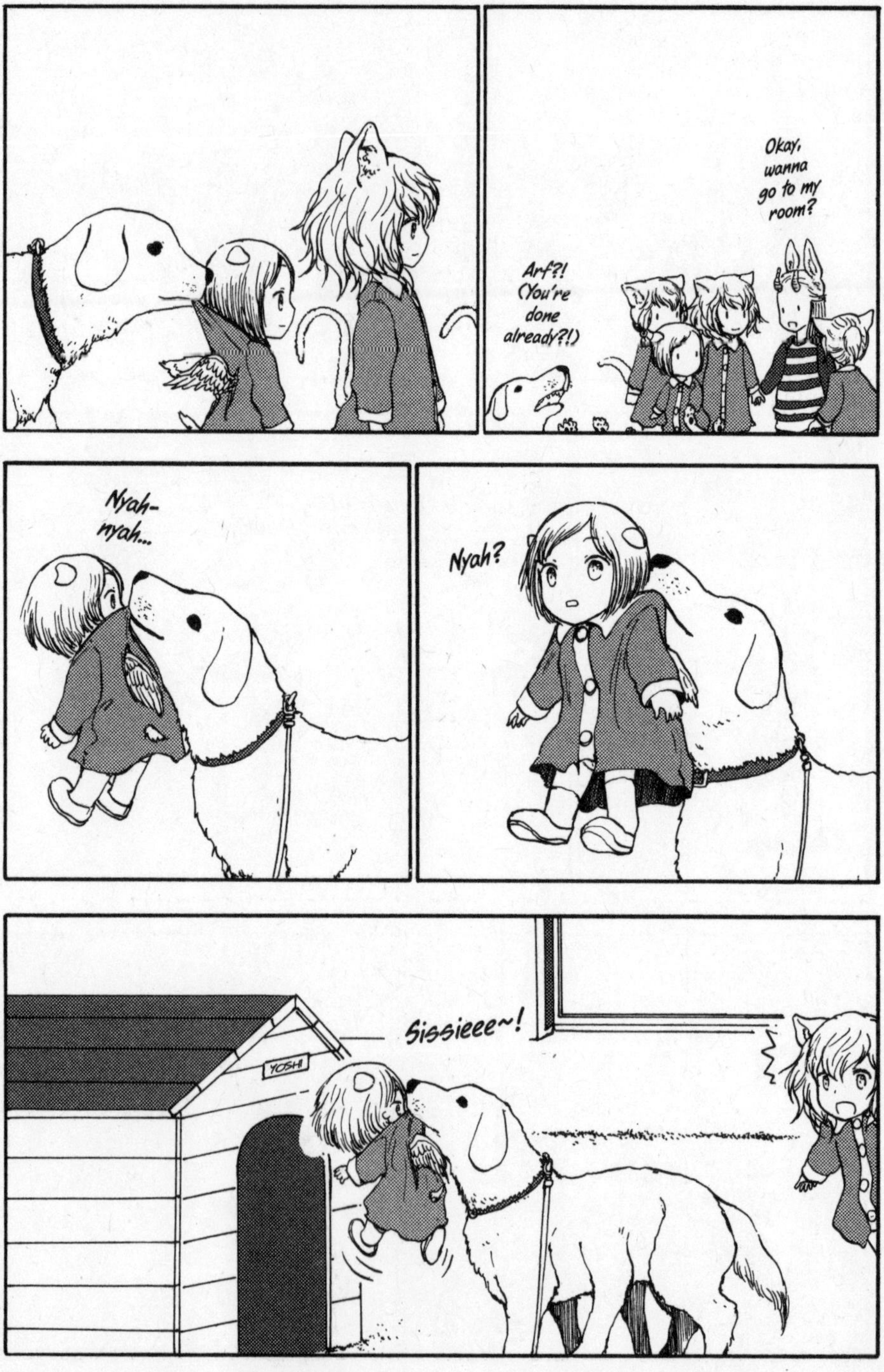
Okay, wanna go to my room?
Arf?! (You're done already?!)
Nyah?
Nyah-nyah...
Sissieee~!
YOSHI

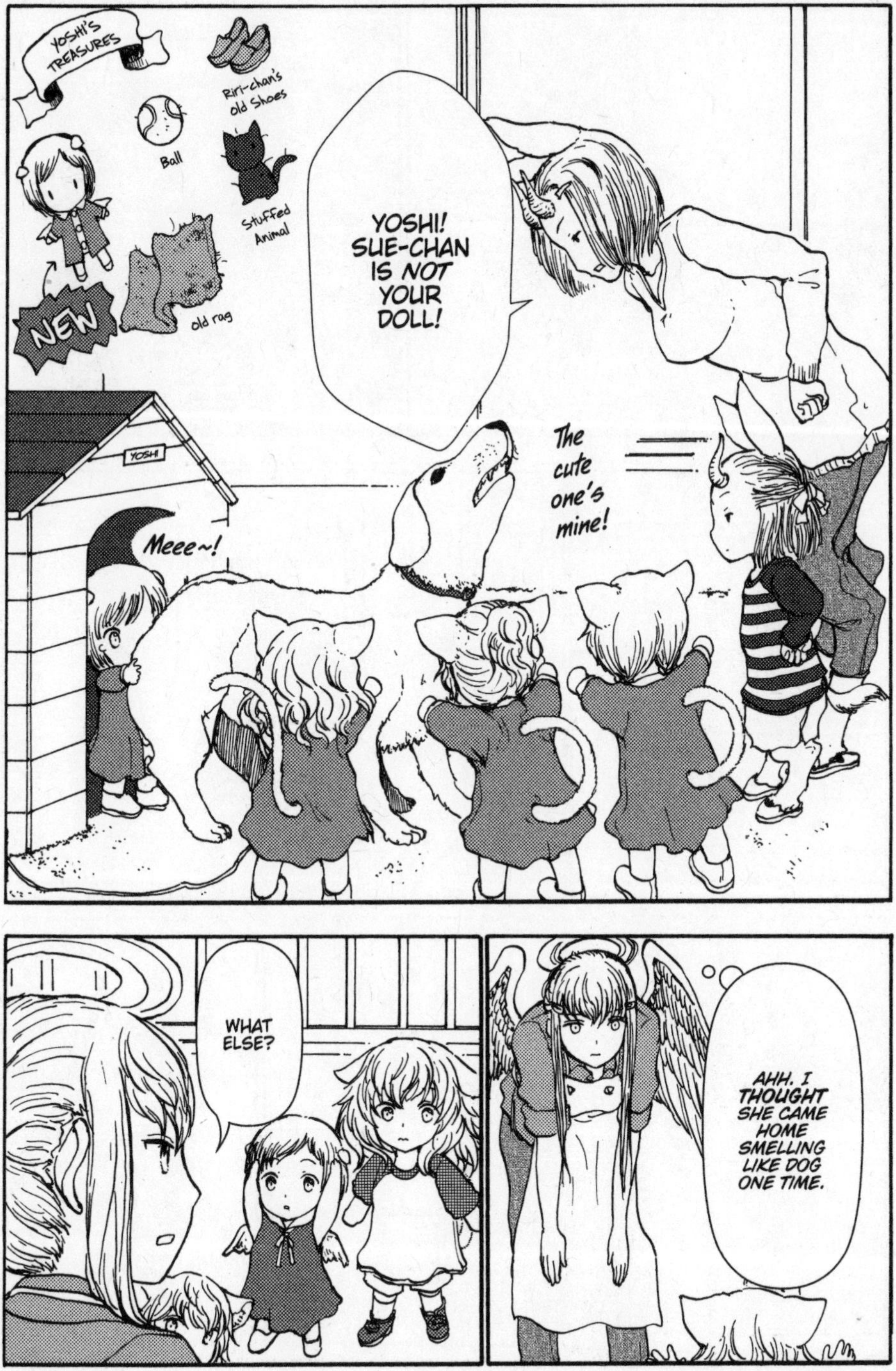
YOSHI! SUE-CHAN IS NOT YOUR DOLL!
YOSHI'S TREASURES
Riri-chan's old Shoes
Ball
Stuffed Animal
old rag
NEW
The cute one's mine!
YOSHI
Meee~!
AHH. I THOUGHT SHE CAME HOME SMELLING LIKE DOG ONE TIME.
WHAT ELSE?

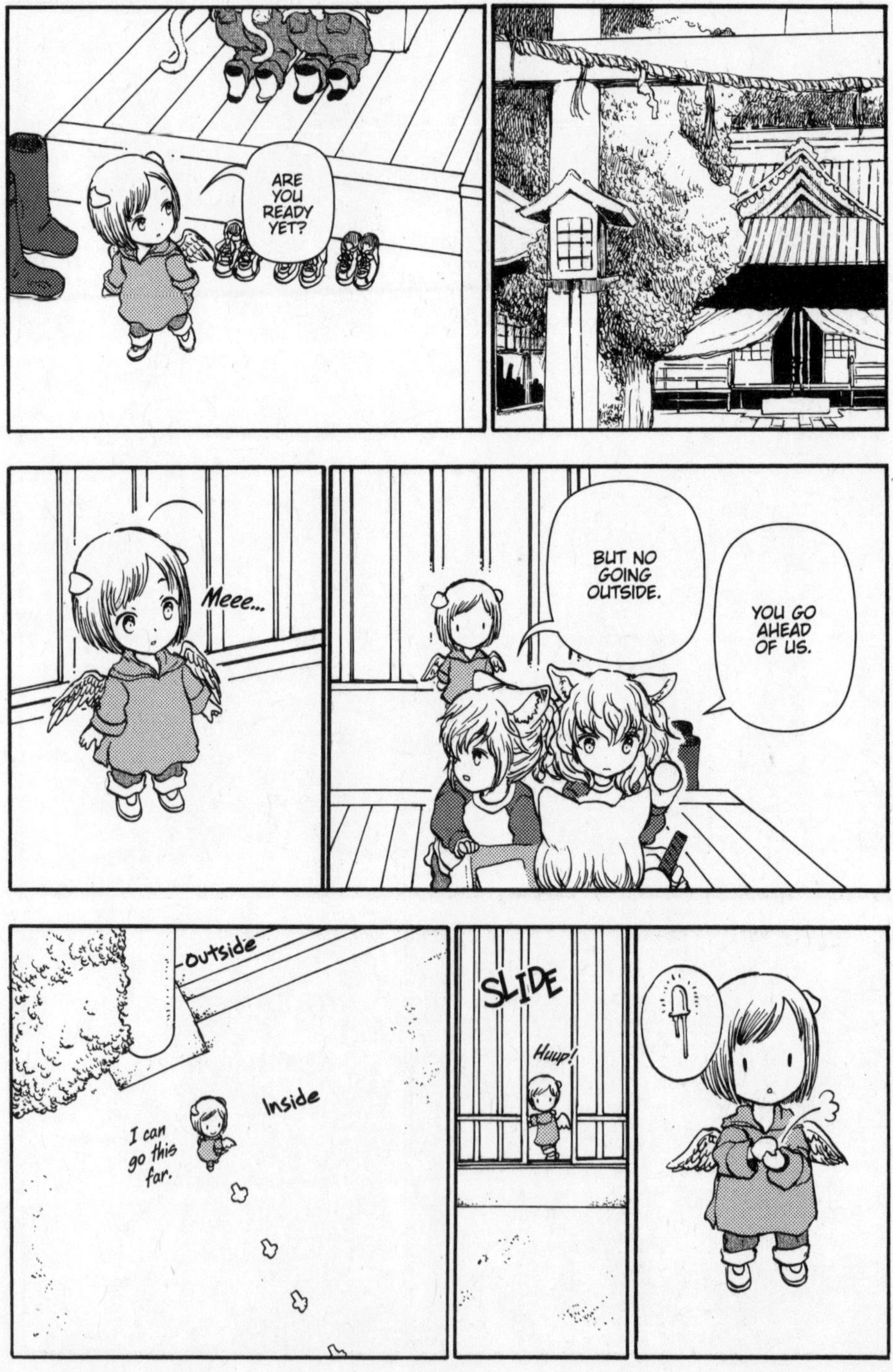

ARE YOU READY YET?
YOU GO AHEAD OF US.
BUT NO GOING OUTSIDE.
Meee...
SLIDE
Huup!
Outside
Inside
I can go this far.

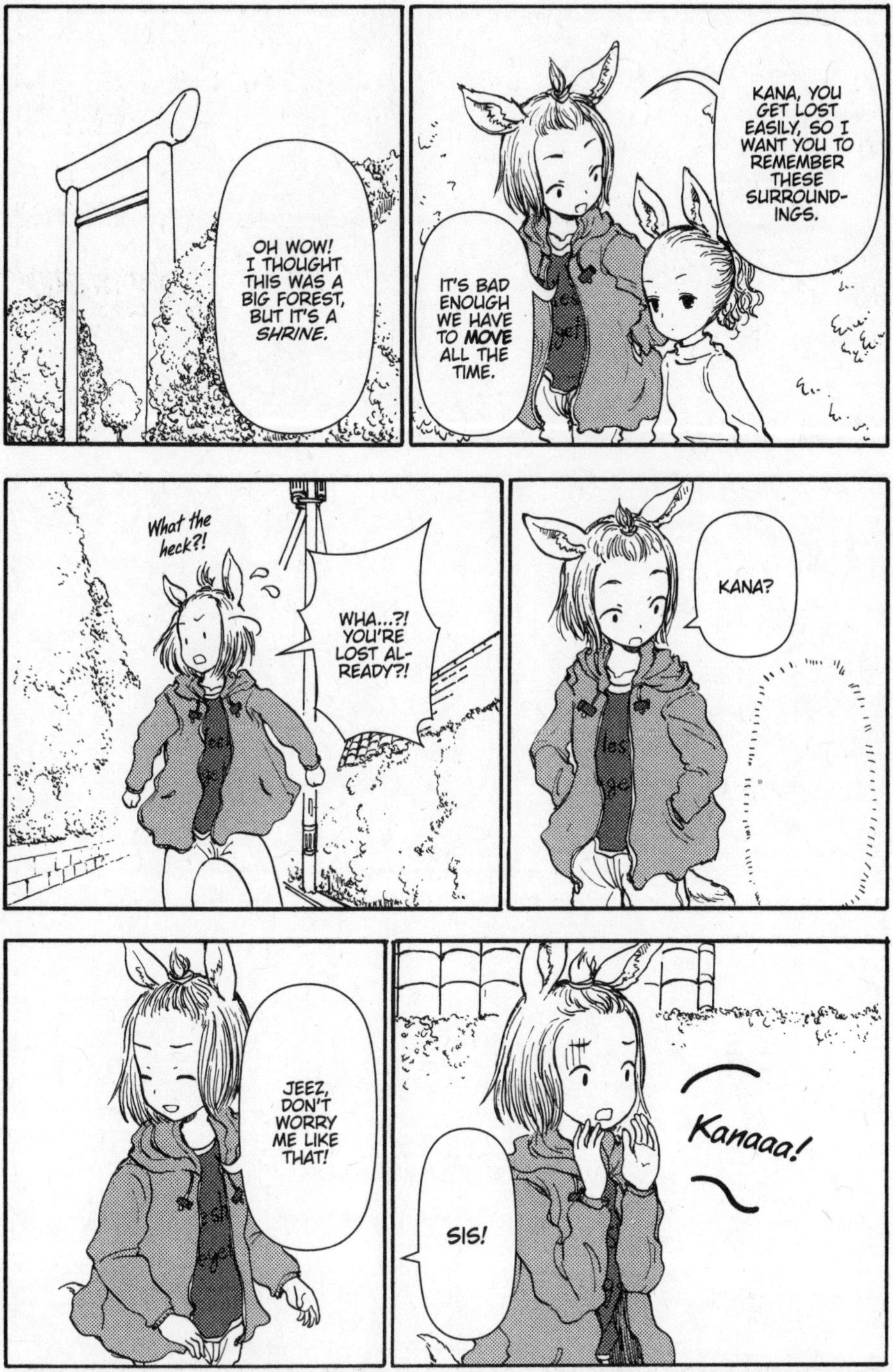
KANA, YOU GET LOST EASILY, SO I WANT YOU TO REMEMBER THESE SURROUND-INGS.
IT'S BAD ENOUGH WE HAVE TO MOVE ALL THE TIME.
OH WOW! I THOUGHT THIS WAS A BIG FOREST, BUT IT'S A SHRINE.
KANA?
WHA...?! YOU'RE LOST AL-READY?!
What the heck?!
Kanaaa!
SIS!
JEEZ, DON'T WORRY ME LIKE THAT!

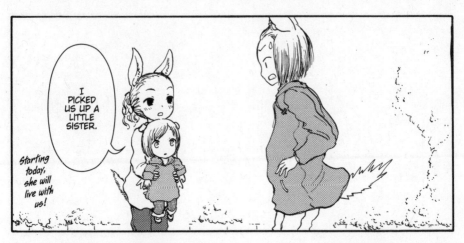

I PICKED US UP A LITTLE SISTER.
Starting today, she will live with us!
H...HEY, WHERE'D YOU GET HER?!
SHE WAS JUST LYING THERE.
Probably abandoned...
SNIFFLE
Myaaah!
Meee~!
There, there.
Now, now, don't cry! Where're you from?

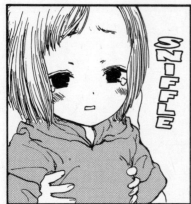

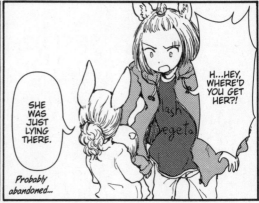

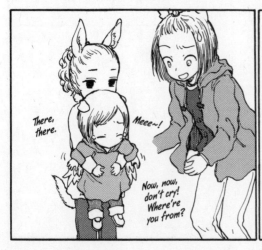

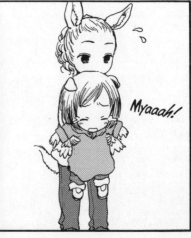

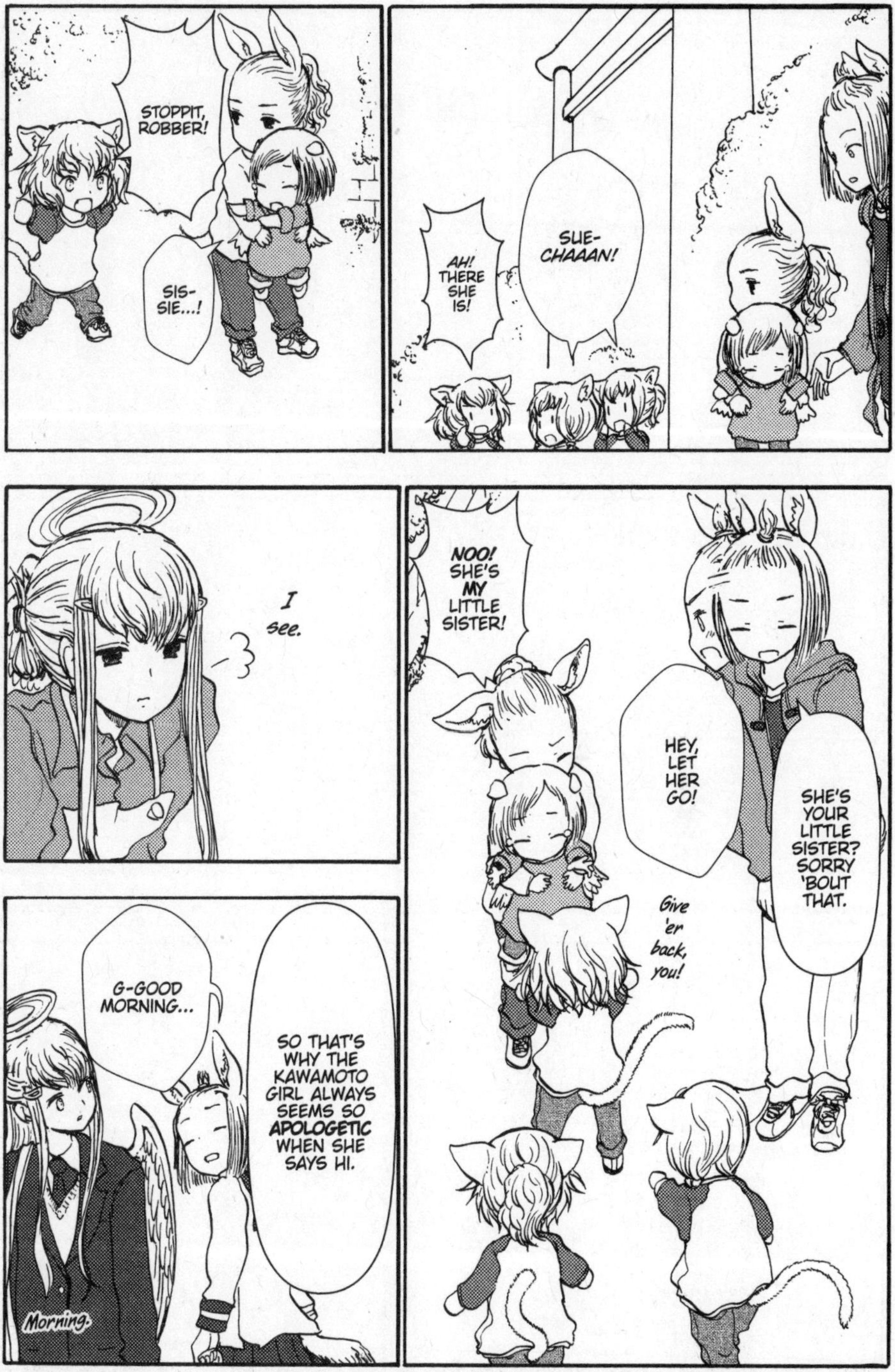

SUE-CHAAAN!
AH! THERE SHE IS!
STOPPIT, ROBBER!
SIS-SIE...!
NOO! SHE'S MY LITTLE SISTER!
HEY, LET HER GO!
SHE'S YOUR LITTLE SISTER? SORRY 'BOUT THAT.
Give 'er back, you!
I see.
SO THAT'S WHY THE KAWAMOTO GIRL ALWAYS SEEMS SO APOLOGETIC WHEN SHE SAYS HI.
G-GOOD MORNING...
Morning.

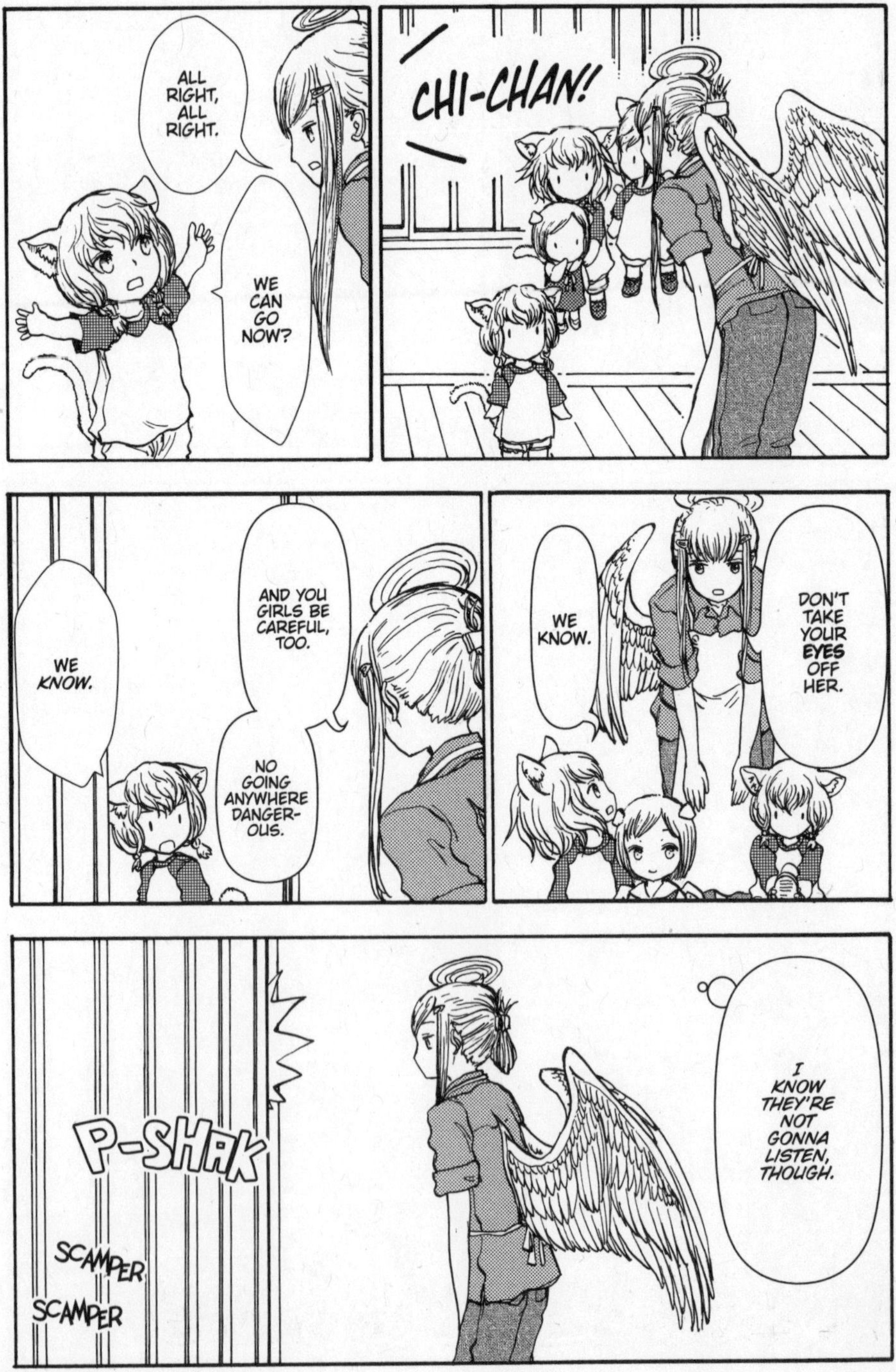
CHI-CHAN!
ALL RIGHT, ALL RIGHT.
WE CAN GO NOW?
DON'T TAKE YOUR EYES OFF HER.
WE KNOW.
AND YOU GIRLS BE CAREFUL, TOO.
NO GOING ANYWHERE DANGER-OUS.
WE KNOW.
I KNOW THEY'RE NOT GONNA LISTEN, THOUGH.
P-SHAK
SCAMPER
SCAMPER

A Centaur's Life

TRADITIONAL DRESS FROM AROUND THE WORLD (COLOMBIA)

THE AMPHIBIANFOLK ARE NATIVE TO TROPICAL RAIN FORESTS SPANNING COLOMBIA, VENEZUELA, AND BRAZIL, PARTICULARLY IN AREAS ADJACENT TO RIVERS. THE DEROGATORY TERM "FROG PEOPLE" HAS GIVEN WAY TO AN IMAGE OF PEOPLE WITH WET, MUCOUSY SKIN, BUT THAT'S NOT PARTICULARLY ACCURATE. IN REALITY, THEIR SKIN RESPIRATION IS COMPARABLE TO THAT OF A MAMMALIAN HUMAN, THOUGH THEY ARE MORE VULNERABLE TO DRY SKIN. THUS, THEY ARE ABLE TO WEAR THE SAME CLOTHES AS MAMMALIAN HUMANS (ALBEIT IN DIFFERENT MEASUREMENTS), AND INDEED YOU ARE LIKELY TO SPOT AMPHIBIANFOLK IN T-SHIRTS OR WAISTCLOTHS. THAT SAID, SINCE AMPHIBIANFOLK LEAD LIVES DIVIDED BETWEEN WATER AND LAND, IT IS NOT COMMON TO SEE THEM WEARING VERY MUCH, AND INDEED THEIR CULTURE HAS NO PARTICULAR RESERVATIONS ABOUT NUDITY.

MORE REMARKABLE ARE THE BITS OF JEWELRY WORN BY AMPHIBIANFOLK AS PERSONAL ORNAMENTS, MOST OF WHICH ARE MADE OF GOLD. THOUGH DIFFICULT TO PRODUCE OR OBTAIN, IT IS LIKELY THAT THEY PREFER GOLD MAINLY BECAUSE IT DOESN'T RUST. HANDMADE MASKS WHICH MIMIC MAMMALIAN HUMAN FACES BEAR A STRONG RESEMBLANCE TO THOSE WORN BY THE ANTARCTICANS LIVING AMONGST MAMMALIAN HUMANS, AND IT IS UNKNOWN IN WHICH CULTURE THEY ACTUALLY ORIGINATED. IN EITHER CASE, THESE MASKS SERVE AS EVIDENCE OF INTERACTION WITH MAMMALIAN HUMANS PRIOR TO THE MODERN AGE. THE GOLDEN JEWELRY, MEANWHILE, WAS RESPONSIBLE FOR THE GREAT MISFORTUNE OF ATTRACTING THE ATTENTION OF EUROPEAN CONQUISTADORS, WHO WOULD LONG PERSECUTE AMPHIBIANFOLK AS "FROGS AND NEWTS RIPE FOR THE KILL," LEADING TO THE MASSIVE LOSS OF PRECIOUS CULTURAL ARTIFACTS.

THOUGH THERE ARE EXAMPLES OF AMPHIBIAN-FOLK, SUCH AS JEAN ROUSSEAU, SECURING POSITIONS OF HIGH ESTEEM WITHIN MAMMALIAN SOCIETY, THE FACT THAT THIS MANNER OF DISCRIMINATION IS STILL SO DEEPLY ROOTED SERVES AS DEPLORABLE EVIDENCE OF ITS OWN FOOLISH INJUSTICE.

CHAPTER 52

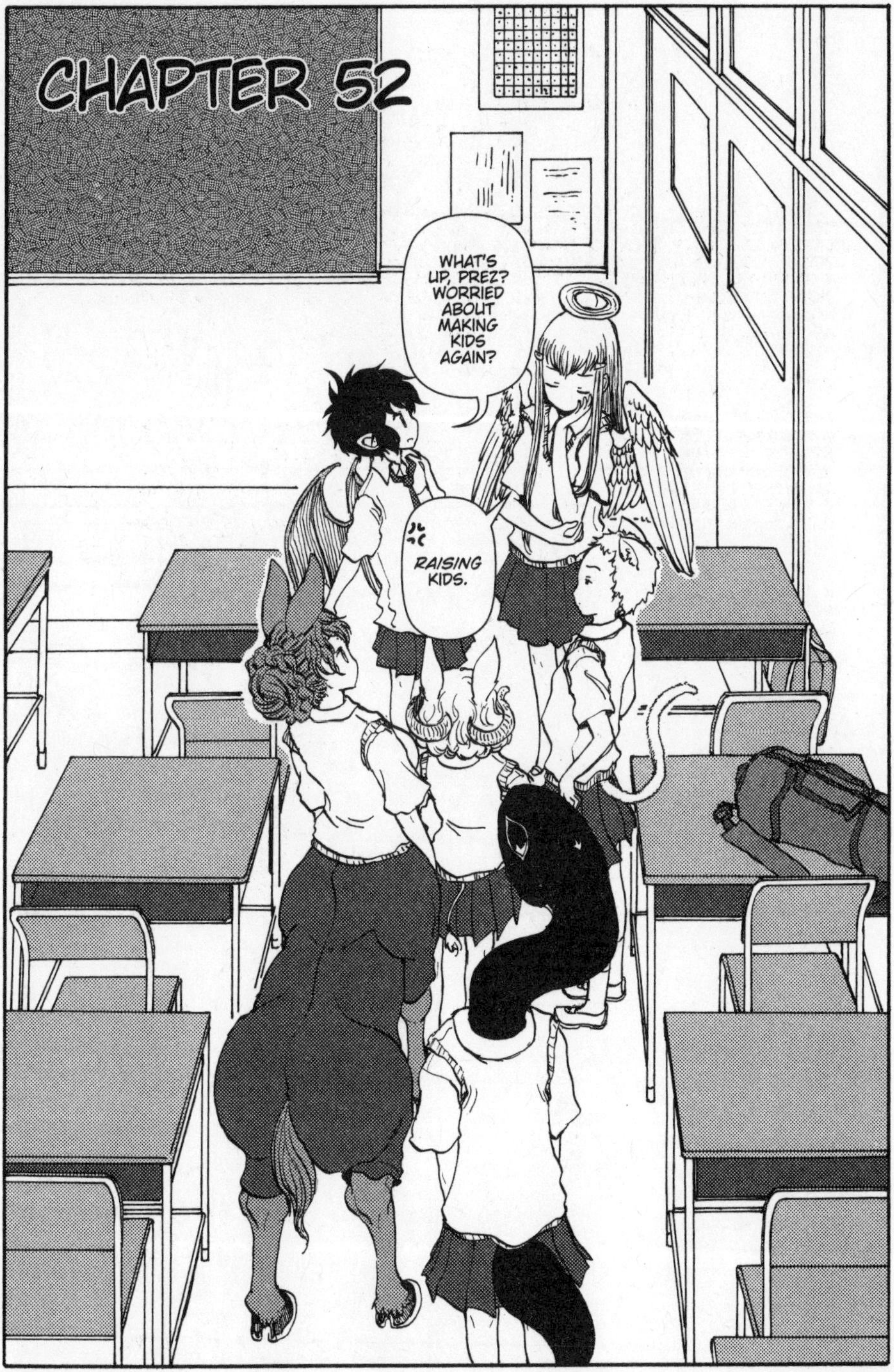
WHAT'S UP, PREZ? WORRIED ABOUT MAKING KIDS AGAIN?
RAISING KIDS.

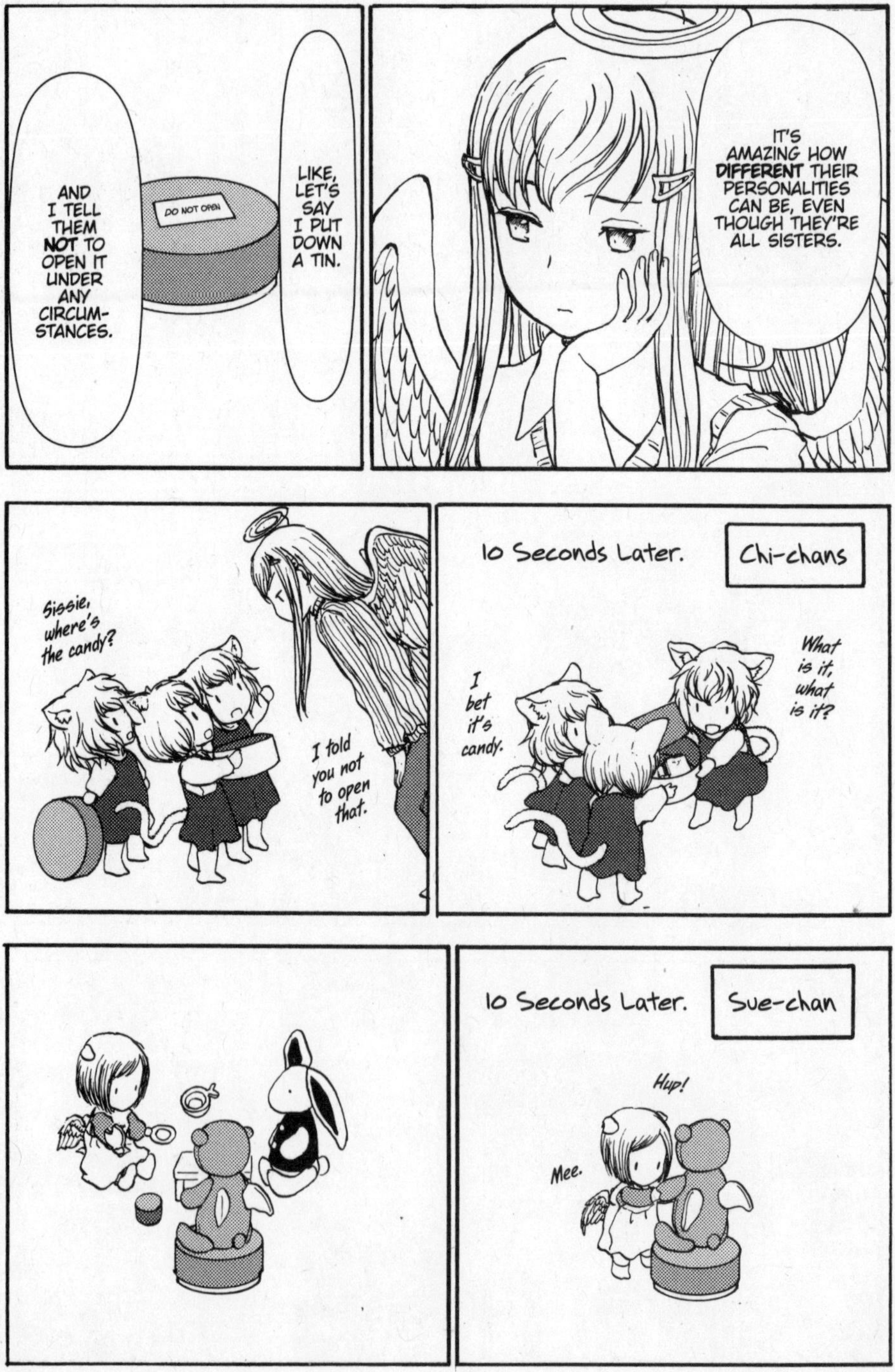
IT'S AMAZING HOW DIFFERENT THEIR PERSONALITIES CAN BE, EVEN THOUGH THEY'RE ALL SISTERS.
LIKE, LET'S SAY I PUT DOWN A TIN.
AND I TELL THEM NOT TO OPEN IT UNDER ANY CIRCUM-STANCES.
DO NOT OPEN
10 Seconds Later.
Chi-chans
What is it, what is it?
I bet it's candy.
Sissie, where's the candy?
I told you not to open that.
10 Seconds Later.
Sue-chan
Hup!
Mee.

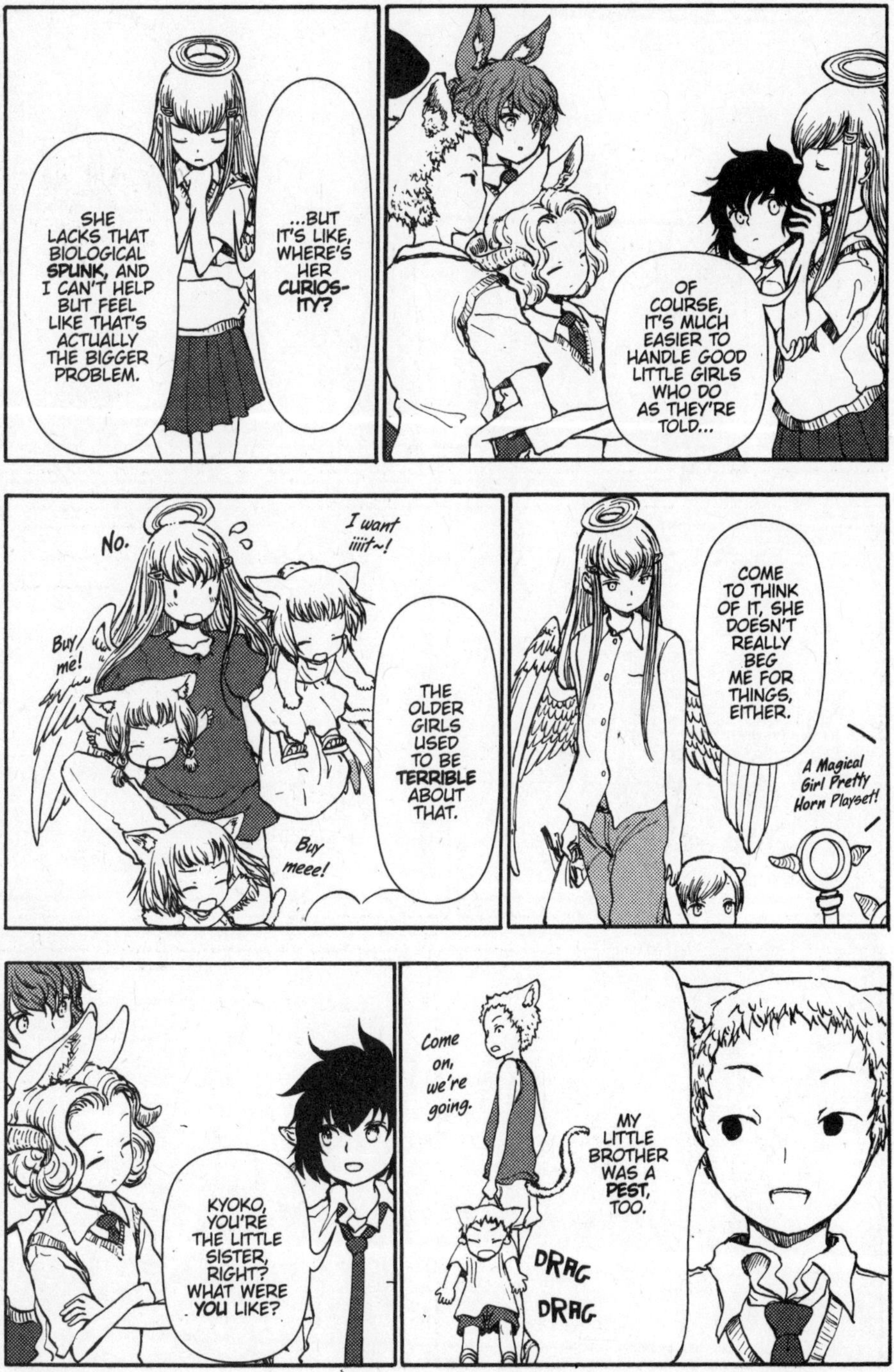
OF COURSE, IT'S MUCH EASIER TO HANDLE GOOD LITTLE GIRLS WHO DO AS THEY'RE TOLD...
...BUT IT'S LIKE, WHERE'S HER CURIOSITY?
SHE LACKS THAT BIOLOGICAL SPUNK, AND I CAN'T HELP BUT FEEL LIKE THAT'S ACTUALLY THE BIGGER PROBLEM.
COME TO THINK OF IT, SHE DOESN'T REALLY BEG ME FOR THINGS, EITHER.
A Magical Girl Pretty Horn Playset!
I want iiiit~!
No.
THE OLDER GIRLS USED TO BE TERRIBLE ABOUT THAT.
Buy me!
Buy meee!
MY LITTLE BROTHER WAS A PEST, TOO.
Come on, we're going.
DRAG
DRAG
KYOKO, YOU'RE THE LITTLE SISTER, RIGHT? WHAT WERE YOU LIKE?

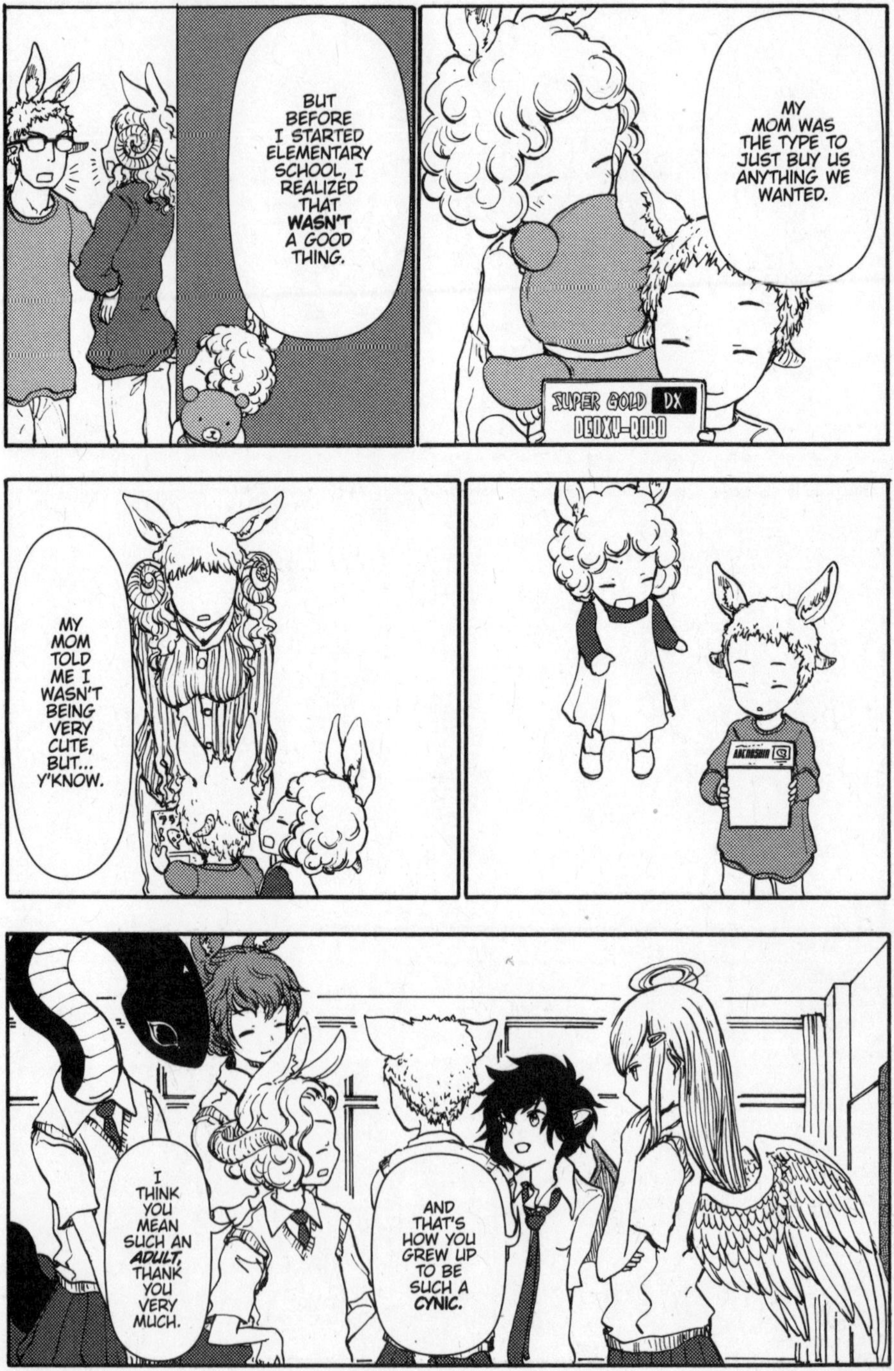
MY MOM WAS THE TYPE TO JUST BUY US ANYTHING WE WANTED.
SUPER GOLD DX
BUT BEFORE I STARTED ELEMENTARY SCHOOL, I REALIZED THAT **WASN'T** A GOOD THING.
MY MOM TOLD ME I WASN'T BEING VERY CUTE, BUT... Y'KNOW.
AND THAT'S HOW YOU GREW UP TO BE SUCH A **CYNIC.**
I THINK YOU MEAN SUCH AN ***ADULT,*** THANK YOU VERY MUCH.

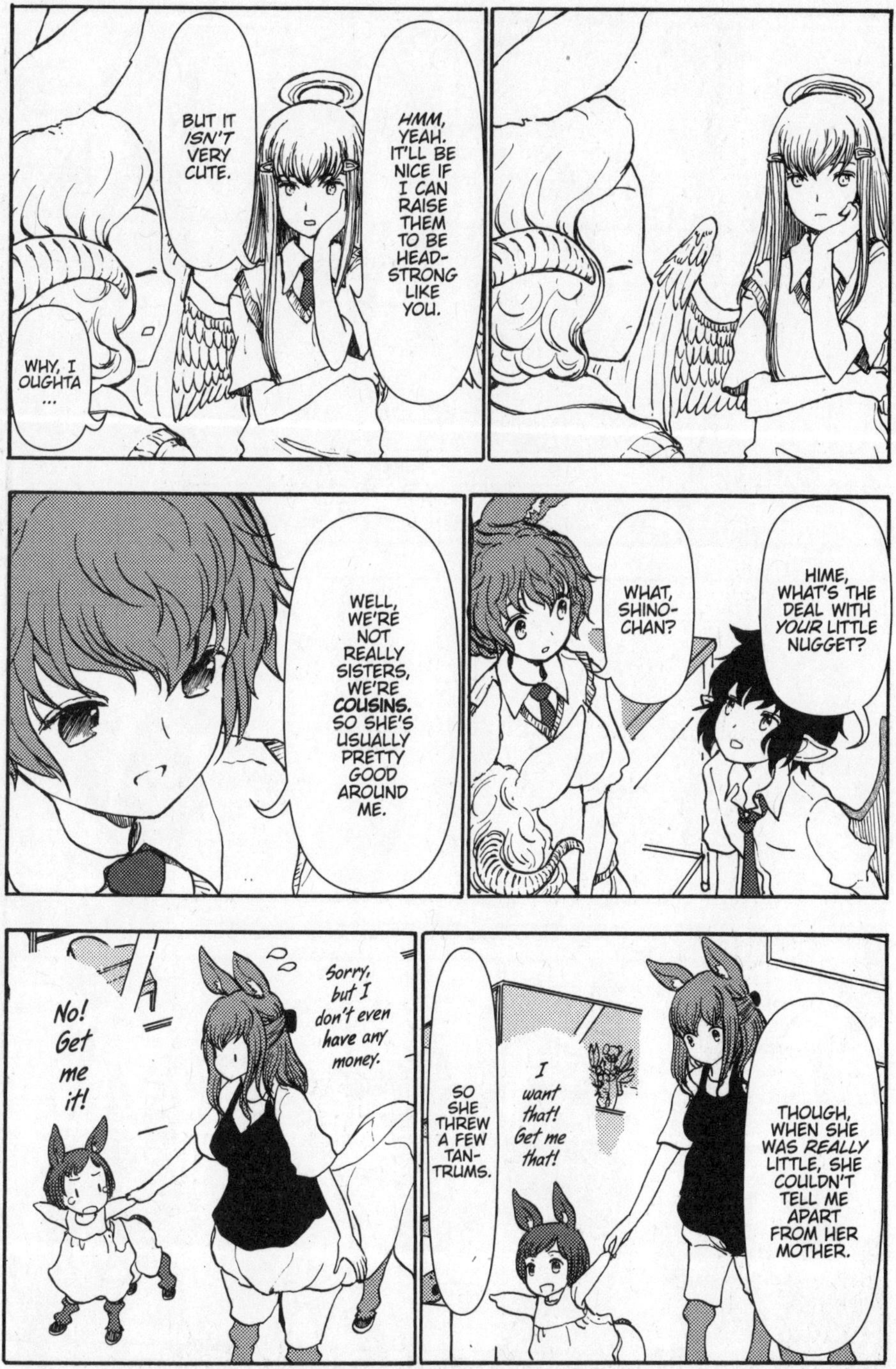
HMM, YEAH. IT'LL BE NICE IF I CAN RAISE THEM TO BE HEADSTRONG LIKE YOU.
BUT IT ISN'T VERY CUTE.
WHY, I OUGHTA ...
HIME, WHAT'S THE DEAL WITH YOUR LITTLE NUGGET?
WHAT, SHINO-CHAN?
WELL, WE'RE NOT REALLY SISTERS, WE'RE COUSINS. SO SHE'S USUALLY PRETTY GOOD AROUND ME.
THOUGH, WHEN SHE WAS REALLY LITTLE, SHE COULDN'T TELL ME APART FROM HER MOTHER.
I want that! Get me that!
SO SHE THREW A FEW TANTRUMS.
Sorry, but I don't even have any money.
No! Get me it!

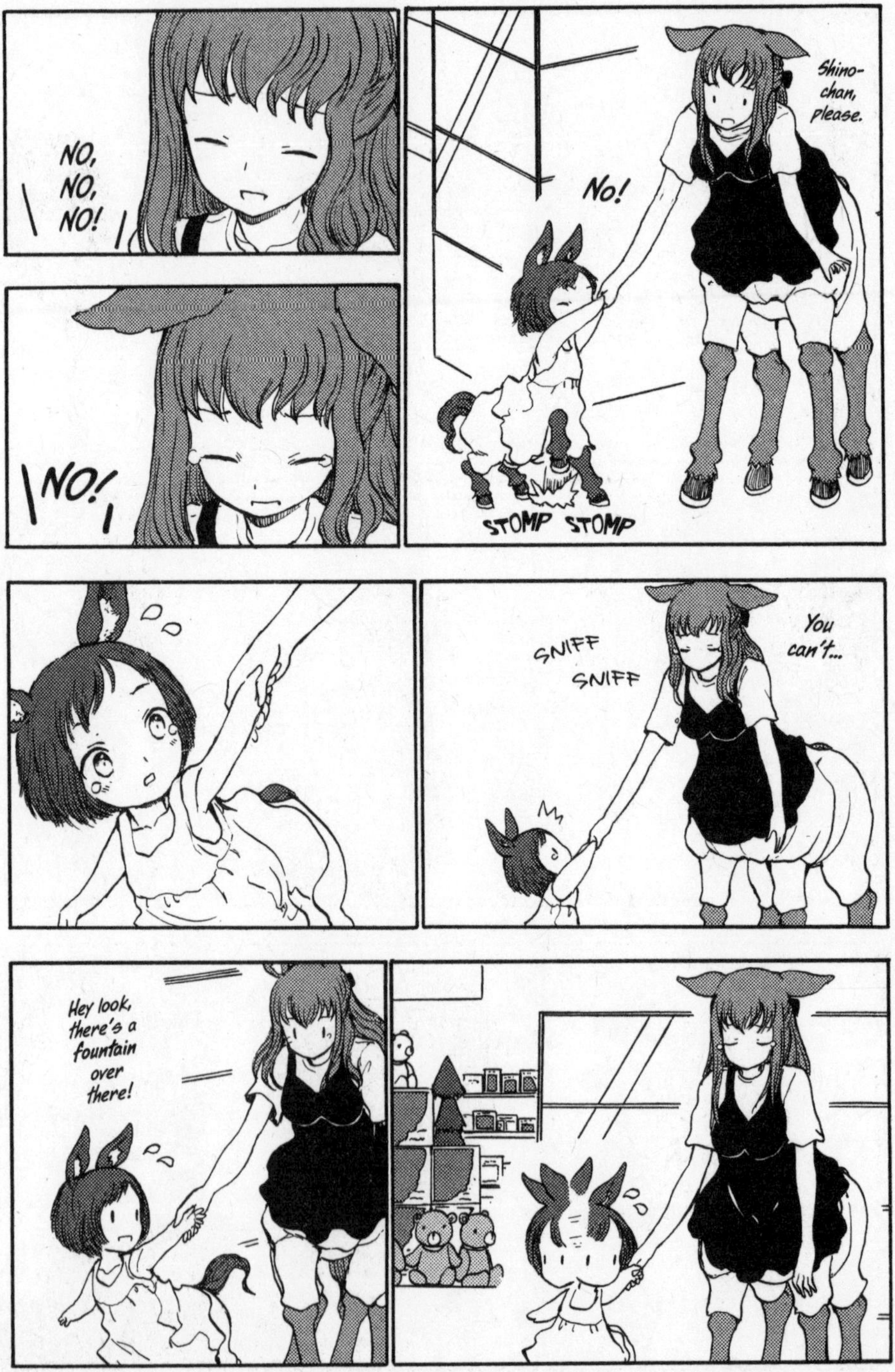
Shino-chan, please.
No!
STOMP STOMP
NO, NO, NO!
NO!
You can't...
SNIFF SNIFF
Hey look, there's a fountain over there!

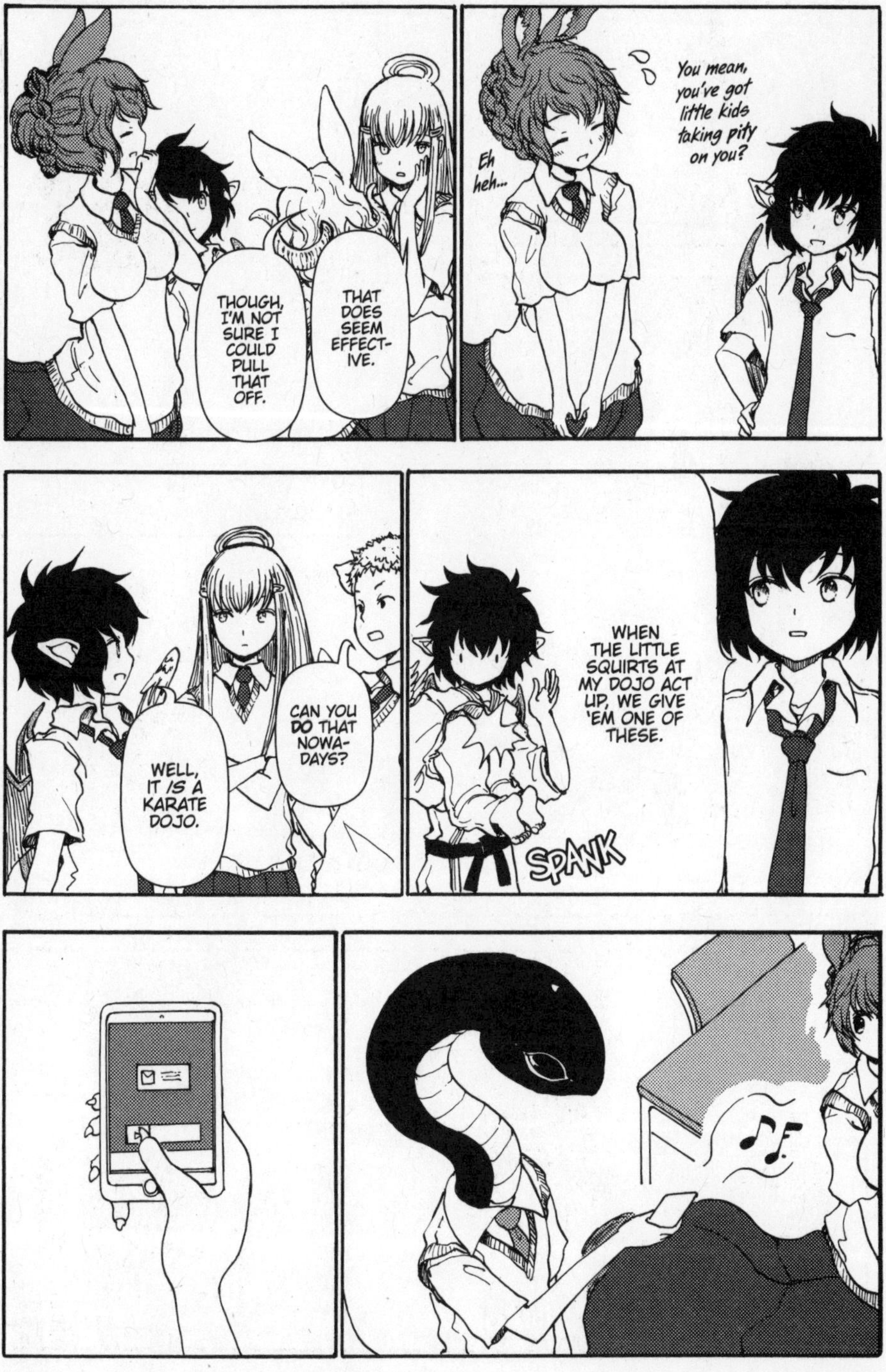
You mean, you've got little kids taking pity on you?
Eh heh...
THAT DOES SEEM EFFECTIVE.
THOUGH, I'M NOT SURE I COULD PULL THAT OFF.
WHEN THE LITTLE SQUIRTS AT MY DOJO ACT UP, WE GIVE 'EM ONE OF THESE.
SPANK
CAN YOU DO THAT NOWADAYS?
WELL, IT IS A KARATE DOJO.

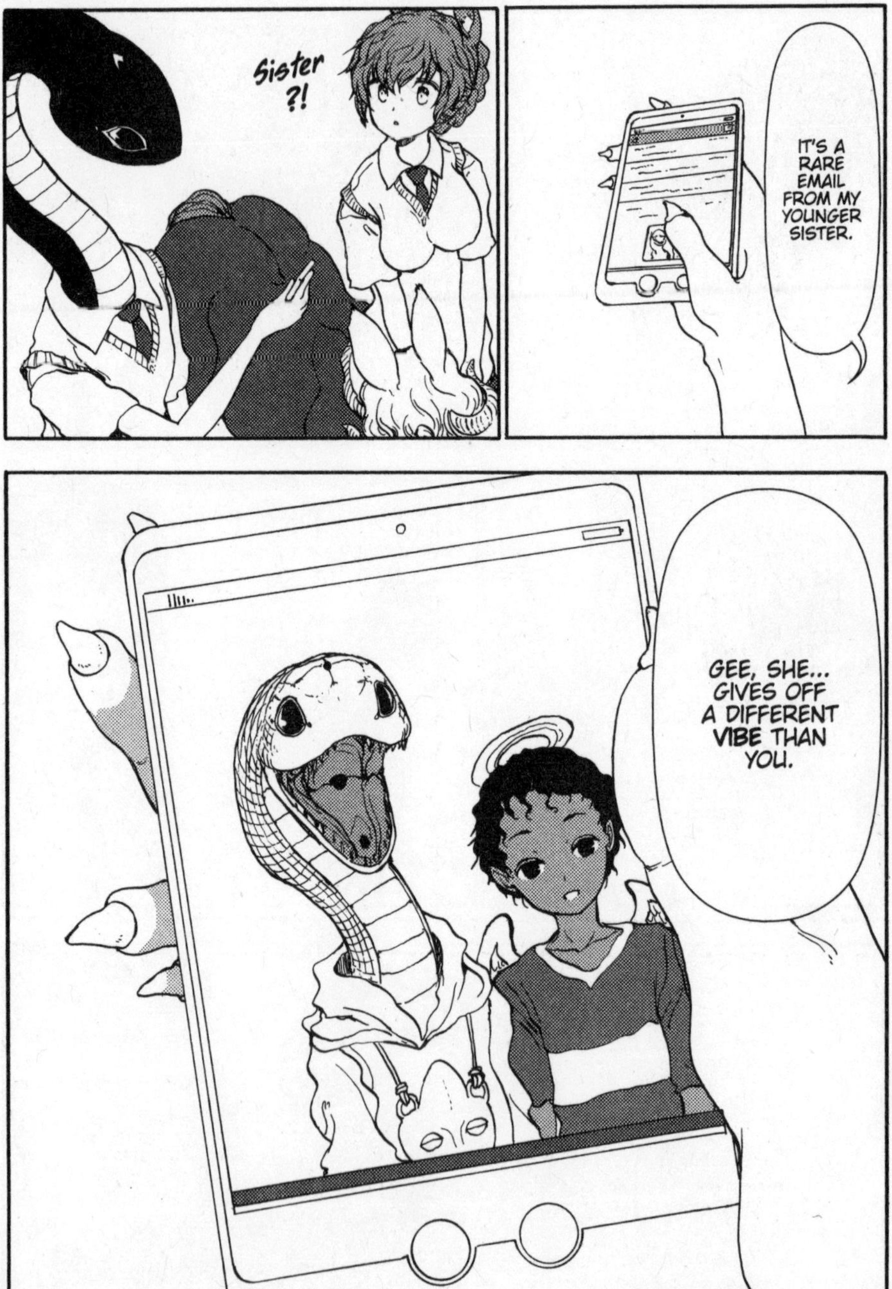
IT'S A RARE EMAIL FROM MY YOUNGER SISTER.
Sister ?!
GEE, SHE... GIVES OFF A DIFFERENT VIBE THAN YOU.

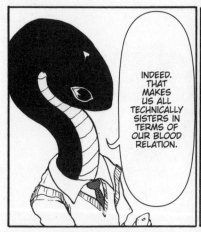

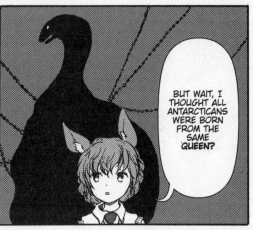

BUT WAIT, I THOUGHT ALL ANTARCTICANS WERE BORN FROM THE SAME **QUEEN?**
INDEED. THAT MAKES US ALL TECHNICALLY SISTERS IN TERMS OF OUR BLOOD RELATION.
BUT DURING OUR MATURATION PROCESS, WE RELY ON MANY PEOPLE.
AND ARE RELIED UPON BY OTHERS, AS WELL.
WE APPLY THE WORD **"SISTER"** TO SUCH PEOPLE.
AND THIS IS ONE OF MY YOUNGER SISTERS.

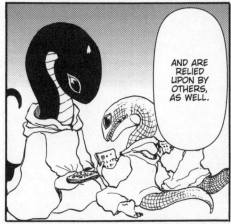

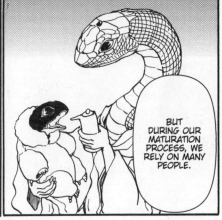

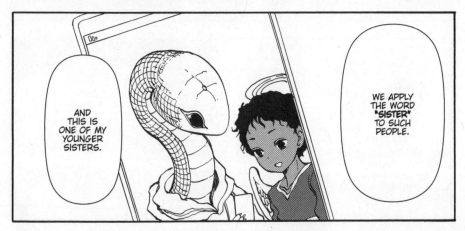

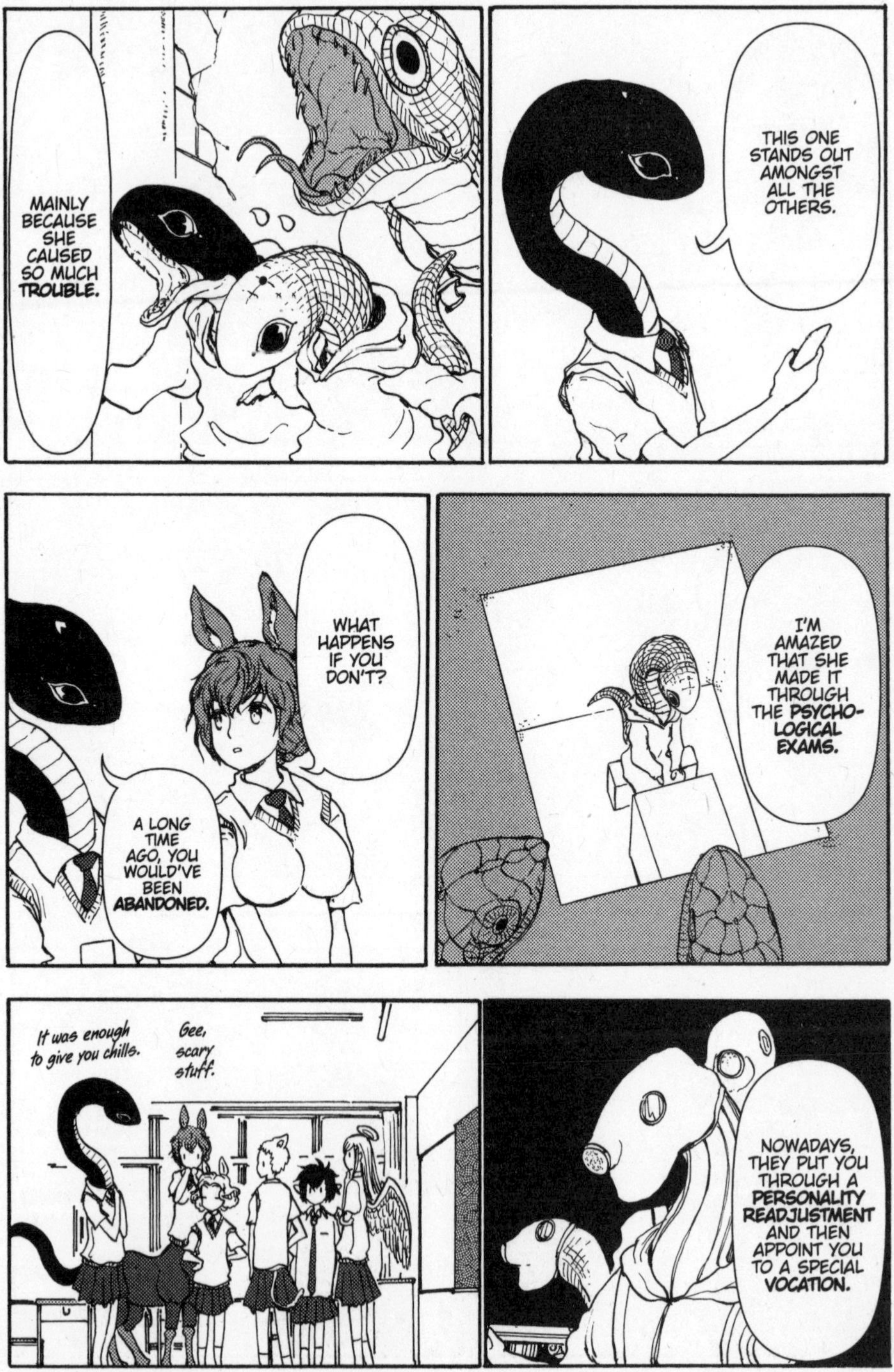
THIS ONE STANDS OUT AMONGST ALL THE OTHERS.
MAINLY BECAUSE SHE CAUSED SO MUCH TROUBLE.
I'M AMAZED THAT SHE MADE IT THROUGH THE PSYCHO-LOGICAL EXAMS.
WHAT HAPPENS IF YOU DON'T?
A LONG TIME AGO, YOU WOULD'VE BEEN ABANDONED.
NOWADAYS, THEY PUT YOU THROUGH A PERSONALITY READJUSTMENT AND THEN APPOINT YOU TO A SPECIAL VOCATION.
Gee, scary stuff.
It was enough to give you chills.

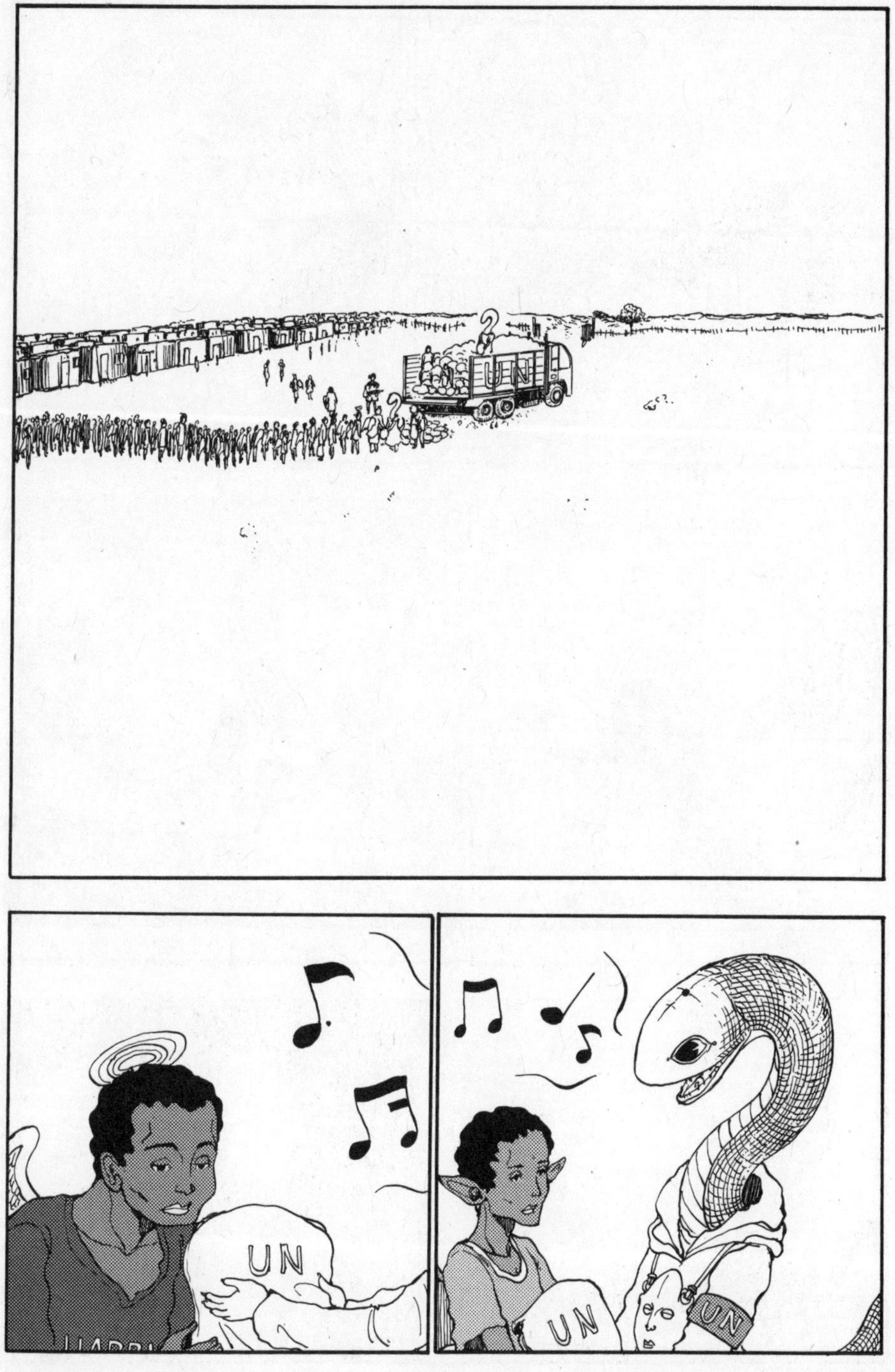
UN
UN
UN
UN

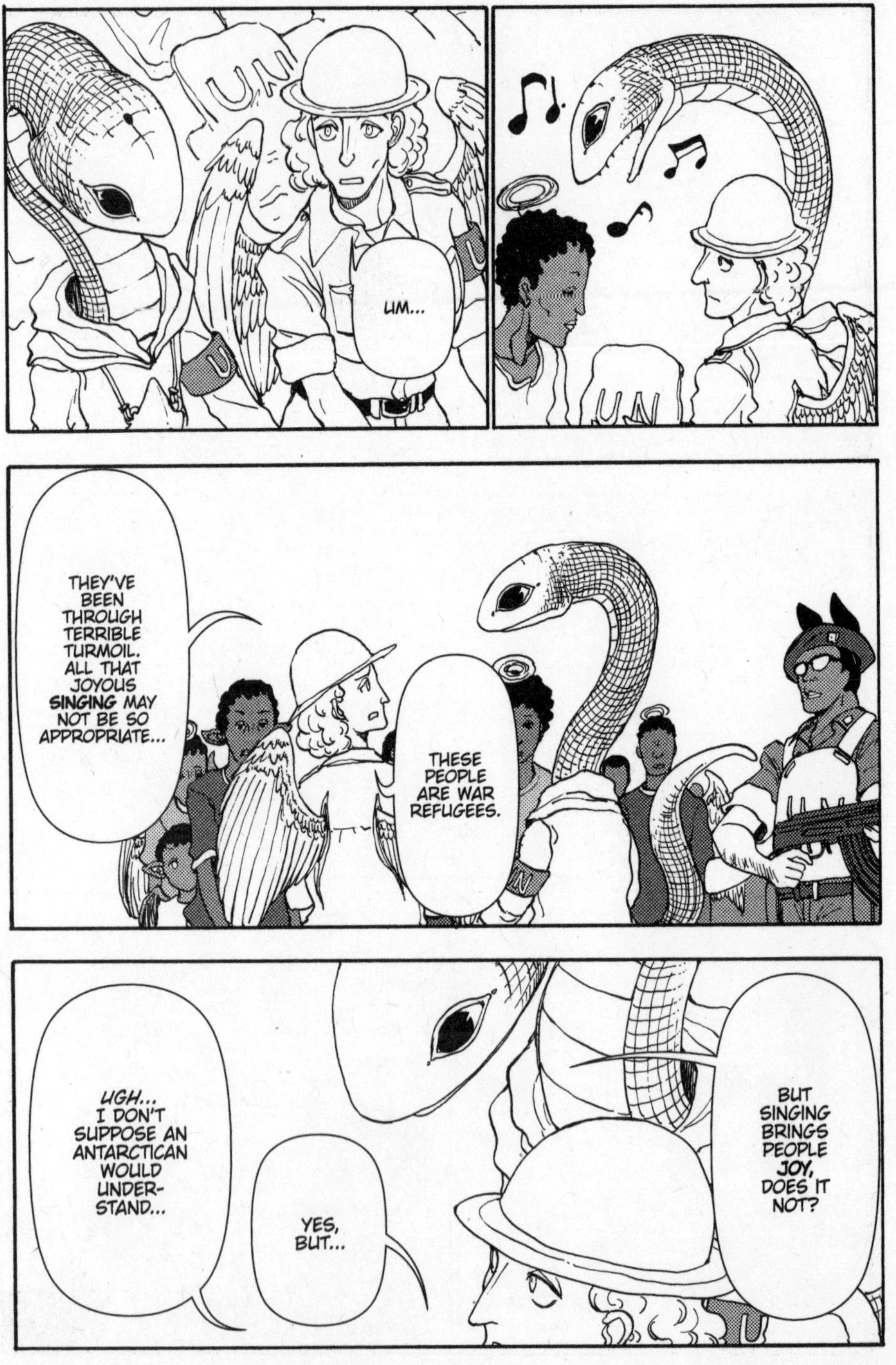
UM...
THESE PEOPLE ARE WAR REFUGEES.
THEY'VE BEEN THROUGH TERRIBLE TURMOIL. ALL THAT JOYOUS **SINGING** MAY NOT BE SO APPROPRIATE...
BUT SINGING BRINGS PEOPLE **JOY,** DOES IT NOT?
YES, BUT...
UGH... I DON'T SUPPOSE AN ANTARCTICAN WOULD UNDER-STAND...

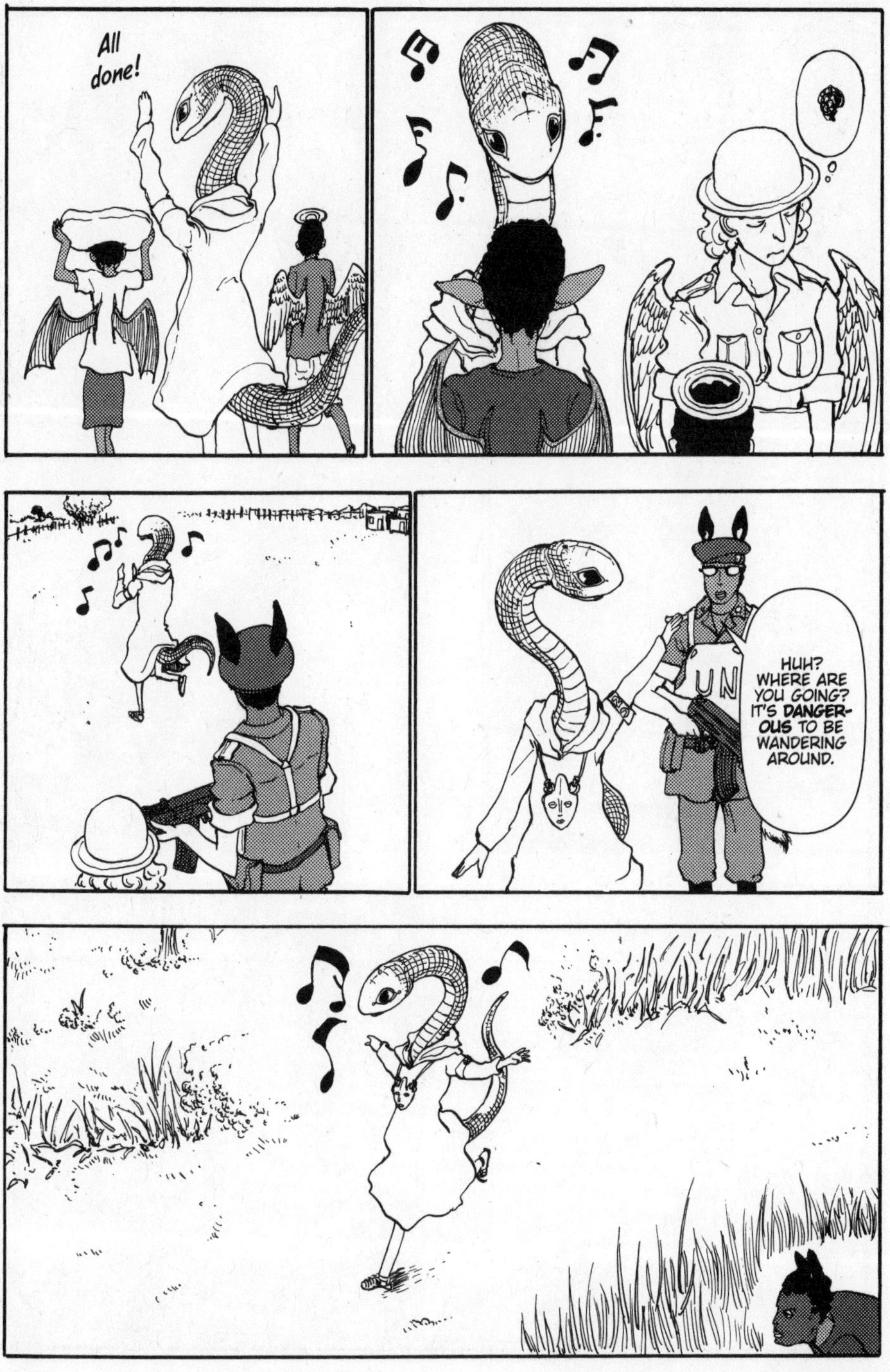
All done!
HUH? WHERE ARE YOU GOING? IT'S **DANGEROUS** TO BE WANDERING AROUND.

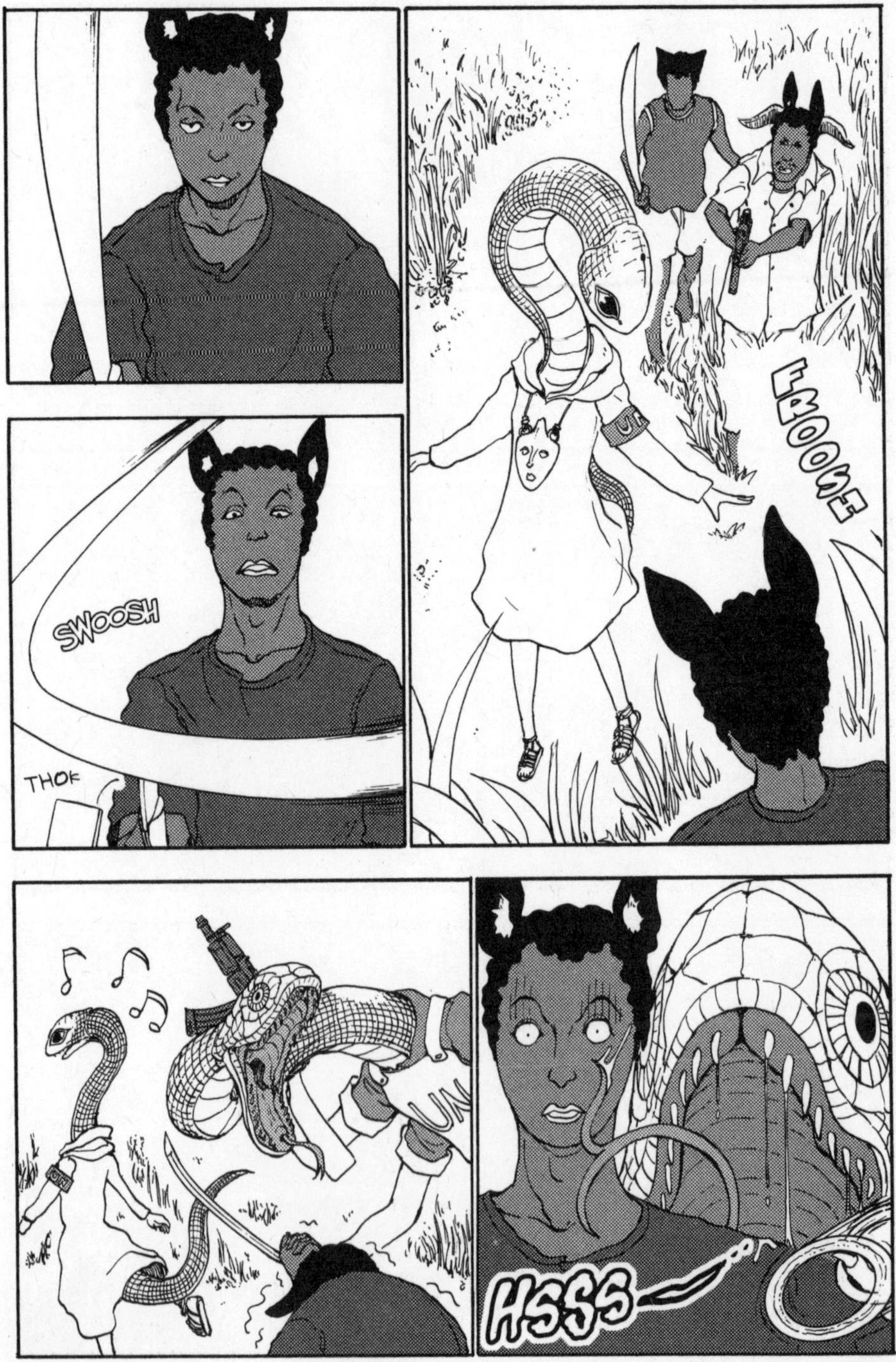
FWOOSH
SWOOSH
THOK
HSSS—

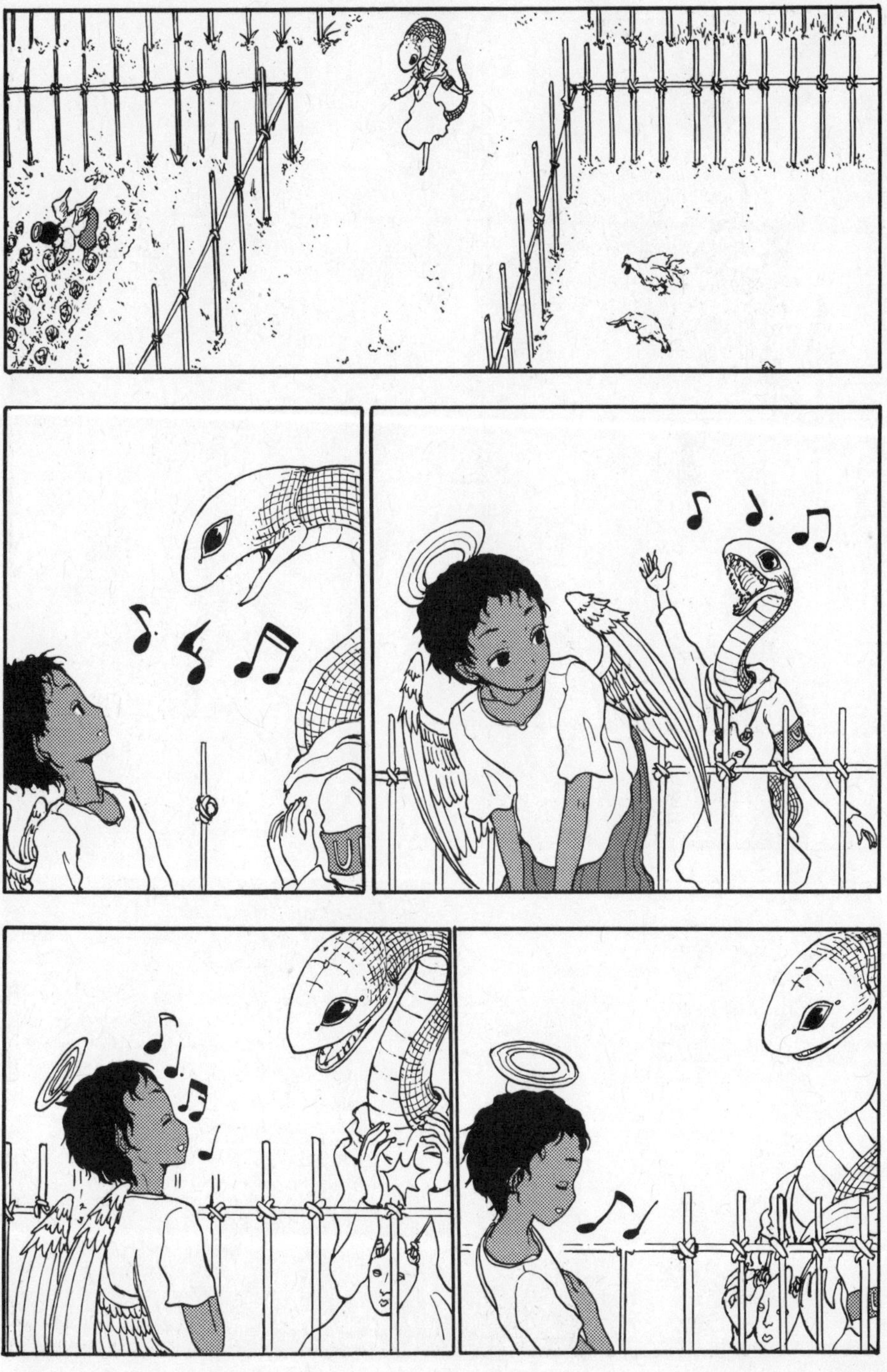

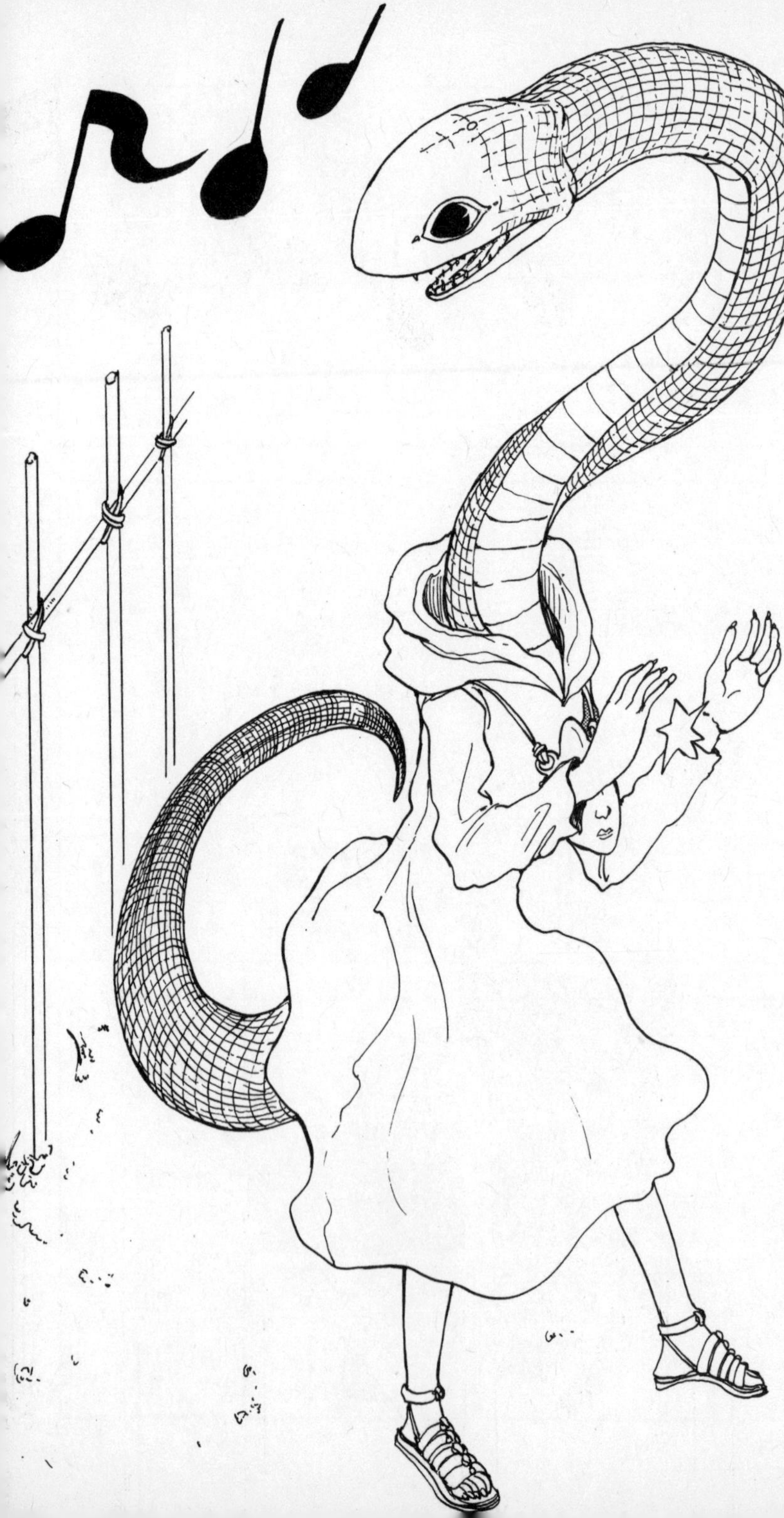

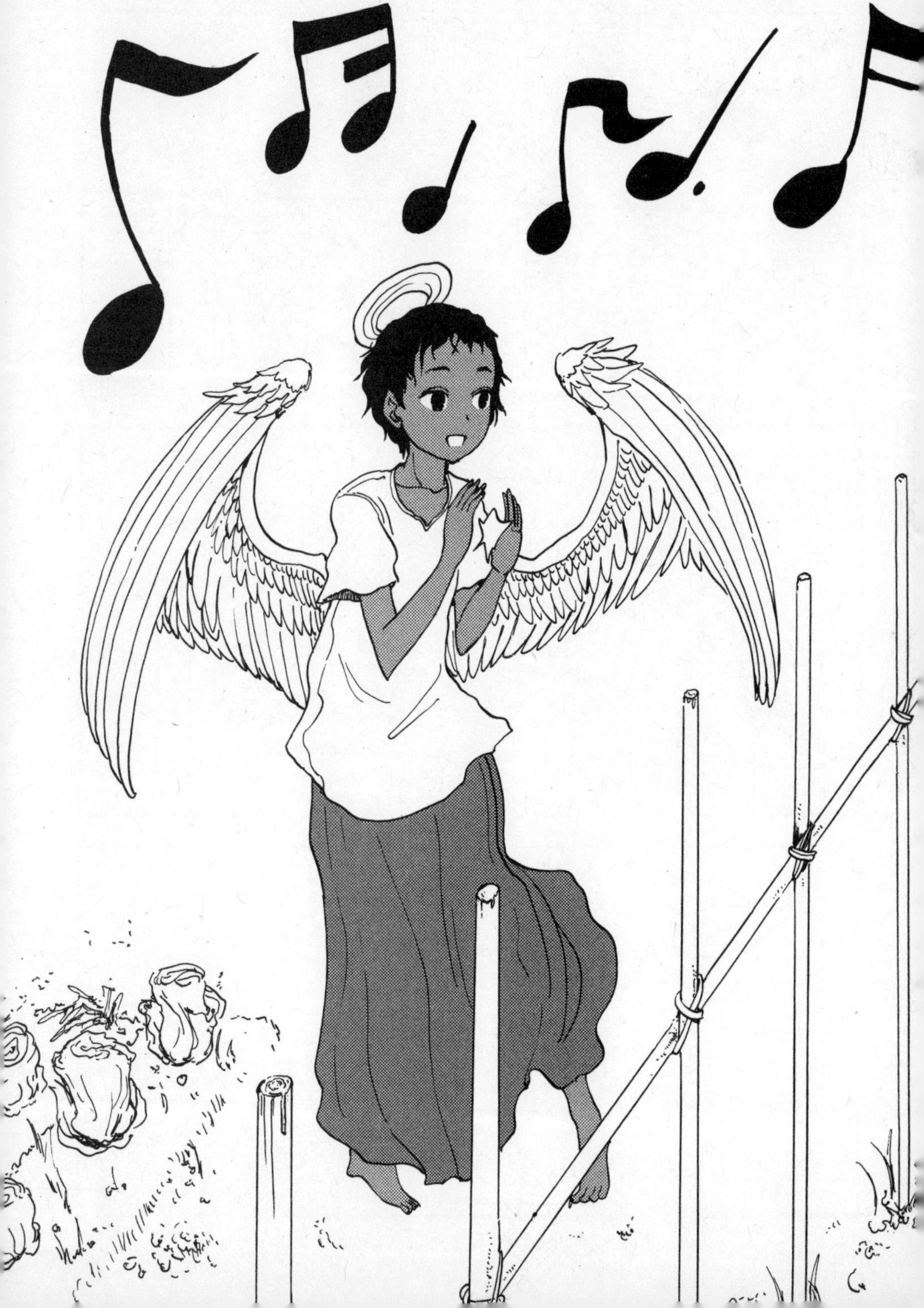

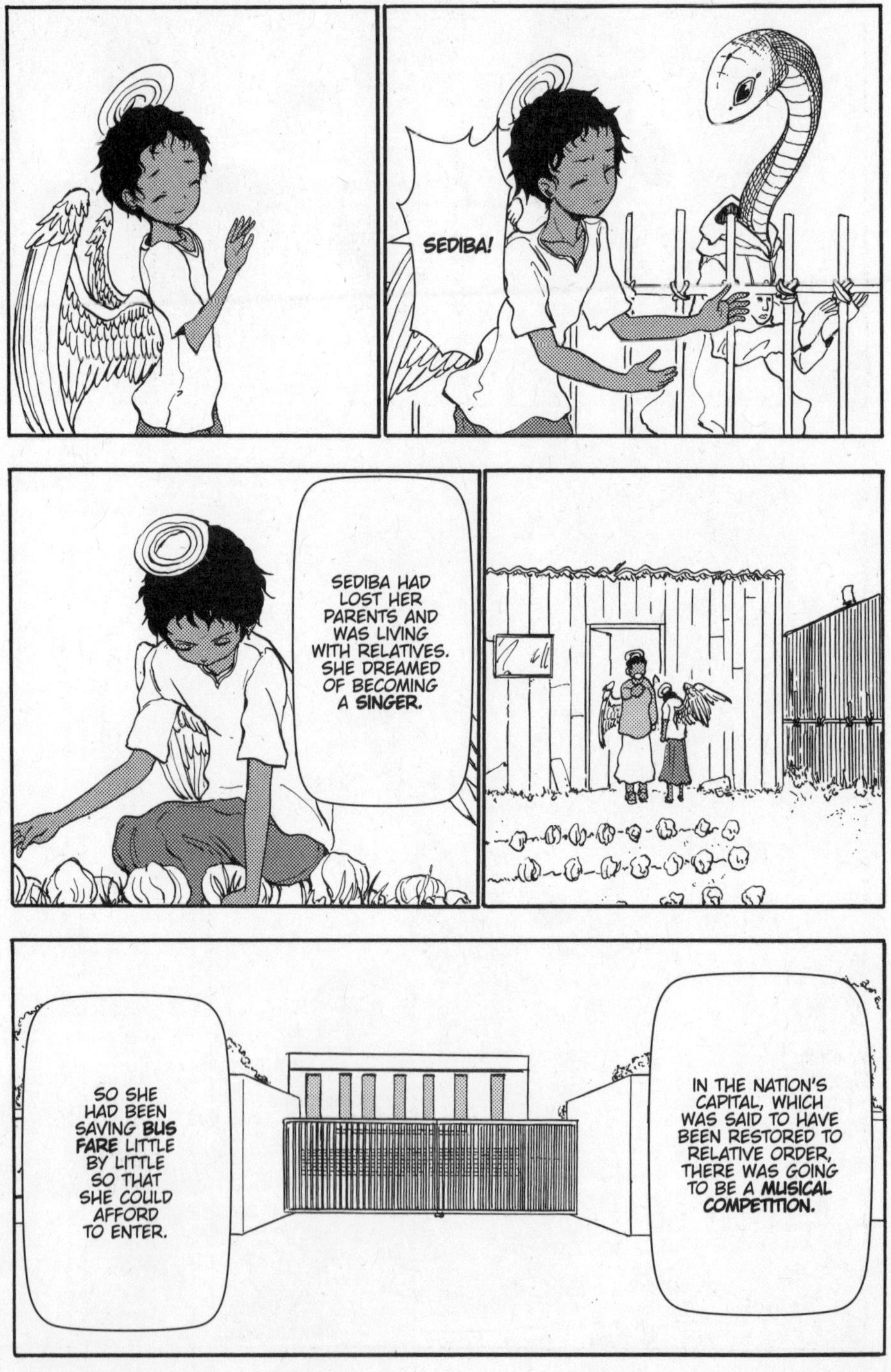
SEDIBA!
SEDIBA HAD LOST HER PARENTS AND WAS LIVING WITH RELATIVES. SHE DREAMED OF BECOMING A SINGER.
IN THE NATION'S CAPITAL, WHICH WAS SAID TO HAVE BEEN RESTORED TO RELATIVE ORDER, THERE WAS GOING TO BE A MUSICAL COMPETITION.
SO SHE HAD BEEN SAVING BUS FARE LITTLE BY LITTLE SO THAT SHE COULD AFFORD TO ENTER.

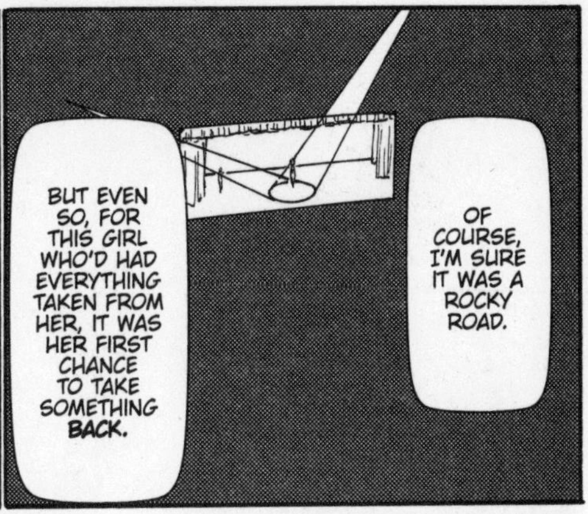
OF COURSE, I'M SURE IT WAS A ROCKY ROAD.
BUT EVEN SO, FOR THIS GIRL WHO'D HAD EVERYTHING TAKEN FROM HER, IT WAS HER FIRST CHANCE TO TAKE SOMETHING BACK.

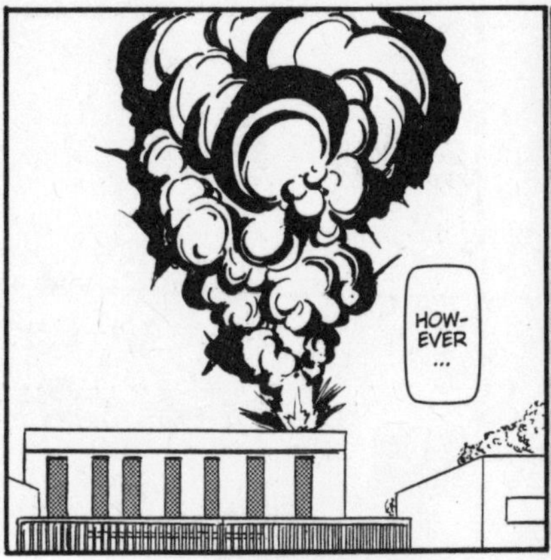
HOW-EVER ...

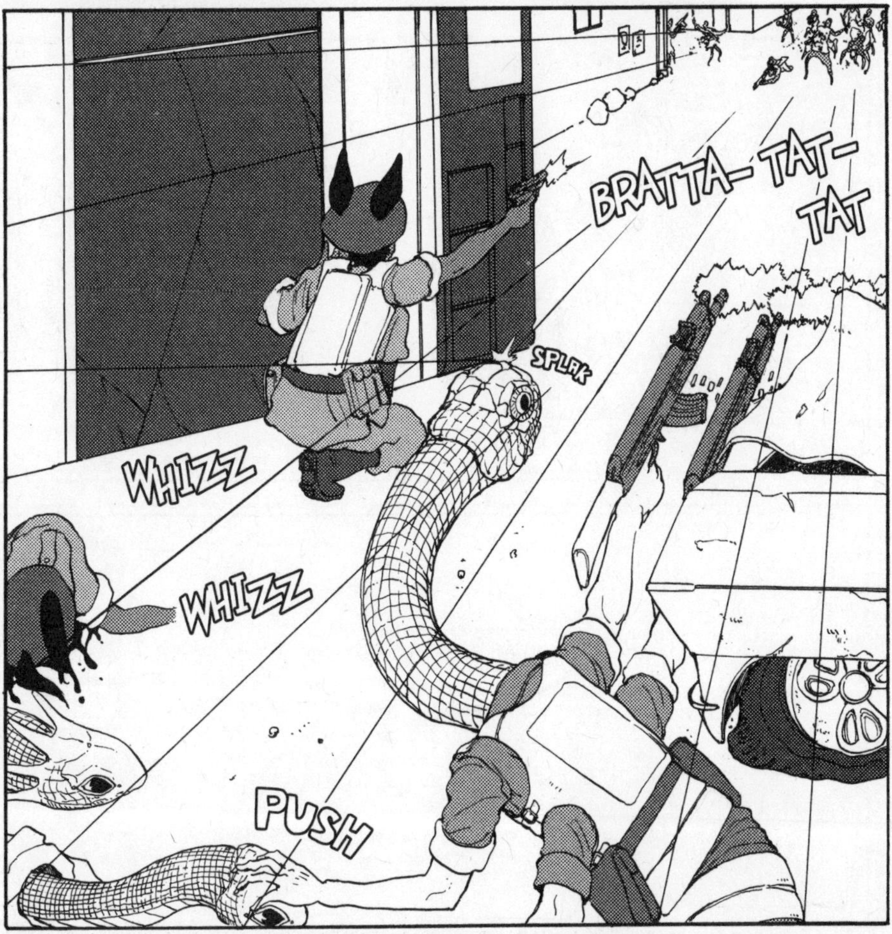
BRATTA-TAT-TAT
SPLAK
WHIZZ
WHIZZ
PUSH

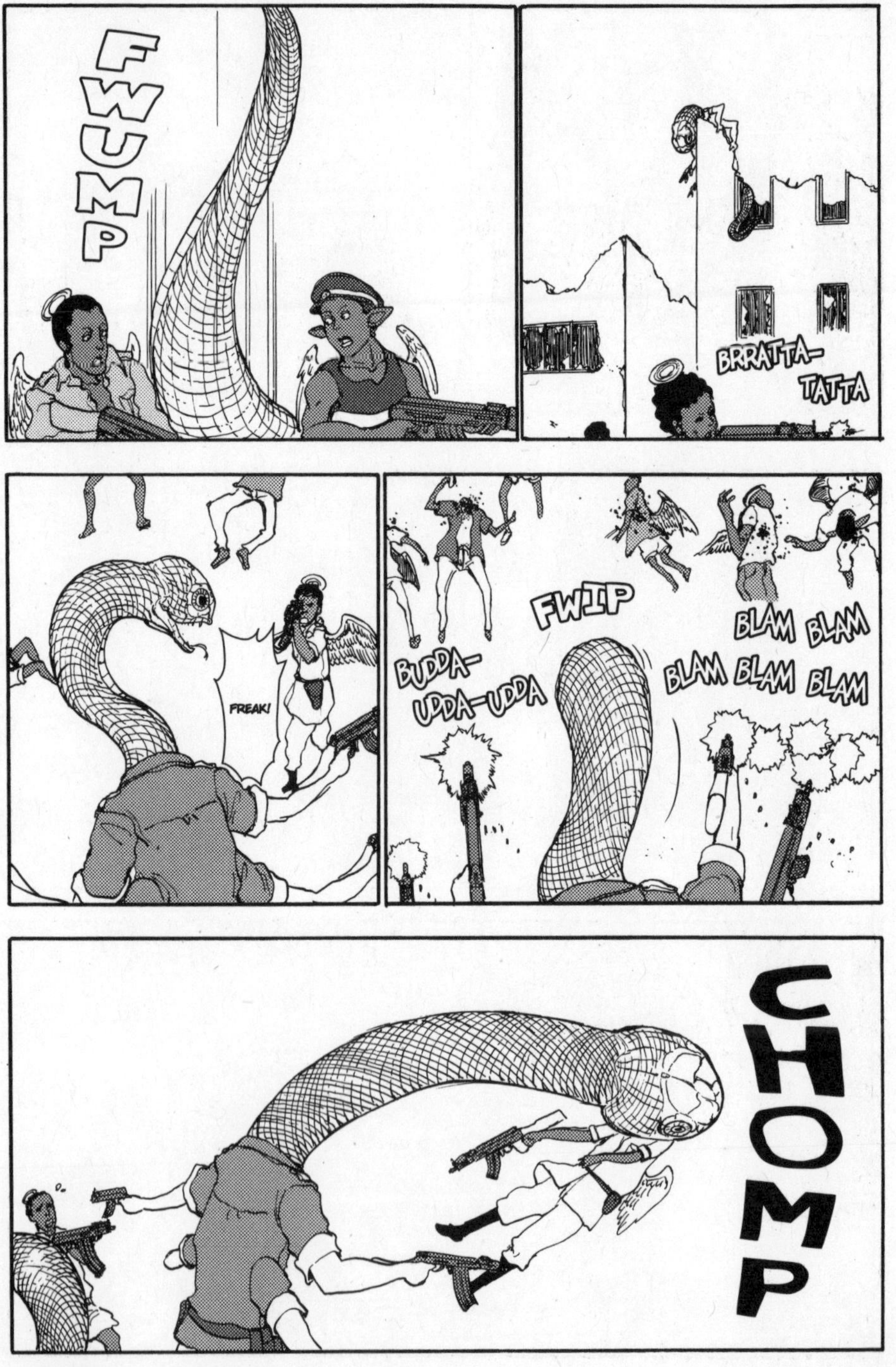
BRRATTA-TATTA
FWUMP
BLAM BLAM
BLAM BLAM BLAM
FWIP
BUDDA-UDDA-UDDA
FREAK!
CHOMP

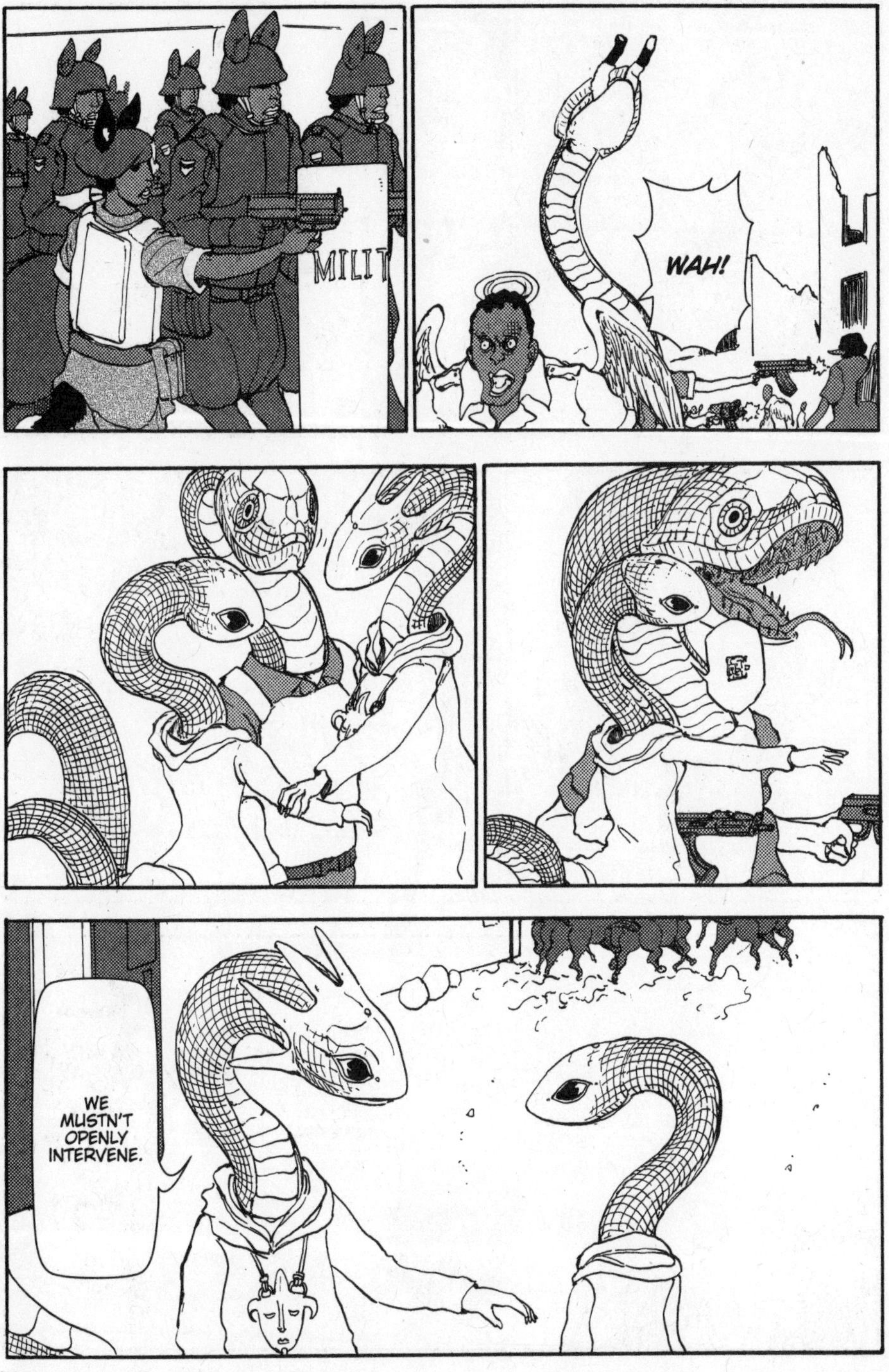
WAH!
MILIT
WE MUSTN'T OPENLY INTERVENE.

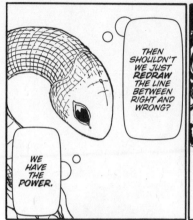

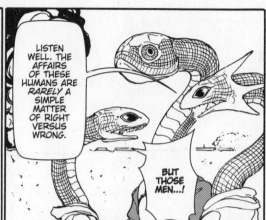

LISTEN WELL. THE AFFAIRS OF THESE HUMANS ARE RARELY A SIMPLE MATTER OF RIGHT VERSUS WRONG.
BUT THOSE MEN...!
THEN SHOULDN'T WE JUST REDRAW THE LINE BETWEEN RIGHT AND WRONG?
WE HAVE THE POWER.
MY SISTER IS--HOW YOU SAY--VERY MAMMALIAN IN HER THINKING, AND IT CONCERNS ME.
HOW EXACTLY IS HUMANKIND PERCEIVED IN ANTARCTICA?
THE EMOTIONS OF THE MAMMAL-HUMANS ARE BOTH WONDERFUL AND DANGEROUS, AND THEY HAVE MANY INHIBITIONS WHEN IT COMES TO TRANSFERRING THOSE EMOTIONS TO ACTIONS.
FEAR OF DEATH OR POVERTY IN THE EVENT OF FAILURE, SYMPATHY FOR THE DEFEATED, SHAME, SLOTH, AMBIVALENCE--NONE OF THESE THINGS EXIST TO ANTARCTICANS.
I'M WORRIED ABOUT MY SISTER NOW. I'M GOING TO TRY CALLING HER.
CULTURAL EDUCATION IS TOUGH STUFF.

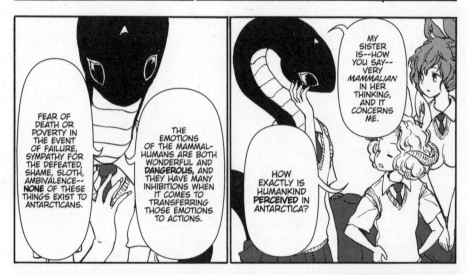

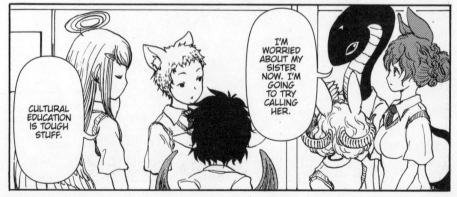

A CentaUr's Life

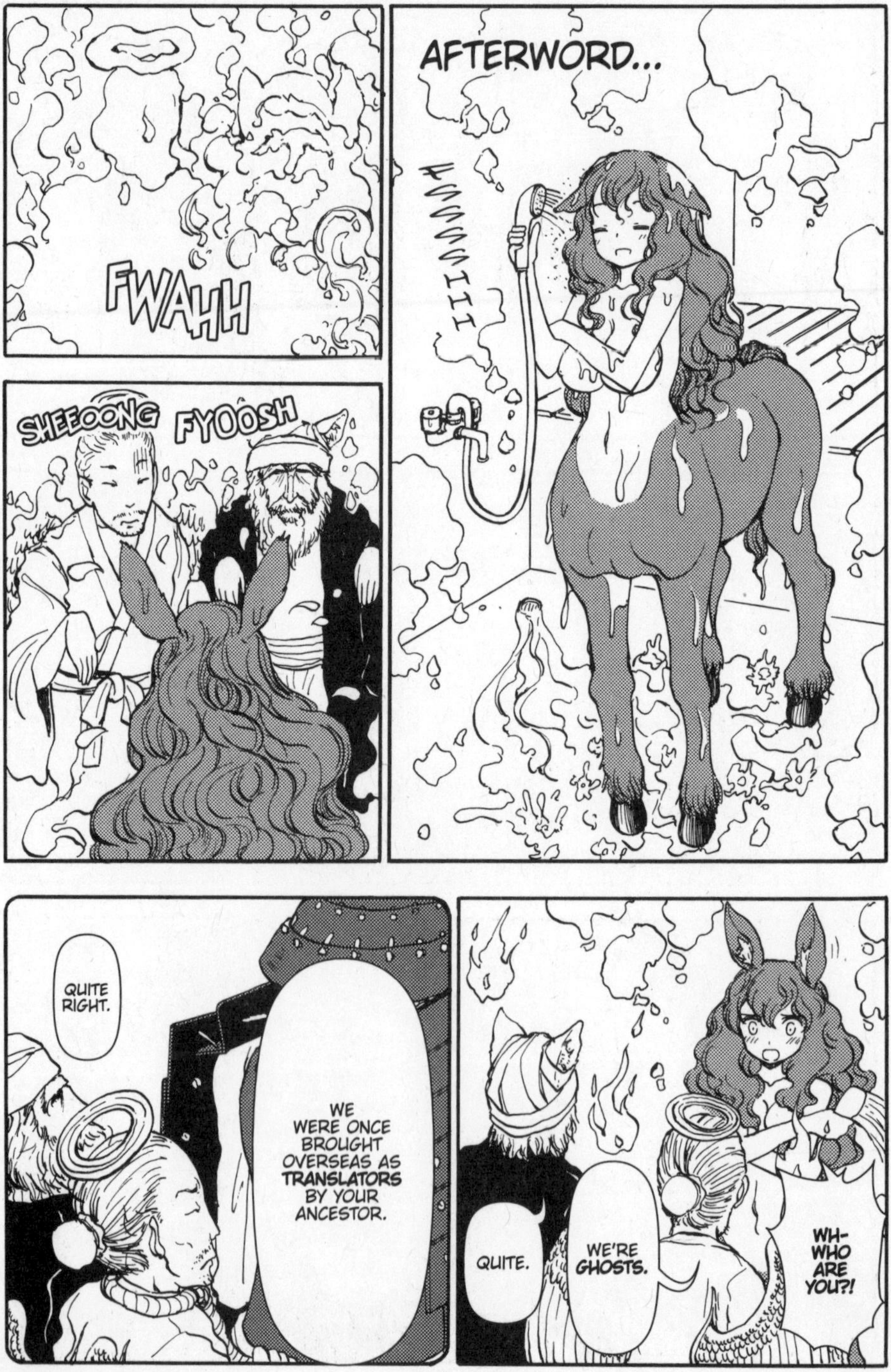
AFTERWORD...
FSSSSHIII
FWAHH
SHEEOONG
FYOOSH
WH-WHO ARE YOU?!
WE'RE GHOSTS.
QUITE.
WE WERE ONCE BROUGHT OVERSEAS AS TRANSLATORS BY YOUR ANCESTOR.
QUITE RIGHT.

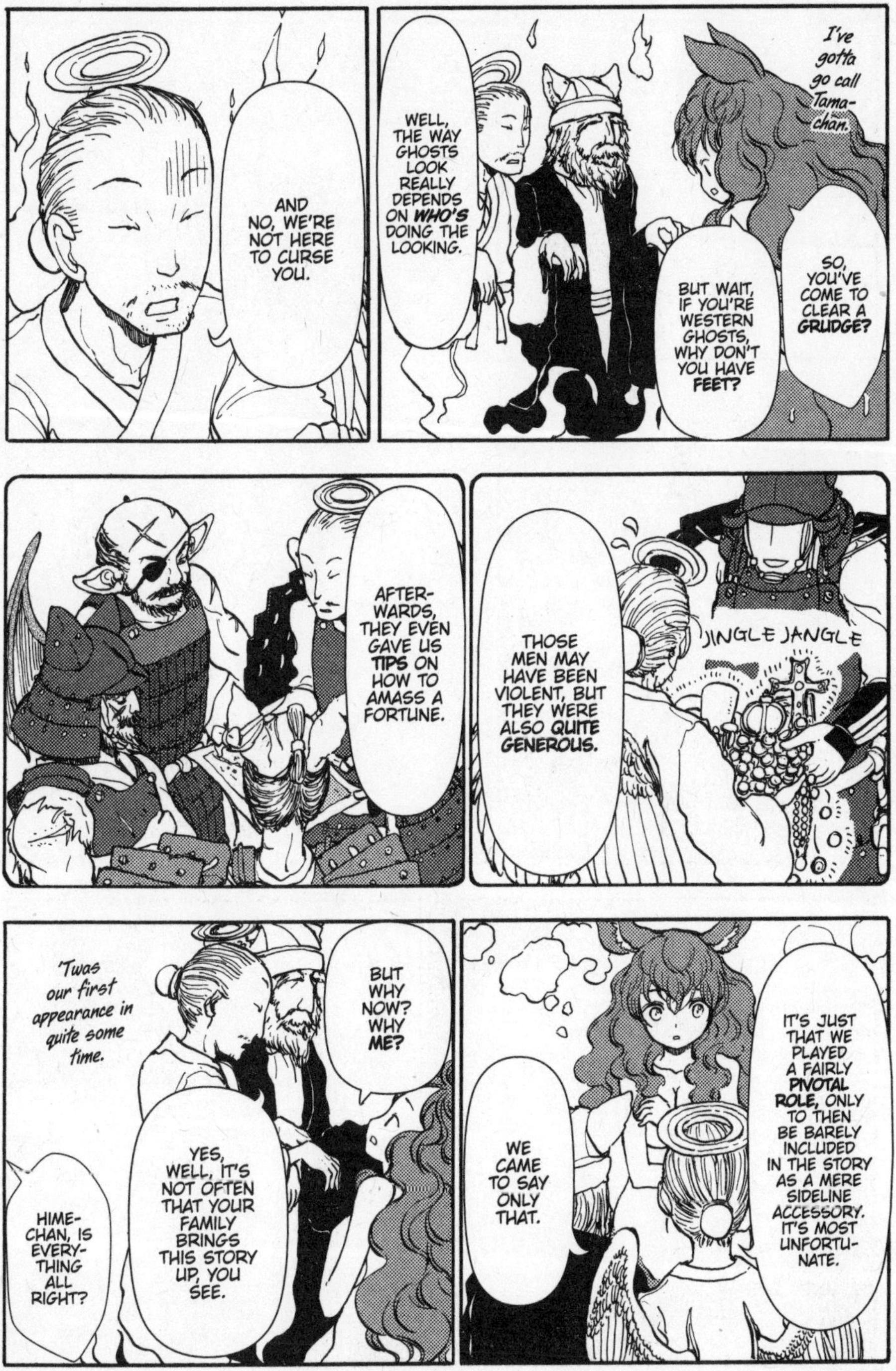
I've gotta go call Tama-chan.
SO, YOU'VE COME TO CLEAR A GRUDGE?
BUT WAIT, IF YOU'RE WESTERN GHOSTS, WHY DON'T YOU HAVE FEET?
WELL, THE WAY GHOSTS LOOK REALLY DEPENDS ON WHO'S DOING THE LOOKING.
AND NO, WE'RE NOT HERE TO CURSE YOU.
THOSE MEN MAY HAVE BEEN VIOLENT, BUT THEY WERE ALSO QUITE GENEROUS.
JINGLE JANGLE
AFTER-WARDS, THEY EVEN GAVE US TIPS ON HOW TO AMASS A FORTUNE.
IT'S JUST THAT WE PLAYED A FAIRLY PIVOTAL ROLE, ONLY TO THEN BE BARELY INCLUDED IN THE STORY AS A MERE SIDELINE ACCESSORY. IT'S MOST UNFORTU-NATE.
WE CAME TO SAY ONLY THAT.
BUT WHY NOW? WHY ME?
'Twas our first appearance in quite some time.
YES, WELL, IT'S NOT OFTEN THAT YOUR FAMILY BRINGS THIS STORY UP, YOU SEE.
HIME-CHAN, IS EVERY-THING ALL RIGHT?

LEARN ABOUT OUR TOWN! KANATA CITY'S PAST, PRESENT, AND FUTURE.

THE TRUE IMAGE OF THE *BUSHI*

Bashaku (old-world hired carriers used for ground transport).

*Bushi** are centaurs--this idea is still strongly held in today's world. Indeed, even in recent history, samurai were all portrayed as centaurs in popular period dramas. And yes, there was an intrinsic belief even amongst *bushi* that the vocation was, at heart, one of a centaur. In reality, however, the *bushi* class comprised a diverse range of humans.

In ancient dynasties, militaries were scraped together from soldiers belonging to powerful aristocratic families; under the *ritsuryou* system, they were formed through mandatory military service. But as occupations eventually became divided by clan, inevitably clans specializing in military affairs emerged. Among them, the En clan and Hou clan were quintessential. These clans were able to repel the horseback guerilla tactics of foreign, northern invaders by establishing a small but elite military consisting solely of swift-footed centaurs armed with bows. It is true that at this point in time, *bushi* were all centaurs. However, as these *bushi* clans were roped into civil disputes within the dynasty, the two pillars of military leadership that were the En and Hou soon began to vie for supremacy. What had previously been militaries composed of several dozen or several hundred units exploded practically overnight into militaries with tens of thousands of units. However, there were considerably fewer centaurs in ancient times than there are in the modern day, and there were simply not enough to fulfill the tremendous demand. Hence, a new class of warrior emerged in the clash between En and Hou--wealthy aristocrats and strong farmers, who were neither centaurs nor *bushi*, mounted horses and took to arms. In return for their service, they were allowed control over territory or *shôen*. But these "overnight soldiers," who now accounted for the majority of each clan's military force, were incapable of engaging in battle tactics which required a great amount of skill with, say, firing a bow. Instead, they began to engage the enemy up close, approaching on horse, grappling, and taking the head of the opponent. The odd image of two intertwined centaurs once common in *Taiga dorama* series** likely originates from this.

After the establishment of the Kamikura Bakufu, the percentage of *bushi* who were centaurs once again rose to some degree. This is likely due to the new class of *bushi* frequently intermarrying with centaur lineage within the En and Hou clans. Centaurs did not account for the majority of *bushi****, but *only* centaurs could claim to be of legitimate military families. There are even accounts of non-centaurs interbreeding with centaurs who were *not* of a *bushi* lineage (or *any* notable lineage, for that matter), or otherwise adopting centaurs as their children.

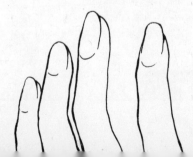

**Bushi: A Japanese warrior; a samurai.*

***Taiga drama, the name of an annual historical fiction TV show broadcast in Japan.*

****Indeed, not all centaurs were bushi. Bushi were actually a minority within the centaur race, while most were, like other humans, simple farmers or members of other occupations. Of particular note, many centaurs traditionally worked as bashaku--hired horses used for transport. This was akin to the merfolk's monopolization of the navy. Likewise akin was this monopoly's collapse in more recent history.*

Research has suggested that a great number of *bushi* family lines were established in this way.

During the *Sengoku* period, the ratio of centaurs to all *bushi* once again declined. The most vital thing demanded of samurai was neither a strong family lineage nor even military prowess-- it was how many men one had under his control. One's ability and experience as a commander was valued above all. In the face of new logical tactics, firearms, and advanced citadel structures, the quick feet and sturdy frames of centaurs no longer provided quite the battlefield advantage that they once had. And indeed, there are not many *Sengoku* daimyo family lines which can be confirmed to have had a multi-generational centaur bloodline. Toyotomi Hideyoshi is well known to have been a draconid*, but even the ultimate ruler of this household, Tokugawa Ieyasu, was in fact goatfolk, despite portraits falsely depicting him as a centaur. It wasn't until the reign of the fifth shogun, Tsunayoshi, that the Tokugawa clan adopted a centaur bloodline**. Even then, the clan continued to frequently bear non-centaur offspring, such as eighth shogun Yoshimune. Nevertheless, the ideal of the centaur bushi, perhaps propagated by literary works such as the *Tale of Houke,* has prevailed to this day.

If one detaches from these popular colloquial myths and simply observes the historical facts, however, one will find that at no point was any one species ever singled out and enslaved by any other. The Western concept of observing history through the lens of "species-based class conflict" was rather born out of the West's morally scarred history of keeping centaurs as slaves and systemized extermination of the merfolk, and in no way applies to our nation. Our nation, with its beautiful history of cooperation and coexistence amongst a diverse people, must, as a world leader, rectify this widespread fallacy and lead others to the truth.

KANATA UNDER THE TOKUGAWA REGIME

After the demise of the Oda clan, Hidachi mostly fell under the rule of the Satake clan, but in 1602 (Keichou 7), the clan underwent *ryôchi-gae* (change of territory), shifting its domain to Idewa and leaving Hidachi behind. Thereafter, control of southern Hidachi, which encompassed the region of modern-day Kanata, would pass through the hands of several long-established daimyo clans. This includes the Yuuki, who would pepper the domain with tens of thousands of small enclaves--retainer domains, Bakufu domains, and religious domains. Oda castle became an abandoned ruin, and Kanata reverted to mere farmland. The tides of change, however, were sure to come.

*Even the famous swordsman Miyamoto Musashi was but a mere ashigaru soldier--the lowest ranking foot soldier-- during his service in the Shimabara Rebellion. Nevertheless, he worked so ceaselessly and humbly, never once boasting his above-average centaur frame or martial art prowess, that he even sustained serious injury from hurling boulders.

**The Oda clan oft referenced in this text, as well as their sworn enemy the Satake clan, did maintain multi-generational centaur bloodlines dating back to the En-Hou period.

SEVEN SEAS ENTERTAINMENT PRESENTS

A Centaur's Life

story and art by KEI MURAYAMA

VOLUME 8

TRANSLATION
Greg Moore

ADAPTATION
Holly Kolodziejczak

LETTERING AND LAYOUT
Jennifer Skarupa

LOGO DESIGN
Courtney Williams

COVER DESIGN
Nicky Lim

PROOFREADER
Patrick King

PRODUCTION MANAGER
Lissa Pattillo

EDITOR-IN-CHIEF
Adam Arnold

PUBLISHER
Jason DeAngelis

CENTAUR NO NAYAMI VOLUME 8
© KEI MURAYAMA 2014
Originally published in Japan in 2014 by TOKUMA SHOTEN PUBLISHING
CO., LTD., Tokyo. English translation rights arranged with TOKUMA SHOTEN
PUBLISHING CO., LTD., Tokyo, through TOHAN CORPORATION, Tokyo.

Seven Seas books may be purchased in bulk for educational, business, or
promotional use. For information on bulk purchases, please contact Macmillan
Corporate & Premium Sales Department at 1-800-221-7945 (ext 5442)
or write specialmarkets@macmillan.com.

Seven Seas and the Seven Seas logo are trademarks of
Seven Seas Entertainment, LLC. All rights reserved.

ISBN: 978-1-626922-36-5

Printed in Canada

First Printing: March 2016

10 9 8 7 6 5 4 3 2 1

DISCARD

FOLLOW US ONLINE: www.gomanga.com

READING DIRECTIONS

This book reads from *right to left*, Japanese style. If
this is your first time reading manga, you start
reading from the top right panel on each page and
take it from there. If you get lost, just follow the
numbered diagram here. It may seem backwards at
first, but you'll get the hang of it! Have fun!!

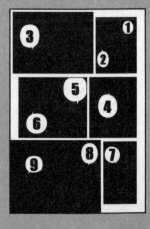